Politics after Neoliberalism

The shift from state-led to market-oriented, neoliberal economic policies has been one of the most important changes in the developing world during the last two decades. Although much existing research has focused on why countries choose these neoliberal policy reforms and how they implement them, Richard Snyder's study breaks new ground by offering an analysis of politics *after* neoliberalism. The book proposes a framework that explains how neoliberal reforms, rather than unleashing market forces, actually trigger "reregulation" processes involving strategic interactions between political entrepreneurs and societal groups. Depending on the strengths and strategies of politicians and societal groups, reregulation results in different types of new institutions for market governance with contrasting consequences for economic efficiency and social justice. This framework is used in conjunction with an innovative subnational comparative method to analyze fresh evidence from four Mexican states about the politics of reregulation. By showing that neoliberal reforms result in different kinds of new regulatory institutions at the subnational level, the book challenges the widely held view that these reforms have set countries on a convergent path toward laissez-faire markets.

Richard Snyder is Associate Professor of Political Science at Brown University. He previously taught at the University of Illinois at Urbana-Champaign. He has been a visiting fellow at the Harvard Academy for International and Area Studies and at the Center for U.S.-Mexican Studies at the University of California, San Diego. His research has been supported by numerous institutions, including the National Science Foundation, the Institute of International Education, and the Institute for the Study of World Politics. He is the editor of three volumes on the political economy of rural Mexico, including Institutional Adaptation and Innovation in Rural Mexico. His articles have appeared in such journals as *World Politics, Comparative Politics, Studies in Comparative International Development*, and *British Journal of Political Science*.

T0382033

Cambridge Studies in Comparative Politics

General Editor
Margaret Levi   *University of Washington, Seattle*

Assistant General Editor
Stephen Hanson   *University of Washington, Seattle*

Associate Editors
Robert H. Bates   *Harvard University*
Helen Milner   *Princeton University*
Frances Rosenbluth   *Yale University*
Susan Stokes   *Yale University*
Sidney Tarrow   *Cornell University*
Kathleen Thelen   *Northwestern University*
Erik Wibbels   *University of Washington, Seattle*

Other Books in the Series
Lisa Baldez, *Why Women Protest? Women's Movements in Chile*
Stefano Bartolini, *The Political Mobilization of the European Left, 1860-1980: The Class Cleavage*
Mark Beissinger, *Nationalist Mobilization and the Collapse of the Soviet State*
Nancy Bermeo, ed., *Unemployment in the New Europe*
Carles Boix, *Democracy and Redistribution*
Carles Boix, *Political Parties, Growth, and Equality: Conservative and Social Democratic Economic Strategies in the World Economy*
Catherine Boone, *Merchant Capital and the Roots of State Power in Senegal, 1930–1985*
Catherine Boone, *Political Topographies of the African State: Territorial Authority and Institutional Change*
Michael Bratton and Nicolas van de Walle, *Democratic Experiments in Africa: Regime Transitions in Comparative Perspective*
Michael Bratton, Robert Mattes, and E. Gyimah-Boadi, *Public Opinion, Democracy, and Market Reform in Africa*
Valerie Bunce, *Leaving Socialism and Leaving the State: The End of Yugoslavia, the Soviet Union, and Czechoslovakia*

(continued after index)

Politics after Neoliberalism

REREGULATION IN MEXICO

RICHARD SNYDER

Brown University

CAMBRIDGE
UNIVERSITY PRESS

CAMBRIDGE
UNIVERSITY PRESS

32 Avenue of the Americas, New York NY 10013-2473, USA

Cambridge University Press is part of the University of Cambridge.

It furthers the University's mission by disseminating knowledge in the pursuit of education, learning and research at the highest international levels of excellence.

www.cambridge.org
Information on this title: www.cambridge.org/9780521688703

First published 2001
First paperback edition 2006

A catalogue record for this publication is available from the British Library

Library of Congress Cataloguing in Publication data
Snyder, Richard (Richard Owen)
Politics after neoliberalism: reregulation in Mexico / Richard Snyder.
p.   cm. – (Cambridge studies in comparative politics)
Includes bibliographical references and index.
ISBN 0-521-79034-4
1. Mexico – Economic policy – 1994 – Case studies.   2. Trade regulation – Mexico – Case studies.   I. Title.   II. Series.

HC135 .S58   2001
380.1′3′09772 – dc21   00-046793

ISBN 978-0-521-79034-5 Hardback
ISBN 978-0-521-68870-3 Paperback

*To my mother and father
and to Margarita*

Contents

List of Illustrations

Acknowledgments

Many people have contributed to and supported this research. First I wish to acknowledge my teachers at the University of California, Berkeley. David Collier has been an exceptional mentor and friend over the last decade. David chaired the doctoral dissertation from which this book evolved, and from the start he saw the value of a subnational comparative analysis. I am grateful for his enthusiasm and support. Ruth Berins Collier also has been a wonderful mentor and friend. I am glad that her fascination with the twists and turns of Mexican politics proved contagious. Peter Evans has been a key source of intellectual support. His ability to frame the big issues and get students focused on important questions is truly remarkable. At several junctures, Peter provided insightful comments on the manuscript that were fundamental for helping me find my way. Ernst Haas fully lived up to his reputation as a "mentor of mentors." Ernie's guidance, humor, and wisdom have been greatly appreciated. Finally, in addition to being a good friend, Elizabeth Perry, now at Harvard, helped me see the importance of in-depth fieldwork with a dual focus on grass-roots actors and political elites.

I also want to express my gratitude to two other senior scholars who have made important contributions to my intellectual development. While I was an undergraduate, I had the privilege to study with Theda Skocpol. In addition to providing a compelling model of what the enterprise of social science should be, Theda played a pivotal role convincing a young, uncertain student that he had what it took to become a university professor. Before entering graduate school, I also had the good fortune to meet Juan Linz. Juan has been a fundamental source of intellectual guidance and support, and I am grateful for the kindness and generosity he has shown me over the years. Although I regret that I never took a formal class with Juan, I like to think that the many informal interactions I have been lucky enough to have had with him do, in fact, make me a Linz student.

A number of other colleagues and friends were good enough to read and comment on portions of the manuscript at various stages. I appreciate valuable feedback from Robert Bates, William Bernhard, Wayne Cornelius, Jorge Domínguez, Jonathan Fox, Stephan Haggard, Frances Hagopian, Judy Harper, Luis Hernández, Peter Houtzager, Pauline Jones-Luong, Robert Kaufman, Timothy Kessler, Atul Kohli, Thomas Lewis, Richard Locke, James Mahoney, Scott Mainwaring, Kevin Middlebrook, Joel Migdal, Paul Pierson, Daniel Posner, David Samuels, Kenneth Shadlen, Matthew Shugart, Judith Tendler, Nicolas van de Walle, and Steven Vogel. Gerardo Munck deserves special mention for his willingness to read and reread multiple drafts of chapters on short notice. Gerry has more than lived up to his reputation as an exemplary colleague.

In Mexico, many *campesinos*, rural development workers, and state and federal government officials trusted my pledge of anonymity and generously shared their experiences and insights with me. In particular, I owe an enormous debt to the members, staff, and leaders of the National Coordinating Network of Coffee Producers' Organizations (CNOC) and its regional affiliates in the states of Oaxaca, Guerrero, Chiapas, and Puebla. This project simply would not have been possible without their help.

Several institutions provided support for my research. Fieldwork in Mexico during 1994 and 1995 was funded by a National Science Foundation Graduate Fellowship, a J. William Fulbright Fellowship from the Institute of International Education, a grant from the Institute for the Study of World Politics, and a grant from the Ejido Reform Research Project of the Center for U.S.–Mexican Studies at the University of California, San Diego. The writing of the manuscript was supported by a Visiting Research Fellowship from the Center for U.S.–Mexican Studies at the University of California, San Diego. I am especially grateful to the Center's Director, Kevin Middlebrook, for providing an exceptional environment for research. A generous and timely postdoctoral fellowship from the Harvard Academy for International and Area Studies also provided crucial support for writing, as did a semester of released time from the Department of Political Science at the University of Illinois at Urbana-Champaign.

Earlier versions of portions of the manuscript appeared as "After Neoliberalism: The Politics of Reregulation in Mexico," *World Politics* 51

Acknowledgments

(January 1999): 173–204; "Reconstructing Institutions for Market Governance: Participatory Policy Regimes in Mexico's Coffee Sector," in Richard Snyder, ed., *Institutional Adaptation and Innovation in Rural Mexico* (La Jolla, California: The Center for U.S.–Mexican Studies, University of California, San Diego, 1999); and "After the State Withdraws: Neoliberalism and Subnational Authoritarian Regimes in Mexico," in Wayne A. Cornelius, Todd A. Eisenstadt, and Jane Hindley, eds., *Subnational Politics and Democratization in Mexico* (La Jolla, California: Center for U.S.–Mexican Studies, University of California, San Diego, 1999).

Outside of the academy, a number of friends have contributed in important ways to this book. David Griswold first opened my eyes to the fascinating world of rural Mexico. He enthusiastically introduced me to his network of contacts in the Mexican coffee sector and thus played a pivotal role helping me get this project off the ground. Paul Butler taught me much about Mexico and was even able to observe a portion of my field research firsthand. In Mexico, Margarita Romo and Ignacio Caballero graciously welcomed me into their home and provided greatly appreciated warmth and support. Three old friends – Sean Elias, John Nimo, and Paul Bryan – deserve special recognition for helping me learn to think outside the box.

One of the greatest rewards of undertaking a research project on Mexico was meeting my wife, Margarita. She has enriched my life in countless ways, and I am truly grateful for her love and companionship.

Finally, and most important, I acknowledge my parents, Margaret and Roger. They have been there since the very start, and, in their own way, each has been a good and devoted parent. I thank them for their sustaining love and support.

Acronyms

ARIC	Asociación Rural de Interés Colectivo / Rural Collective Interest Association
BANAMEX	Banco Nacional de México / National Bank of Mexico
BANRURAL	Banco Nacional de Crédito Rural / National Rural Credit Bank
BUAP	Benemérita Universidad Autónoma de Puebla / Autonomous University of Puebla
CARTT	Cooperativa Agropecuaria Regional "Tosepan Titataniske" / "We Shall Overcome" Regional Agricultural Cooperative
CCI	Centro Coordinador Indigenista / Indigenous Coordinating Center
CEPCO	Coordinadora Estatal de Productores de Café de Oaxaca / Statewide Coordinating Network of Coffee Producers of Oaxaca
CESCAFE	Consejo de Empresas Sociales de Cafetaleros de Chiapas / Social Enterprise Council of Coffee Producers of Chiapas
CIOAC	Central Independiente de Obreros Agrícolas y Campesinos / Independent Central of Agricultural Workers and Peasants
CMPC	Confederación Mexicana de Productores de Café / Mexican Confederation of Coffee Producers
CNC	Confederación Nacional Campesina / National Peasants' Confederation
CNOC	Coordinadora Nacional de Organizaciones Cafetaleras / National Coordinating Network of Coffee Producers' Organizations

CNPP	Confederación Nacional de Pequeños Propietarios / National Confederation of Smallholders
CNPR	Confederación Nacional de Propietarios Rurales / National Confederation of Rural Smallholders
COCEI	Coalición Obrero Campesino Estudiantil del Istmo / Coalition of Workers, Peasants, and Students of the Isthmus
COESCAFE	Consejo Estatal del Café del Estado de Chiapas / State Coffee Council of Chiapas
CONASUPO	Compañía Nacional de Subsistencias Populares / National Basic Foods Company
COPLADE	Comité de Planeación para el Desarrollo del Estado / State Planning Commission
COR	Consejo Operativo Regional / Regional Operating Council
CORFO	Corporación Forestal de Chiapas / Chiapas Forestry Corporation
COVEI	Comité para la Organización y Vigilancia de Elecciones Internales / Committee for Organization and Oversight of Internal Elections
CTM	Confederación de Trabajadores de México / Confederation of Mexican Workers
FDC	Frente Democrático de Coyuca / Coyuca Democratic Front
FDN	Frente Democrático Nacional / National Democratic Front
FIDECAFE	Fideicomiso del Café / National Coffee Trust Fund
FNOB	Federación Nacional de Organizaciones Bolcheviques / National Federation of Bolshevik Organizations
FUDT	Frente Unico Democrático de Tlacolula / Authentic Democratic Front of Tlacolula
GON	Grupo Operativo Nacional / National Operating Group
GOR	Grupo Operativo Regional / Regional Operating Group
GTC	Grupo de Trabajo Colectivo / Collective Work Group
ICA	International Coffee Agreement

Acronyms

ICO	International Coffee Organization
IEPES	Instituto de Estudios Políticos, Económicos y Sociales / Institute of Economic, Political, and Social Sciences
IMF	International Monetary Fund
IMSS	Instituto Mexicano del Seguro Social / Mexican Social Security Institute
INEGI	Instituto Nacional de Estadística, Geografía e Informática / National Institute of Statistics, Geography, and Informatics
INFONAVIT	Instituto del Fondo Nacional de la Vivienda para los Trabajadores / National Worker Housing Institute
INI	Instituto Nacional Indigenista / National Indigenous Institute
INMECAFE	Instituto Mexicano del Café / Mexican Coffee Institute
ISMAM	Indígenas de la Sierra Madre de Motozintla / Organization of Indigenous People of the Sierra Madre of Motozintla
ITAO	Instituto Tecnológico Autónomo de Oaxaca / Autonomous Technological Institute of Oaxaca
MERCOSUR	Mercado Común del Sur / Common Market of the South
NAFINSA	Nacional Financiera, S.A. / National Development Bank
NAFTA	North American Free Trade Agreement
NGO	nongovernmental organization
OIT	Organización Independiente Totonaca / Independent Totonaco Organization
PAN	Partido Acción Nacional / National Action Party
PCM	Partido Comunista Mexicano / Communist Party of Mexico
PECE	Pacto para la Estabilidad y Crecimiento Económico / Pact for Stability and Economic Growth
PR	proportional representation
PRD	Partido de la Revolución Democrática / Party of the Democratic Revolution
PRI	Partido Revolucionario Institucional / Institutional Revolutionary Party

PRONASOL	Programa Nacional de Solidaridad / National Solidarity Program
SAGAR	Secretaría de Agricultura, Ganadería y Desarrollo Rural / Ministry of Agriculture, Livestock, and Rural Development
SAM	Sistema Alimentario Mexicano / Mexican Food System
SARH	Secretaría de Agricultura y Recursos Hidráulicos / Ministry of Agriculture and Water Resources
SEDESOL	Secretaría de Desarrollo Social / Ministry of Social Development
SNTE	Sindicato Nacional de Trabajadores de la Educación / National Union of Education Workers
SPP	Secretaría de Programación y Presupuesto / Ministry of Budget and Planning
SSA	Secretaría de Salubridad y Asistencia / Ministry of Health and Welfare
SSS	Sociedad de Solidaridad Social / Social Solidarity Society
TNC	transnational corporation
UCI "Cien Años"	Unión de Comunidades Indígenas "Cien Años de Soledad" / Union of Indigenous Communities "One Hundred Years of Solitude"
UCIRI	Unión de Comunidades Indígenas de la Región del Istmo / Union of Indigenous Communities of the Isthmus
UCIZONI	Unión de Comunidades Indígenas de la Zona Norte del Istmo / Union of Indigenous Communities of the Northern Isthmus
UEPC	Unidades Económicas de Producción y Comercialización / Economic Units for Production and Marketing
UEPC-CNC	Unión Estatal de Productores de Café–Confederación Nacional Campesina / State Union of Coffee Producers–National Peasants' Confederation
UNAM	Universidad Nacional Autónoma de México / National Autonomous University of Mexico

Acronyms

UNORCA	Unión de Organizaciones Regionales Campesinas Autónomas / National Union of Autonomous Regional Peasant Organizations
URICAA	Unión Regional Independiente de Cafetaleros Autónomos / Independent Regional Union of Autonomous Coffee Producers
WTO	World Trade Organization

PART I

The Framework and Comparative Analysis

1

Rethinking the Consequences of Neoliberalism

The neoliberal wave has crested and broken. During the last two decades, virtually all developing countries shifted from state-led to market-oriented economic strategies. This global wave of policy reform, which affected the lives of literally billions of people across the developing world, stands as perhaps the most remarkable economic event of the late twentieth century.[1]

In the wake of this policy revolution, an ideologically charged debate has raged about the consequences of neoliberal reforms. Proponents of neoliberalism herald the triumph of free markets over government control. They euphorically predict new levels of prosperity as market forces are liberated from the fetters of government intervention.[2] By contrast, opponents of neoliberalism warn of developmental disaster. They argue that market-oriented reforms set countries on a pernicious "race to the bottom" as they compete to attract footloose global capital by lowering environmental and workplace standards.[3]

This study aims to get beyond the apocalyptic rhetoric by analyzing fresh evidence about the effects of neoliberal policy reform. The evidence challenges a fundamental assumption shared by both friend and foe of these reforms, who converge in the belief that they result in laissez-faire markets. I find instead that neoliberal policies, rather than unleashing market forces, trigger the construction of new institutions for market governance.

---

[1] For a vivid overview of this wave, see Yergin and Stanislaw (1998).
[2] See, for example, De Soto (1989); Friedman (1990); and Schwartz and Leyden (1997).
[3] See, for example, Clark (1991, esp. ch. 13); Walton and Seddon (1994); Collins and Lear (1995); Green (1995); and Wallach and Sforza (1999).

By vacating institutionalized policy domains, neoliberal reforms create opportunities for political incumbents to expand their authority and their support bases by "reregulating" sectors of the economy.[4] Organized societal groups have a stake in how markets are reregulated and can mobilize to support or challenge politicians' reregulation projects. Neoliberal reforms thus trigger two-step reregulation processes: First, political entrepreneurs launch projects to build support coalitions by reregulating markets; second, societal actors respond to these projects by mobilizing to influence the terms of reregulation. The varying strengths and strategies of politicians and societal groups, in turn, determine the various types of new institutions for market governance that will result from these reregulation processes. In short, rather than ending government intervention in markets and narrowing the range of the political, neoliberal reforms result in a new politics of reregulation.

Recognizing that neoliberal reforms create opportunities and incentives for institution building raises a further issue: What kinds of new institutions replace those destroyed or displaced by neoliberal policies? Because these institutions are likely to have a crucial impact on how countries perform in the global economy, it is imperative to understand their origins and dynamics.[5] To achieve this objective, I propose a framework for explaining the different types of new institutions for market governance that emerge after neoliberal reforms.

In sum, this book has three overarching goals. First, by showing that neoliberal policies can result in new institutions for market governance instead of unregulated markets, it challenges expectations rooted in neoliberal economic theory. Second, it provides a framework for explaining the different kinds of institutions that replace those destroyed by neoliberal reforms. Finally, by shifting the focus from the politics of neoliberal reform to the politics of reregulation, it moves beyond the well-studied questions

---

[4] The term "reregulation" has been employed since the early 1980s by students of regulatory reform in the United States and other advanced industrial countries. For an early use of the term, see Weingast (1981). See also Vogel (1996). The *locus classicus* of the idea that free-market reforms can result in new regulations is Polanyi (1944). Polanyi (1944:140) observed that "the introduction of free markets, far from doing away with the need for control, regulation, and intervention, enormously increased their range." The present study confirms Polanyi's basic insight, yet offers a new, political explanation for reregulation.

[5] In an important shift away from its earlier focus on structural adjustment and neoliberal reform, the World Bank has increasingly recognized the importance of institutional reconstruction after neoliberalism. See Burki and Perry (1998).

4

of why countries choose neoliberal policies and how they implement them. In taking this step, the book develops a new agenda for comparative political economy: the study of politics *after* neoliberalism.

Beyond Neoliberalism: How Far Do Existing Studies Go?

The study of neoliberal reform has dominated work on the political economy of development during the last decade. Because most analyses treat market-oriented policies as a dependent variable, however, few explore the political effects of these policies. Many scholars seek to explain why countries choose neoliberal policies.[6] Within this focus on policy choice, some try to account for cross-national variation in the timing of reforms (Nelson 1990b). Others analyze differences in the composition of policy packages, attempting to explain, for example, why countries pursue orthodox or heterodox policies (Kahler 1990). Scholars have also focused on issues of policy implementation, identifying political and social conditions that help or hinder implementation of neoliberal reforms.[7] Such studies mainly try to explain what makes neoliberal reforms possible, rather than explain their political consequences.

Previous work offers important insights about the factors that induce politicians to support or oppose neoliberal policies and about how political institutions affect their implementation. These insights help explain why countries have had varied success at achieving macroeconomic stabilization and structural adjustment. Because they focus on the dismantling of ancien régimes based on state-led, inward-oriented development strategies, however, existing analyses shed little light on how institutions for market governance are reconstructed after transitions away from statism.

The few analyses of developing countries that look beyond the dismantling of old statist regimes have been curiously apolitical. Scholars have increasingly noted that states acquire new capabilities in the course of implementing neoliberal reforms. However, they have focused mainly on capabilities linked either to technical requirements of neoliberal policies, such as preparing state enterprises for sale and improving control of public expenditures, or to global market pressures, such as providing sophisticated information about export markets to domestic producers to

---

[6] See, for example, Nelson (1990a) and Bates and Krueger (1993).
[7] Callaghy (1990); Przeworski (1991); Haggard and Kaufman (1992); Haggard and Webb (1994); Naím (1995); and Grindle (1996).

help boost their competitiveness abroad.[8] These analyses underemphasize the possibility that neoliberal reforms can trigger *politically motivated* institution building, driven not by technical or market exigencies but by ambitious politicians looking to control policy areas vacated by state downsizing.

Perhaps because most advanced industrial countries embraced neoliberal reforms earlier than their counterparts in the developing world,[9] students of those countries have focused considerable attention on policy dynamics after the implementation of such reforms. Most notably, they have shown that the shift to market-oriented policies in countries such as Britain and the United States actually increased government regulation in high-technology sectors like telecommunications and financial services.[10] Although studies of reregulation in advanced industrial countries do go beyond the implementation of neoliberal reforms, they deemphasize the distributive effects of regulatory policy and instead portray reregulation as a relatively apolitical process led by technocrats who strive to promote economic performance, codify rules, or expand their bureaucratic prerogatives.[11] Consequently, these studies offer weak leverage for understanding how reregulation works in developing countries.

In developed and developing countries alike, the distributive effects of regulatory policy generate powerful incentives for political action.[12] In most developing countries, however, autonomous bureaucratic agencies insulated from "capture" by political actors are nonexistent or scarce.[13] Hence the impulse to reregulate often stems from politicians, not from technocrats. Understanding the dynamics of reregulation in such contexts requires a perspective that highlights politicians' efforts to gain and keep power.

In short, existing work in comparative political economy offers few insights about the politics of reregulation, leaving us, consequently, without a satisfactory framework for explaining the reconstruction of insti-

---

[8] Kahler (1990); Evans (1992); Waterbury (1992); Haggard and Kaufman (1995:310–14). Pastor and Wise (1999) include a focus on social policy and the state's potential role in promoting human capital.

[9] Chile is a notable exception. See Foxley (1983).

[10] On reregulation in advanced industrial countries, see Weingast (1981); Borrus et al. (1985); Moran (1991); and Vogel (1996).

[11] According to Vogel (1996:19), the "core agenda of regulatory reform" consists of efforts by bureaucrats to generate revenue and design new mechanisms for policy implementation.

[12] Bates (1983); Noll (1989). [13] Migdal (1988). See also Schneider and Maxfield (1997).

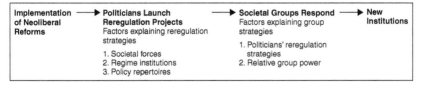

Figure 1.1. Framework for Analyzing the Politics of Reregulation.

tutions for market governance after neoliberalism. Building such a framework requires new conceptual and analytic tools.

The Politics of Reregulation: A Framework

This section develops a framework for analyzing the politics of reregulation. The framework combines a focus on politicians' choices of regulatory policies with a focus on subsequent bargaining between politicians and societal groups over the terms of reregulation. Together, these two perspectives help explain varied reregulation processes and the divergent institutions for market governance that result from them. Figure 1.1 summarizes the core components of the framework.

Reregulation Projects: A Politician-Centered Perspective

The distributive consequences of market regulation give politicians strong incentives to harness regulatory policy to political purposes. Regulation makes it possible to distribute "rationed favors, privileged access, and individual exceptions to general rules," thereby helping "generate the resources by which to govern" (Bates 1983:131). In contexts where bureaucratic agencies insulated from political control are scarce, we should expect regulatory policy to serve frequently as a tool that incumbent politicians deploy to build support and compete for power.

Neoliberal reforms give incumbents further reasons to regulate. First, such reforms often impose high costs on organized interest groups (e.g., industrial labor, government employees), thus creating difficult coalitional challenges for politicians.[14] Because regulatory policy generates divisible benefits and targetable rewards, reregulation can be a potent instrument for maintaining or restructuring support coalitions strained by neoliberal

---

[14] Collier (1992); Levitsky and Way (1998); and Burgess (1999).

reforms. Second, neoliberal shocks evacuate policy domains, and, from the perspective of ambitious politicians, these vacant domains may represent opportunities for increasing their authority. Reregulation can thus serve not only as a means to preserve power in situations of coalitional crisis caused by neoliberal reforms but also as a way to expand power.

Combined with the distributive consequences of regulatory policy, the characteristic political challenges and opportunities posed by neoliberal reforms give incumbents compelling incentives to reregulate. Thus there is a strong basis for expecting reregulation to serve as a coalition-building tool wielded by politicians in the paradigmatic "soft states" of developing countries that lack robust autonomous bureaucracies.[15]

The recognition that the impetus for reregulation stems from ambitious politicians, rather than from insulated technocrats, puts incumbents' strategic calculations at the center of the analysis. Yet politicians are not completely free in their choice of reregulation strategies. Their policy choices are constrained by societal forces and political institutions. Furthermore, politicians often have ideas and beliefs that prescribe a course of policy choice and implementation. To explain reregulation strategies, we need a framework that links societal and institutional constraints as well as politicians' ideas and values to the shaping of policy choice.[16]

Societal Forces. The configuration of societal interests in a policy area constrains politicians' reregulation strategies by delimiting the range of feasible policy options. Mapping the policy preferences of societal actors thus serves as an important first step for explaining reregulation strategies.

However, the distribution of societal preferences cannot by itself explain these strategies. As students of collective action have long observed, group preferences do not necessarily translate into group demands. Moreover, even if societal groups do organize to defend their interests, it is politicians, not interest groups, that are authorized to make regulatory policy. And, as we shall see, the responsiveness of politicians to interest-group demands depends on political institutions.

In sum, focusing on societal forces helps explain the menu of policy options. However, such a focus, while important, serves more to narrow the range of possible strategies than to explain actual strategies. To account

---

[15] The term "soft state" is from Myrdal (1968:66).
[16] Previous efforts to develop a multilevel, integrated analysis of policy choice include Gourevitch (1986) and Haggard (1990).

for politicians' reregulation strategies, we thus need to consider additional factors.

Regime Institutions. Regimes are the formal and informal rules of a political system that determine how authoritative decisions are made and who may participate in the decision making process (Collier 1979:402–3). Regime institutions have an important impact on reregulation because they define *who holds authority to make regulatory policy.* In federal regimes, for example, state and local governments may have authority over aspects of regulatory policy in their jurisdictions, which means that reregulation processes can unfold differently across subnational units and may involve intergovernmental competition to control policy areas abandoned by the federal government. In unitary regimes, by contrast, potentially autonomous policy jurisdictions usually do not exist at the subnational level, and reregulation is thus likely to be a territorially more uniform process than in federal systems. Nevertheless, a unitary system, too, can experience varied reregulation dynamics, with variation occurring across economic sectors, rather than administrative units, and involving interagency, rather than intergovernmental, bargaining.

Regime institutions also shape reregulation strategies by defining *the structure of the policymaking process.*[17] This structure helps determine the political tasks incumbents need to accomplish in order to achieve their policy objectives. In regimes with multiple veto points (e.g., systems in which executive power is checked by a legislature and judiciary), politicians may face complex challenges in securing consent from actors empowered to overturn or modify their policy initiatives. Regulatory policy in such contexts is likely to be a collective output that reflects the preferences of multiple actors from different government agencies and organizations. By contrast, in regimes with few veto points (e.g., systems in which policy can be made or changed by executive fiat), regulatory policy often reflects the preferences and political styles of a handful of leaders and their advisers.[18]

Finally, regime institutions influence regulatory policy by determining *the responsiveness of politicians to societal interests.* Regime institutions shape incumbents' career incentives by defining those to whom they are

---

[17] Immergut (1992); Tsebelis (1995).
[18] Such centralized regimes are exemplified by "delegative" and "majoritarian" democracies. See O'Donnell (1994) and Lijphart (1984).

accountable. In competitive multiparty democracies, for example, elected officials often face strong incentives to represent citizens in their districts because their career fortunes hinge on winning reelection (Mayhew 1974). In such contexts, incumbents are downwardly accountable and thus highly responsive to societal interests. In other types of regimes, by contrast, incumbents may be upwardly accountable to political elites and, hence, relatively unresponsive to societal groups. For example, in nondemocratic systems and in democracies with highly centralized parties or constitutional prohibitions against immediate reelection, performing constituency service can mean pleasing political elites, not societal interests.

Because they shape the responsiveness of politicians to societal pressures, regime institutions help explain how much their reregulation projects reflect the preferences of societal groups. If regime institutions give politicians compelling incentives to respond to societal demands, interest groups may exert decisive influence over reregulation strategies. By contrast, if regime institutions generate only weak incentives to serve societal interests, incumbents can have more freedom choosing reregulation strategies.

Policy Repertoires.   Although I assume politicians are motivated mainly by the goals of gaining and retaining office, regulatory policies are not necessarily optimal career boosters. Politicians often have distinct *policy repertoires* that condition their policy decisions and may lead them to support regulatory policies that do not enhance their career fortunes. Policy repertoires are coherent frameworks of beliefs, values, and ideas that prescribe a course of policy choice and implementation. These repertoires include conceptions about the proper role for government and the appropriate means of government intervention. They can also include specific understandings and expectations about the political effects of different regulatory policies. Policy repertoires shape incumbents' perceptions of both the types of policy tools at their disposal and the methods available for manipulating these tools to create political dividends.[19]

Policy repertoires consist of more than just expert knowledge transmitted by policy analysts and professional economists. In addition to embodying such *pure* policy knowledge, politicians' repertoires are anchored in practical, *applied* knowledge, based on their accumulated expe-

---

[19] On ideas and policymaking, see Hall (1997).

rience in government and potentially distorted interpretations of expert prescriptions. Policy repertoires may be shaped in profound and enduring ways by a politician's formative career experiences. Consequently, rather than mirroring current expert consensus, policy repertoires may reflect outdated, past prescriptions.

Data about incumbents' career paths and memberships in political cohorts or generations should help explain the content of their policy repertoires. For example, incumbents with extensive experience administering statist policies may have distorted understandings of how neoliberal reforms should be implemented. These understandings can lead them to interpret core neoliberal imperatives, such as achieving macroeconomic stabilization and increasing exports in sectors with comparative advantages, not as mandates for shrinking the state's role, but rather as tasks that require expanding it.

By recognizing how beliefs, values, and ideas can shape policy choices, a politician-centered perspective need not reduce incumbents to faceless calculators of costs and benefits. Although it is a helpful and powerful simplification to assume that incumbents seek mainly to maximize their career fortunes, these efforts are framed by historically constructed, potentially idiosyncratic understandings about the range and consequences of policy options. A focus on policy repertoires thus illuminates *how* incumbents pursue political survival and helps explain why, for example, politicians seeking support from similar constituencies may have quite different policy agendas.

The influence of repertoires on policy choice should increase with the degree of autonomy incumbents have from societal forces. If politicians enjoy significant autonomy from societal pressures, their beliefs and ideological orientations can play a decisive role in their choice of reregulation strategies.

Institutional Outcomes: An Interactive Perspective

At the most general level, I argue that the politics of reregulation leads to two institutional outcomes: *oligarchic* policy frameworks that generate monopoly rents for a narrow group of elites, or, alternatively, *mass-based* policy frameworks that distribute benefits widely to nonelite groups. Oligarchic frameworks are as inefficient as they are exclusionary. If neoliberal reforms always resulted in oligarchic outcomes, it would be difficult not to condemn them as a disastrous hoax. By contrast, mass-based frameworks are inclusionary and can potentially promote cooperation between societal organizations and government that improves economic efficiency and performance. If neoliberal reforms always led to this kind of outcome, even their harshest critics might find merits in such policies. As we shall see, both oligarchic and mass-based outcomes are in fact possible, as are a number of intriguing intermediate outcomes between these two extremes.

To explain these contrasting outcomes, I focus initially on reregulation projects launched by incumbent politicians. Scholars have correctly emphasized the disorganizing effects of neoliberal policies and economic crisis on societal groups, especially organized labor.[20] Coupled with the powerful incentives neoliberal reforms give incumbents to deploy regulatory policy as a political weapon, these effects provide a strong basis for inferring that reregulation projects are launched by politicians, not by interest groups.[21] A focus on politicians should thus offer the best vantage point for explaining reregulation initiatives.

As noted, however, politicians are not completely free in their choice of reregulation projects: Political institutions and societal forces constrain their policy options. If the institutions of government give politicians only weak incentives to serve societal interests, they can have significant freedom when choosing reregulation strategies. By contrast, if these institutions generate compelling incentives to respond to societal demands, the configuration of societal interests has an important influence on politicians' strategies. When private elites dominate the political arena, incumbents face strong incentives to launch *crony capitalist* reregulation projects that create monopoly advantages for these elites. If implemented successfully, crony capitalist projects result in oligarchic outcomes.[22] Alternatively, when mass-based groups dominate, politicians have compelling incentives to pursue *neocorporatist* reregulation projects that

---

[20] See, for example, Zermeño (1990); Geddes (1995); and Hagopian (1998a).

[21] Of course, politicians often try to anticipate how societal actors will respond to their policy choices, especially if regime institutions give them incentives to attend to societal interests. Hence, even in the absence of organized societal pressures, political incumbents may try to incorporate societal preferences into their policy decisions.

[22] The term "crony capitalism" was commonly used to refer to the political economy of the Philippines under the patrimonial regime of Ferdinand Marcos. See, for example, Hutchcroft (1998). The literature on the important role of oligarchs in Latin American politics is also relevant here. See, for example, Collier (1976); Cardoso and Faletto (1979); Collier and Collier (1991); and Hagopian (1996).

deliver economic benefits to such groups.[23] If implemented successfully, neocorporatist projects lead to mass-based outcomes. In contexts where neither elite nor mass actors dominate, the configuration of societal forces cannot predict reregulation strategies. Rather, politicians' policy repertoires help explain whether they choose crony capitalist or neocorporatist strategies.

Although societal actors may not make the first move in reregulation processes, they can have a decisive impact on the institutional outcomes of such processes. Societal groups have stakes in how markets are reregulated, and politicians' reregulation projects can supply incentives and focal points that help them surmount barriers to collective action and mobilize to defend their interests. Hence, depending on the strengths and strategies of societal groups, the new institutions for market governance that result from politicians' reregulation strategies can deviate significantly from what these politicians had intended.[24]

For example, when politicians launch crony capitalist projects, a mass-based outcome is possible if strong grassroots movements mobilize and can find allies to help them offset the power of societal elites. By contrast, if grassroots organizations are weak, an oligarchic outcome is likely. In the face of neocorporatist projects, powerful societal elites may be able to block a mass-based outcome. Consequently, neocorporatist projects are most likely to succeed when societal elites are weak. Even if these elites are weak, however, conflict can nevertheless occur between politicians and mass-based organizations over the terms of reregulation. To reward their supporters and punish their opponents, politicians may try to restrict the distribution of benefits created by neocorporatist projects. These projects can thus spark intense struggles over access to benefits because excluded groups may mobilize to gain inclusion.

The strategies of groups excluded by neocorporatist projects have a decisive impact on the outcomes of reregulation. If such groups engage and seek to modify the neocorporatist project, they may be able to achieve robust institutions for market governance that help improve their welfare. By contrast, if excluded groups try to defeat the project, reregulation is

---

[23] The concept of neocorporatism has played an important role in work on European political economy. See, for example, Schmitter and Lehmbruch (1979); Goldthorpe (1984); and Katzenstein (1984, 1985).

[24] As we shall see in the case material analyzed in subsequent chapters, reregulation projects often had the unintended consequence of galvanizing societal opposition that forced politicians to modify their projects.

likely to result in political polarization and weak economic institutions that contribute little to welfare.

In sum, to explain the institutional outcomes of reregulation, we should analyze strategic interactions between politicians and societal groups as they negotiate the terms of reregulation.[25] This interactive perspective connects reregulation projects launched "from above" by political incumbents to responses to these projects "from below" by societal groups. As we shall see in subsequent chapters, making this connection is a crucial step toward explaining the new institutions for market governance that replace those destroyed by neoliberal reforms.

A Subnational Comparative Method

The following chapters apply the politics of reregulation framework to the case of Mexico, a country that between the late 1980s and 1995 was widely regarded as a textbook example of successful neoliberal reform.[26] The analysis focuses on the deregulation of coffee, Mexico's most important agricultural export. That deregulation, which involved the dismantling of a massive state-owned enterprise, was orchestrated by the same technocratic team responsible for earning the country's reputation as a neoliberal success story. The Mexican coffee sector thus represents an interesting case of government withdrawal from agricultural markets in the context of a neoliberal policy shock.

More important, the Mexican coffee sector provides an excellent opportunity for showing how the politics of reregulation framework presented above can explain the different kinds of new institutions that result from neoliberal reforms. Instead of unleashing free markets, neoliberal reforms in the coffee sector led to new institutions for market governance, as actors who previously had not intervened in the regulation of coffee moved to control policy areas abandoned by the old state-owned enterprise. Most notably, the governments of Mexico's coffee-producing states sought to

---

[25] In its dual focus on political actors and societal groups, this interactive perspective is similar to the "state in society" approach developed in Migdal, Kohli, and Shue (1994). For related approaches, see Collier and Collier (1991); Skocpol (1992); Fox (1993); and Evans (1995, 1996a, b).

[26] Upbeat assessments of Mexico's neoliberal reforms prior to the peso devaluation of December 1994 include Nelson (1990a) and esp. Córdoba (1994).

establish subnational regulatory frameworks and essentially reregulate what federal law had deregulated.[27] The new institutions that resulted from these state-level reregulation processes had dramatically different distributive and developmental consequences.

To explain these divergent outcomes, this book employs a subnational comparative method, which proves to be an especially powerful way to analyze the politics of reregulation. By focusing on the politics of reregulation across four of Mexico's most important coffee-producing states, I use *intranational* comparisons of hypothesized explanatory variables to highlight causal patterns and regularities.[28] Moreover, interviews with over two hundred state and federal government officials and local coffee producers anchored my understanding of the goals and strategies of the actors involved in reregulation processes. The interviews helped situate the actors in the context of the institutions and structures of strategic interaction that constrained them. By setting the motives and actions of specific individuals at the center of analysis, the interviews also helped me detect the causal mechanisms that generate the observed associations among the explanatory variables.[29]

---

[27] Mexico is a federal system with 31 states.

[28] Because they have potentially autonomous policy jurisdictions at the subnational level, federal political systems are especially appropriate settings for making comparisons across subnational units. Indeed, students of federal countries, such as Brazil, Germany, India, Russia, Spain, and the United States, have already put the subnational comparative method to good use. See, for example, Linz and de Miguel (1966); Kohli (1987); Anderson (1992); Skocpol (1992); Brace (1993); Hagopian (1996); Herrigel (1996); Stoner-Weiss (1997); Tendler (1997); and Varshney (in press). Although Mexico's federal structure also offers excellent opportunities for comparing state and municipal units, few have exploited these possibilities (Fox 1996; Rubin 1996, 1997; and Graham 1971 are exceptions). The paucity of comparative studies of subnational units probably reflects conventional scholarly wisdom about the highly centralized nature of the Mexican political system. See, for example, Reyna and Wienert (1977) and Centeno (1997). My research challenges this view by showing that political regimes with distinct dynamics exist at the subnational level. This finding suggests that the comparative analysis of state politics offers a powerful, if underutilized, methodological tool for understanding Mexico's ongoing political and economic transformation.

[29] On the fundamental role of mechanisms in social science explanation, see Hedström and Swedberg (1998) and Elster (1999, esp. ch. 1). According to Hedström and Swedberg (1998:7), "The search for mechanisms means that we are not satisfied with merely establishing systematic covariation between variables or events; a satisfactory explanation requires that we are also able to specify the social 'cogs and wheels' that have brought the relationship into existence." In the present study, the behavior and choices of politicians and producer organizations are these cogs and wheels.

Although the subnational comparative method combines controlled case comparisons with a close sensitivity to case material in much the same way as the well-known "small-N" comparative method,[30] the focus on subnational political units offers two critical advantages for studying the politics of reregulation. First, by making it easier to establish control over cultural, historical, ecological, and socioeconomic conditions, a focus on subnational units helps pinpoint how different kinds of institutions channel political ambition. Indeed, because the four Mexican states I have selected – Oaxaca, Guerrero, Chiapas, and Puebla – are all located in southern Mexico, have large indigenous populations, and are among the poorest in the country, I am able to establish control over nonpolitical variables to a far greater extent than is usually possible in conventional small-N analyses.[31] Thus my subnational focus is especially appropriate for the politician-centered perspective that this book adopts to explain reregulation projects.

Second, the subnational comparative method helps overcome a major limitation of existing work on the politics of neoliberal reform: extreme dependence on aggregate, national-level data. This striking "whole-nation bias" has obscured the possibility that neoliberal reforms, rather than unleashing market forces, can trigger reregulation processes at the subnational level.[32] Looking below the national level by disaggregating countries along territorial lines makes it easier to see that neoliberal reforms in fact result in different kinds of new institutions for market governance. This novel perspective, in turn, highlights why we need to move beyond previous work by shifting the focus from the politics of neoliberal reform to the politics of reregulation.

In addition to comparing subnational political units, this study reflects another key methodological decision: I have chosen to analyze a single economic sector. A multisectoral study that, in addition to coffee, also included petroleum, automobiles, and corn would provide a stronger basis for drawing conclusions about broad trends in Mexico's economy.

---

[30] On the small-N comparative method, see Lijphart (1971) and Collier (1993).

[31] The subnational comparative method does not necessarily improve control over such nonpolitical variables, however, as there may be as much, if not more, variation within countries as between them. For example, states in southern Mexico may have more in common with subnational units in neighboring Guatemala than with states in northern Mexico. Consequently, the use of the subnational method does not in itself guarantee greater control over potential explanatory variables.

[32] On "whole-nation bias" see Rokkan (1970:ch. 2) and Lijphart (1975:166–9). See also Locke (1995) for an insightful critique of the "national models" perspective in comparative political economy.

Although the transformation of the Mexican economy is a fascinating topic,[33] the aim of this book is not to explain that transformation, but rather to develop a set of general concepts, propositions, and arguments about the politics of reregulation. To achieve this goal, a *one sector, many places* research strategy that compares political rather than sectoral units proved essential. Implementing this research strategy required a territorially widespread industry. Because coffee production plays a major economic role across several southern Mexican states with contrasting interest groups, political institutions, and party systems, the coffee sector provided an ideal sectoral lens for studying the politics of reregulation.

In its reliance on a one-sector, many places research design, this book resembles important cross-national studies in political economy by scholars such as Robert Bates, Peter Evans, Terry Karl, and Jeffrey Paige.[34] These studies have shown that making comparisons across distinct territorial units in a single sector is an effective way to analyze how political variables shape outcomes such as economic performance and policy choice. Although the present analysis also compares cases that are matched in terms of the economic sector, it deals differently with the inescapable trade-off between (1) the ability to hold nonpolitical conditions constant and (2) the ability to generalize. On the one hand, as stated above, this book combines a focus on one sector with a focus on subnational territorial units in a single country, a research design that is better able to control for nonpolitical factors. On the other hand, because the cases are drawn from one country, this research design is less able to test the generalizability of my explanations. To mitigate this trade-off, the concluding chapter shows how my subnational cases bear crucial similarities to types of national cases and can thus be treated as proxies for national ones.[35] These similarities strengthen the overall generalizability of my argument about the politics of reregulation because they provide a basis for inferring that the causal patterns and mechanisms that I have found in subnational units also occur in national units.

---

[33] A number of studies have focused on the overall transformation of the contemporary Mexican economy. See, for example, Lustig (1992); Ros (1994); and Teichman (1995).

[34] Bates (1997); Evans (1995); Karl (1997); and Paige (1997).

[35] Przeworski and Teune's (1970) "substitution" rule illustrates one way to employ this technique. Another strategy for potentially increasing the generalizability of subnational studies involves comparing subnational units from *different* countries. On how game-theoretic tools can help strengthen the generalizability of single-country studies, see Bates et al. (1998:230–8).

In sum, this book employs an innovative method that combines a focus on a single economic sector with controlled comparisons across subnational political units. Because it highlights how neoliberal reforms, rather than unleashing market forces, result in different types of new institutions for market governance, this method provides a new way of looking at the consequences of neoliberalism. Thus the subnational comparative method serves as an essential tool for shifting the focus from the politics of neoliberal reform to the politics of reregulation.

Looking Ahead

The chapters that follow provide a subnational comparative analysis of the politics of reregulation in Mexico. The analysis starts by comparing four Mexican states. This cross-case perspective highlights the key variables that account for the contrasting institutional outcomes of reregulation. The book then turns to an in-depth study of the *process* of reregulation in each of the four states. By setting the motives, strategies, and choices of specific actors (that is, politicians and producers) at the center of analysis, this within-case perspective highlights the causal mechanisms that generate and explain the politics of reregulation. Finally, the focus shifts to a broadly comparative viewpoint by exploring how the framework and findings presented here can be extended to other cases.

Chapter 2 applies the politics of reregulation framework to the case of the Mexican coffee sector. The chapter shows how the dismantling of a massive, state-owned enterprise triggered projects by subnational politicians to reregulate coffee markets. The varying responses of grassroots organizations of small producers, in turn, determined the various types of new institutions for market governance that resulted from these reregulation projects. These contrasting outcomes had dramatically different consequences for the welfare of producers and their ability to compete in global markets. By utilizing controlled comparisons across four major coffee-producing states, Chapter 2 also underscores why the subnational comparative method is an especially strong tool for analyzing the politics of reregulation.

Chapters 3 to 6 analyze distinct reregulation scenarios by focusing on the politics of reregulation in four Mexican states. Chapter 3 analyzes the case of Oaxaca, where the state government launched an authoritarian, neocorporatist reregulation project. A powerful grassroots producers' movement mobilized against the project, pursuing a strategy that combined a focus on economic development goals with efforts to modify the project. Because this strategy emphasized nonpartisan economic objectives that did not pose a political threat to the state government, the government was eventually willing to accommodate the producers' organizations. The accommodation resulted in an inclusionary, mass-based outcome that enhanced welfare by making producers more competitive in export markets. Thus the case of Oaxaca raises the intriguing possibility that the task in contemporary Mexico, as well as in the many other developing countries with authoritarian corporatist heritages, may be to make corporatism work by making it inclusive and participatory, rather than to get rid of it. This case also shows how politicians in pursuit of power can unintentionally supply institutional raw materials that grassroots organizations may be able to transform into institutions for market governance that help them compete in global markets.

Chapter 4 analyzes the case of Guerrero, where producers' organizations joined a broader struggle for political democracy in Mexico, thereby choosing a partisan strategy aimed at defeating the state government's neocorporatist project. This strategy narrowed the possibilities for accommodation between the government and the producers' organizations, a process that resulted in exclusionary institutions for market governance that delivered virtually no benefits to the farmers. Thus the case of Guerrero highlights the difficulties of achieving inclusionary forms of corporatism in the context of an authoritarian political regime pursuing neoliberal economic reforms. In such a situation, one of the costs of choosing to be a democrat first and a producer second may be losing the opportunity to construct new economic institutions that could help improve welfare.

Chapters 5 and 6 show why neoliberal reforms in contexts with powerful private-sector elites, rather than resulting in unregulated markets, are likely to trigger crony capitalist reregulation projects intended to generate monopoly rents for oligarchs. Chapter 5 analyzes the case of Chiapas, where alliances between strong grassroots organizations and reformist, federal government officials offset the power of private elites, thereby making it possible to build inclusionary institutions for market governance even in a polarized context with powerful oligarchs. When neoliberal policies are implemented in places with strong oligarchs, such coalitions between grassroots movements and external allies are probably a necessary condition for a mass-based outcome.

The alternative scenario is seen in Chapter 6, an analysis of the case of Puebla, where reformist federal officials lacked organized pressure from below and thus failed in their efforts to prevent an oligarchic outcome. This failure shows the difficulties of building and sustaining reformist coalitions where grassroots movements are not strong. The case of Puebla thus serves as a sobering reminder that, rather than leading to the efficient allocation of resources by competitive markets, neoliberal reforms in contexts with powerful oligarchies and weak grassroots organizations are likely to result in new regulatory institutions that generate monopoly rents for private elites.

The final chapter synthesizes the argument and explores how the four reregulation scenarios seen in the Mexican case can help us understand the politics of reregulation in other countries. The chapter concludes with a broad research agenda for a comparative political economy of post-neoliberalism.

Chapter 2

From Deregulation to Reregulation in the Mexican Coffee Sector

At the end of the 1980s the Mexican government launched a massive deregulation of agriculture. For the mostly foreign-trained technocrats who designed these neoliberal economic reforms, the coffee industry posed perhaps the easiest target for deregulation. Although an entrenched state-owned enterprise – the Mexican Coffee Institute (INMECAFE) – dominated the industry, a powerful grassroots movement of small coffee producers had already mobilized against it.[1] Thus, neoliberal reformers had strong societal allies, making government retrenchment in the coffee sector an easy task.[2]

Yet this easy retrenchment had surprising consequences. Rather than leading to unregulated markets, as the neoliberal reformers had anticipated, the dismantling of INMECAFE resulted in the formation of new institutions for market governance. Actors who had not previously intervened in coffee sought to control policy areas vacated by the old state-owned enterprise. Most notably, the governments of Mexico's coffee-producing states established new regulatory frameworks and essentially

---

[1] Ejea and Hernández (1991); Santoyo Cortés et al. (1994); and Krippner (1997).

[2] In Mexico's rural sector, the neoliberal reformers consisted mainly of a team of technocrats in the Ministry of Agriculture and Water Resources (SARH) led by a U.S.-trained economist, Luis Téllez Kuenzler, who served as undersecretary for planning in the early 1990s. Between 1989 and 1994, this team succeeded in implementing reforms that dramatically cut government subsidies to the rural sector, ended the special legal status of communal lands farmed by peasants, and dismantled massive state-owned companies, of which INMECAFE was a prime example. Téllez explicitly sought to "modernize" the Mexican countryside via market-oriented reforms (see Téllez Kuenzler 1994). On the implementation of neoliberal reforms in rural Mexico, see Fox (1994a); Encinas et al. (1995); de Grammont (1996); Cornelius and Myhre (1998); Snyder and Torres (1998); and Snyder (1999a).

reregulated what federal law had deregulated. As a result, by 1994, Mexico's coffee producers found themselves confronting a new and complex regulatory environment and not the free markets that had been anticipated.[3]

In the states of Oaxaca and Chiapas the politics of reregulation led to *participatory policy frameworks* that gave organizations of small producers central roles in policymaking. In addition to meeting producers' demands for a voice in the policy process, these participatory frameworks fostered partnerships between the public sector and producer organizations that helped improve the welfare and market competitiveness of small coffee farmers. In the states of Guerrero and Puebla, by contrast, the politics of reregulation resulted in *exclusionary policy frameworks* that denied small producers access to the policy process. These exclusionary frameworks generated spoils for political and economic elites, undermining the efficiency of coffee production.

Why did reregulation in Oaxaca and Chiapas result in institutions that promoted the welfare of small farmers and offered them new channels for participating in policy decisions? Why did reregulation in Guerrero and Puebla yield institutions that served elite interests and reproduced long-standing patterns of exclusionary, top-down policymaking? This chapter explains these divergent outcomes by deploying the analytic framework developed in Chapter 1. The first part of the chapter focuses on the reregulation projects pursued by Mexico's state governments. It shows how the three variables emphasized by the politician-centered perspective that I introduced in Chapter 1 – regime institutions, societal forces, and policy repertoires – explain the different reregulation projects launched by the governments of Mexico's coffee-producing states. In analyzing societal forces, this section also provides important information on the economics of the coffee sector. The second part of the chapter shifts to an interactive perspective in order to explain how bargaining between politicians and producer organizations over the terms of reregulation resulted in distinct policy frameworks across the four states. A concluding section sum-

---

[3] The present analysis covers the period 1980–96. This time frame encompasses the period preceding the implementation of the neoliberal reforms, the episode of reform itself, and the period of institutional reconstruction after neoliberalism. As of 1996 the institutional outcomes analyzed in this study were firmly in place. Although the time frame does not allow an assessment of the long-term durability of these institutions, this study's focus on the shorter-term institutional outcomes of the neoliberal reforms does provide important insights about the politics of reregulation.

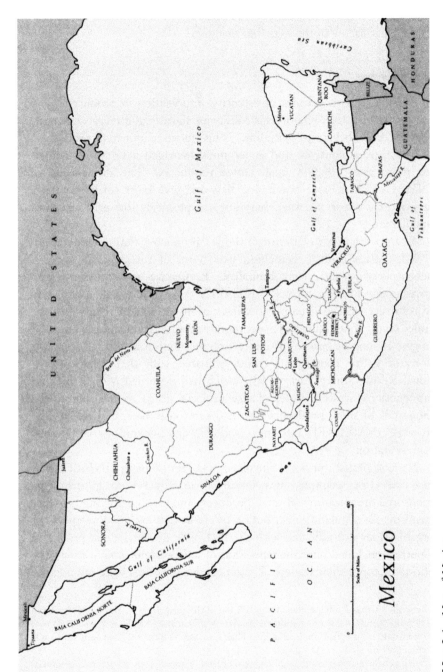

Map 2.1 Map of Mexico

23

marizes the comparative analysis and provides an introduction to the case studies that follow in the next four chapters.

Reregulating Coffee

In 1989, after two decades of extensive intervention in production and marketing of coffee, one of Mexico's major sources of foreign exchange,[4] INMECAFE began to withdraw. This move eliminated production supports, price controls, and government-managed marketing channels for more than 190,000 small coffee producers.[5] The dismantling of INMECAFE's massive purchasing network gave most small producers few options but to sell their harvests at exploitively low prices to local middlemen.

The governments of the major coffee-producing states responded to INMECAFE's exit by launching two types of reregulation projects: neocorporatism and crony capitalism. In Oaxaca and Guerrero state government officials took INMECAFE's departure as an opportunity to resurrect weakened corporatist institutions of political control in the coffee sector. They launched neocorporatist reregulation projects intended to give monopoly control of interest representation to official organizations of coffee producers – those affiliated with the ruling Institutional Revolutionary Party (PRI), which had governed Mexico without interruption for six decades. These projects aimed to incorporate the thousands of small producers who had previously been tied to the PRI through INMECAFE into new authoritarian institutions of interest representation.

Neocorporatist projects involved (1) transferring INMECAFE's resources (for example, agro-industrial machinery) to government-sponsored organizations of small producers and (2) constructing new mechanisms for regulating distribution of credit that excluded independent organizations not affiliated with the PRI. The neocorporatist project in Guerrero included outright repression of independent organizations and efforts to coopt their leaders. These coercive measures were intended to

---

[4] Between 1970 and 1989, coffee averaged 5.1% of the total value of Mexico's exports and 34% of the total value of agricultural exports. Approximately 2 million Mexicans depend on income from coffee production. See Díaz Cárdenas et al. (1991) and Santoyo Cortés et al. (1994).

[5] Small producers have less than 20 hectares of land (approximately 50 acres). The official proposal for INMECAFE's dismantling is found in INMECAFE (1989a).

24

force the organizations to renounce their independent status and affiliate with the PRI's National Peasants' Confederation (CNC).

In Chiapas and Puebla, by contrast, state governments pursued crony capitalist reregulation projects designed to benefit the coffee oligarchy. These projects sought to turn the clock back to the period preceding the intervention of INMECAFE, when local elites had dominated the coffee economy. In contrast to neocorporatist projects, which focused on building new institutions of interest representation for small producers, crony capitalist projects focused on resurrecting the monopoly control by local elites over coffee processing and marketing.

Crony capitalist projects involved efforts to create marketing boards managed by the coffee oligarchy. The government of Chiapas, for example, sought to give prominent members of the oligarchy control over licenses to export coffee. In addition to creating a major source of rents and income for these private elites, this new regulatory power promised to help keep small producer cooperatives out of export markets and thus force them to sell at low prices to elite-owned exporting firms.

What explains these different responses to the withdrawal of INMECAFE? Why did the governors of Oaxaca and Guerrero pursue neocorporatist strategies focused on smallholders, while the governors of Chiapas and Puebla chose crony capitalist policies oriented toward oligarchs? The analysis below shows how Mexico's federal regime institutions gave state governors powerful incentives to reregulate policy areas vacated by neoliberal reforms. Although institutional factors help explain *why* governors reregulated, such factors do not explain *how* they reregulated. To account for their different reregulation strategies, we need to focus on societal forces and policy repertoires. In states where small producers or oligarchs dominated the coffee sector, such as Guerrero and Puebla, societal forces explain governors' strategies: The goal was to benefit the dominant group. By contrast, in states with no dominant producer group, such as Oaxaca and Chiapas, policy repertoires played the decisive role: Governors chose strategies that fit their ideological orientations.

Regime Institutions: Federalism and Upward Accountability

In federal systems, subnational units are potentially autonomous policy jurisdictions. Mexico's federal institutions empowered politicians at the subnational level, especially state governors, to reregulate what federal law had deregulated.[6] Governors had the authority to establish public agencies at the state level that often played important regulatory roles. During the mid-1980s, for example, when the federal government was starting to dismantle public enterprises at the national level, the governor of Guerrero formed twenty-eight new public enterprises which intervened across a range of key economic sectors (Estrada Castañón 1994a:51). Federalism thus helped define the politics of reregulation in the coffee sector as an essentially subnational process.

Other core regime institutions structured accountability in ways that gave Mexican governors autonomy from societal interests. A constitutional prohibition against immediate reelection to the same office weakened incentives for elected officials to perform constituency service. Furthermore, virtually all governors were directly appointed by the president, who could also dismiss them.[7] Because governors could not run for reelection and typically hoped to move on to high-level federal posts after completing their terms, their career futures depended on loyalty to actors at the "center" (that is, to the president, or a national-level political faction). Hence, governors were *upwardly* accountable to national political elites, not *downwardly* accountable to voters and interest groups. But if such upwardly accountable governors had autonomy from interest groups inside their states, why would they seek to deliver targeted benefits to such groups and respond so eagerly and decisively to opportunities for reregulating markets? To answer these questions requires more knowledge about governors' motivations than can be deduced from the formal rule prohibiting reelection.

Until the late 1990s Mexico had a hegemonic party system in which virtually all governors were affiliated with the PRI (Cornelius 1996). Ruling party elites expected governors to maintain political stability and deliver quotas of votes to the PRI in local and federal elections. Governors who failed to accomplish these tasks saw their career fortunes plummet, and many were dismissed by the president, as illustrated vividly by the case of Guerrero, where since 1917 only six governors had completed a full, six-year term.[8] To get out the vote and maintain political

---

[6] Rodríguez (1997:ch. 2) and Snyder (1999b).

[7] Martínez Assad and Arreola Ayala (1987). Although state governors in Mexico were formally elected, these elections were not free, fair, and competitive under the old PRI regime.

[8] González Oropeza (1987) and Estrada Castañón (1994a:75). Similarly, the state of Chiapas has had an average of approximately one governor per year since its creation 170 years ago. See Castro Aguilar (1995:41).

Table 2.1. *Institutional Context of Gubernatorial Decision Making in Mexico (1940–1995)*

Rules of Office	Incentives for Governors
Formal rule	
No reelection	Upward accountability to political masters; ignore societal groups
Informal rules	
Appointed by the president	Upward accountability to political masters; ignore societal groups
Future career prospects depend on national-level elites (e.g., the president and PRI leaders)	Upward accountability to political masters; ignore societal groups
Maintain political stability	Downward responsiveness to societal interests; seek alliances with societal groups
Secure quotas of votes for PRI	Downward responsiveness to societal interests; seek alliances with societal groups

Note: With the exception of no reelection, these rules of office did not apply to the handful of governors in several northern states after 1988 who were affiliated with the center-right opposition National Action Party (PAN). None of those states produces significant amounts of coffee.

stability, governors faced pressures to ally with local groups such as traditional elites who controlled patronage networks and political bosses from the PRI's corporatist confederations. Even in the absence of a direct electoral connection, then, the unwritten rules of Mexico's political system gave governors strong incentives to forge support coalitions, at least to the extent necessary to maintain stability and deliver sufficient votes for the ruling party on election day.[9] Paradoxically, upward accountability to political elites at the center created pressures for downward responsiveness by governors to local interest groups.

Hence, as summarized in Table 2.1, although most governors entered office with autonomy from societal interests, their autonomy was bounded by the dual imperatives of securing votes for the PRI and maintaining stability. When the federal government implemented neoliberal reforms, reregulation offered a potent new tool for governors to build the selective alliances with societal groups they needed to manage these

---

[9] The term "electoral connection" is from Mayhew (1974).

imperatives and protect their career fortunes. Moreover, the economic reforms coincided with a period of growing pressures for democratization and escalating political instability across Mexico. This timing made reregulation an especially important political weapon at the subnational level.[10]

These political pressures against the national PRI regime help explain an intriguing paradox: If governors were upwardly accountable to presidents, how were they able to pursue regulatory policies that cut against the neoliberal agenda set at the national level by President Carlos Salinas de Gortari (1988–94)? Because of the growing threat to the PRI's hegemony from opposition parties, Salinas had strong incentives to allow state governors to choose policies that helped secure electoral majorities and maintain political stability, whether or not these policies conformed to orthodox neoliberal prescriptions. In fact, Salinas did not merely tolerate subnational deviations from the neoliberal line, he selectively promoted them. At the height of his government's neoliberal reforms, for example, Salinas gave his support to a populist governor in Oaxaca whose policies diverged dramatically from neoliberal orthodoxy.[11] Despite the president's strong preference for neoliberalism, the political imperatives of mobilizing support for his party and maintaining social stability inhibited him from using his power to impose those preferences universally on subnational governments.[12]

Taken together, federalism and upward accountability help us understand why reregulation in Mexico was a process led by state governors. However, regime institutions by themselves cannot explain governors' reregulation strategies: Although governors labored under similar institutional constraints, they chose strikingly different strategies. To account for this variation, we need to turn from regime institutions to societal forces and the policy repertoires available to governors.

---

[10] On these pressures for democratization, see, for example, Cornelius, Gentleman, and Smith (1989) and Cook, Middlebrook, and Horcasitas (1994).

[11] Similarly the National Solidarity Program (PRONASOL), a national program of poverty alleviation and social provisions implemented by the Salinas administration, has been understood as an illiberal counterpart to the neoliberal project that was intended to help generate the political support necessary for the economic reforms to proceed. See, for example, Cornelius, Craig, and Fox (1994).

[12] Ironically, the capacity of Mexico's federal government to implement and sustain neoliberal reforms at the national level actually may have depended on the ability of state governors to mobilize political support by reregulating at the subnational level.

Societal Forces: Coffee and Power

Chapter 1 argued that societal forces help define the menu of reregulation strategies available to politicians. In the four Mexican states analyzed in this book, the configuration of societal forces was shaped in crucial ways by the economics of coffee and the old policy regime that existed under INMECAFE. An explanation for the different reregulation strategies pursued by governors thus requires that we explore how each of these two factors influenced the power and interests of societal actors.

The Economics of Coffee. To understand how the economics of coffee shaped societal forces across Mexico's coffee-producing states, we need to consider three key aspects of coffee: production, processing, and marketing. In terms of *production*, coffee is an ideal peasant cash crop. It requires little except land and labor, and it can be profitably grown by peasants with extremely small plots of land. Farmers can invest in coffee one tree at a time, and although coffee trees take three to five years to bear fruit, they can easily be interspersed with food and other crops. This possibility helps peasants weather the start-up phase of coffee production.[13] Because of these low economic barriers to entry by peasants, coffee production systems can support a very large number of small producers. In Mexico, for example, more than 190,000 smallholders grow coffee, and some 2 million people rely on income from this crop (Santoyo Cortés et al. 1994:3–5). As we shall see, the large number of small producers makes coffee a politically strategic sector in Mexico.

Although coffee has a strong affinity with smallholder cultivation, it can also be grown using a variety of other production techniques. Most notably, coffee is profitably cultivated on large, specialized estates with mechanized production technologies. Many coffee-producing countries thus have a dual production profile where large estates with high yields and high input costs coexist with small holdings that use low-cost production techniques.[14] Mexico's coffee sector has such a dual profile. In 1991, 270 large, specialized estates of more than 50 hectares accounted for 13.5 percent of total national production, whereas approximately 190,000

---

[13] De Graaf (1986:75–9); Shafer (1994:190–2). According to Shafer (1994:190), "sweat equity is the peasants' main investment."

[14] Pieterse and Silvis (1988:8–10); De Graaf (1986:77–81).

smallholders with less than 10 hectares accounted for 66 percent of overall production.[15]

Coffee *processing* – which basically involves separating the pulpy "cherry" from the hard bean inside, then cleaning and drying the bean – requires considerable capital.[16] Nevertheless, peasants are not excluded from coffee processing. Low-cost, rustic processing techniques are one option for peasants, although such techniques usually result in a low-grade product. Alternatively, peasants can join together in cooperatives to build sophisticated, modern processing facilities that are able to mill high-grade coffee.[17]

In Mexico's coffee-producing states, the question of who would control the processing of coffee grown by smallholders was a defining axis of conflict. Prior to the neoliberal reforms, the struggle over processing was essentially a three-way contest among (1) an "agrarian-industrial" oligarchy comprising large coffee farmers who owned processing machinery;[18] (2) the federal government agency, INMECAFE; and (3) peasant-owned cooperatives (Nolasco 1985). The implementation of neoliberal reforms at the end of the 1980s transformed the structure of conflict by eliminating the federal government as a participant. As we shall see, a pivotal issue in the politics of reregulation involved whether agrarian-industrial oligarchs or, alternatively, peasant-owned cooperatives would emerge as the dominant processors of smallholder coffee.

With regard to *marketing*, coffee is primarily an export crop. On average, 70 percent of Mexico's national coffee production is exported, making coffee an important source of foreign exchange.[19] Like the issue

---

[15] Approximately 3,700 producers with 10 to 50 hectares accounted for the remaining 20% of total production (Santoyo Cortés et al. 1994:26).

[16] Processing, and especially marketing, are the most profitable areas of the coffee industry. One study estimated that only 16% of the final price paid by a European consumer of Mexican coffee reaches the actual producer; the bulk of the value-added is retained by processing and marketing agents (Santoyo Cortés et al. 1994:127).

[17] The two main processing methods are "unwashed," or "dry processing," and "washed," or "wet processing." Wet processing produces higher quality coffee but is more complicated and requires more capital. Although both techniques are employed in Mexico, wet processing is far more common. On the various techniques for processing coffee, see Marshall (1983:33–6).

[18] See Paige (1997:ch. 2) for a nuanced discussion of "agrarian" and "agro-industrial" coffee elites in Central America. My use of the term "agrarian-industrial" reflects the frequent fusion of these two factions into a single, cohesive elite in southern Mexico. See, for example, Guillén Rodríguez (1994).

[19] As noted above, between 1970 and 1989, coffee averaged 5.1% of the total value of Mexico's exports and 34% of the total value of agricultural exports (Díaz Cárdenas et al.

of who would control processing, control over access to export markets was also a major area of conflict in the coffee sector. Until 1989 the federal government held control over access to export markets because INMECAFE managed the quotas allocated to Mexico by the International Coffee Organization (ICO), which regulated international trade in coffee. The collapse of the ICO's global quota system in June and July 1989 combined with INMECAFE's dismantling pitted peasant cooperatives against coffee oligarchs in a struggle for access to international markets.[20] The cooperatives saw INMECAFE's exit as an opportunity to move smallholders closer to international markets, whereas the oligarchs sought to force smallholders to sell at low prices to their export firms. How this conflict between peasants and oligarchs would be resolved was a central issue in the politics of reregulation.

Because coffee is an export crop, to understand the configuration of societal forces in Mexico's coffee-producing states we need to consider the structure of the international coffee market.[21] The most striking feature of the market is its extreme price volatility: Prices change often and swing widely. This volatility is rooted in inelastic demand and strong fluctuations of supply due largely to the vagaries of weather in Brazil, the world's largest coffee producer.[22] According to Shafer, "the problem is on the supply side" because a grower's yield in good years can be ten times those in bad ones (Shafer 1994:194). Moreover, the effects of booms and busts in coffee prices create a long-run tendency toward oversupply and price stagnation. During a bust, farmers offset low prices with more intensive picking, which tends to depress prices further. During a boom, farmers typically engage in new planting. However, supply is price inelastic in the medium run because coffee trees require at least three years to bear fruit and at least

---

1991:67). The overwhelming majority of Mexico's coffee exports are to the United States (e.g., 87% in 1992 and 1993). Germany is the second most important destination for Mexican coffee. See Martínez Morales (1996:139–44) and Santoyo Cortés et al. (1994:115–19).

[20] See Bates (1997) on the functioning and collapse of the ICO.

[21] See Bates (1997:176–7) for a succinct summary of this market structure. See also Pieterse and Silvis (1988) and Shafer (1994:194–5).

[22] Brazil currently accounts for an average of 20–30% of world coffee exports. The second largest producer is Colombia, with an average of 10–20% of the market. Mexico accounts for approximately 4% of world exports (Bates 1997:22; Santoyo Cortés et al. 1994:9). On price elasticities of supply and demand in the world coffee market, see Bates (1997:196) and Santoyo Cortés et al. (1994:125–6). See also the econometric studies by Adams and Behrman (1976) and Winters and Sapsford (1990).

six years to reach their maximum production levels. This lag means that increases in quantity are not proportionate to increases in price. Because coffee trees produce for well over a decade, farmers are reluctant to uproot them when prices plunge, a situation that further exacerbates the problems of oversupply and price instability.[23]

The politics of reregulation in Mexico occurred during a five-year bust in international coffee prices (1989–94) that resulted from the collapse of the ICO's quota system in the middle of 1989.[24] As seen in Table 2.2, this low-price conjuncture saw a severe drop in the price of Mexican coffee, which plunged to its lowest level in fifteen years.[25] Paradoxically, low prices actually helped *strengthen* peasant-owned processing and marketing cooperatives. When prices are high, peasant cooperatives are prone to lose members because they often lack sufficient working capital to compete with deep-pocketed multinational and large-scale private buyers. Consequently, cooperatives tend to face serious problems of defection at the grassroots level during price booms. By contrast, when prices are low, small coffee farmers have a strong incentive to join cooperatives because alternative marketing channels are less readily available. Thus, hard times can greatly strengthen solidarity among small coffee farmers, helping them

[23] The imperfectly competitive structure of the international coffee market further contributes to the instability of prices. The coffee market can be characterized as an oligopoly with a "competitive fringe." Because Brazil and Colombia control approximately 40% of total production, they can strongly influence prices by retaining or releasing stockpiled coffee. By contrast, the other producing countries (including Mexico) are "price takers" who must sell at the price set by supply, demand, and the two dominant producers. Nevertheless, these other countries are able to free ride on the efforts of Brazil and Colombia to manage supply, thereby undercutting the capacity of the big two to raise and stabilize prices (Shafer 1994:194–5). Although the ICO was intended to help stabilize world coffee prices, it is unclear whether it actually had this effect because the few studies of the ICO's impact on prices suffer from methodological problems that appear to have resulted in erroneous estimates (Bates 1997:16–19).

[24] On July 3, 1989, the economic clauses of the International Coffee Agreement (ICA) were suspended, thus ending the ICO's global system of quotas regulating coffee prices. The immediate consequence was a frenzy of indiscriminate exporting by producer countries, which caused a severe oversupply of coffee and a sharp drop in prices, which fell approximately 40% between June and August 1989. Low prices continued during the next several years (Santoyo Cortés et al. 1994:13). See also Bates (1997).

[25] Four major types of coffee are traded in the international market: Colombian, Brazilian, "Other Milds," and Robusta. Coffee from Colombia tends to command the highest price. Coffee from Brazil fetches a middle-range price. Mexican coffee falls into the category of Other Milds, which are also produced in Central America. Other Milds command a price that is between Brazilian and Colombian coffee. Robusta coffees are produced mainly in Africa, and they command the lowest price (Bates 1997:22).

32

Table 2.2. *International Price of "Other Milds" Coffee (1975–1995)*

Year	Average International Price (U.S. Cents per Pound)
1975	65.41
1976	142.75
1977	234.67
1978	162.82
1979	173.53
1980	154.20
1981	128.09
1982	139.87
1983	131.69
1984	144.25
1985	145.56
1986	192.74
1987	112.29
1988	135.10
1989	106.96
1990	89.15
1991	84.97
1992	63.64
1993	69.91
1994	148.53
1995	149.30

Notes: Four major types of coffee are traded in international markets: Colombian, Brazilian, Other Milds, and Robusta. Mexican coffee falls into the category of Other Milds, which are also produced in Central America.

Source: Martínez Morales (1996:103).

overcome the barriers to collective action posed by their large numbers.[26] As we shall see, the bust of 1989–94 saw a remarkable proliferation of new organizations of small coffee producers across Mexico.[27] This explosion of peasant organizing altered the distribution of power between

[26] On the collective action problems facing smallholders, see Bates (1981:87–90) and Shafer (1994:210–13).
[27] Moreover, many older organizations saw their membership bases expand during this period. As discussed below, peasant organizing in the coffee sector was also spurred by the withdrawal of INMECAFE.

smallholders and oligarchs in ways that had an important impact on the politics of reregulation.[28]

Although the international coffee market clearly had a significant influence on the politics of reregulation, it was by no means a determining factor. First, the price of coffee alone does not predict the distribution of power among societal forces. For example, cooperatives of small producers in the state of Puebla remained weak despite the incentives for collective action associated with the price bust of the early 1990s. More importantly, actors in each of the four Mexican states faced the same international market, yet the institutional outcomes of reregulation varied in complex and dramatic ways across the cases. As we shall see, to explain these contrasting outcomes we need to look beyond the economics of coffee by focusing on the distinct political profiles of each state.

The Old Policy Regime: INMECAFE's Regulatory Framework. In an effort to strengthen political control in the countryside and increase foreign exchange earnings, Mexico's federal government began to intervene heavily in the coffee sector in the early 1970s. The principal instrument of government intervention was the state-owned enterprise, INMECAFE, which in addition to controlling export quotas for all producers,[29] organized and dramatically expanded smallholder production.[30] By opening alternative, government-managed processing and marketing channels that guaranteed small producers a set minimum price, INMECAFE competed with the agrarian-industrial oligarchy that had traditionally controlled the processing and exporting of peasant-grown coffee. In the 1970s, INMECAFE built a widespread network of collection centers that it used to purchase coffee directly from small producers. These collection centers were frequently placed near the warehouses of the private elites to whom small producers previously had sold their crops,

---

[28] It is interesting to consider a counterfactual scenario: Had the politics of reregulation in Mexico unfolded during a price *boom* small-producer cooperatives might have been far weaker, thereby increasing the likelihood of exclusionary policy frameworks favoring the coffee oligarchy.

[29] As noted, export quotas were part of the ICO's regulatory regime.

[30] Between 1970 and 1983, the number of coffee farmers with 10 hectares or less increased by nearly 30%, from approximately 88,000 to 113,000 (Nolasco 1985:42). The same period saw a 57% increase in the total land planted with coffee, from 328,573 hectares in 1970 to 581,025 hectares in 1983 (Nolasco 1985:32). INMECAFE played a key role in these increases.

a choice of location that symbolized the potential threat INMECAFE posed to these elites (Nolasco 1985:195).

In addition to purchasing and marketing coffee, INMECAFE also provided subsidized loans to small producers. These credits posed a further threat to the hegemony of local elites, because their control over the coffee economy often depended on the ability to make loans that small producers were obliged to repay with their crops. To distribute its loans, INMECAFE organized small producers into a vast network of Economic Units for Production and Marketing (UEPCs) (Nolasco 1985:185). The UEPCs operated as credit associations in which all members were collectively responsible for repaying the loans from INMECAFE. To obtain a loan, producers were usually obliged to sell their harvest to INMECAFE, a requirement that guaranteed its supply of coffee.[31] By 1984, most of Mexico's small coffee farmers were organized into 2,671 UEPCs (Nolasco 1985:187). In the early 1980s, INMECAFE's network of UEPCs and collection centers enabled it to purchase annually more than 40 percent of total national coffee production (Nolasco 1985:186–7).

In the late 1970s and throughout the 1980s, thousands of small farmers also organized autonomously, forming cooperatives that aimed to open new marketing channels free from the control of both the agrarian-industrial elite and INMECAFE (Ejea and Hernández 1991). Indeed, dissatisfaction with INMECAFE fueled much of this organizing. During the early 1980s, for example, peasant producers seeking higher guaranteed prices launched major protests against INMECAFE. The producers also wanted credits to arrive on time, fair weighting of their crops, and an end to the frequent cooptation of local INMECAFE staff by private elites. Ironically – in light of INMECAFE's populist mission to end the dependence of peasant producers on private-sector middlemen – many of the new producer organizations saw INMECAFE as "the biggest middleman of all"![32]

In the course of mobilizing against the state-owned enterprise, many small producers shifted their energies from trying to improve

---

[31] Hernández and Celis (1994:220). Besides covering the costs of production inputs, these loans often helped small producers survive until their crops were ready to harvest.

[32] Interviews with participants in the mobilizations of the early 1980s, Mexico City, 1995. As Nolasco (1985:194) notes, INMECAFE was most successful when it "reproduced, step by step, a [production and marketing] structure that was virtually identical to the private sector scheme."

INMECAFE's performance to the goal of building their own autonomous marketing cooperatives. In 1988 many of these independent cooperatives formed a national-level umbrella organization, the National Coordinating Network of Coffee Producers' Organizations (CNOC).[33] The collapse of international coffee prices the following year contributed to a wave of grassroots organizing that helped CNOC rapidly establish itself as Mexico's most important independent federation of small coffee producers, thus ending the longstanding hegemony of official producer federations affiliated with the PRI. As we shall see, the varied strengths and strategies of the grassroots producers' organizations affiliated with CNOC had a decisive impact on how coffee markets were reregulated after the dismantling of INMECAFE.

In sum, INMECAFE radically transformed the balance of societal forces in Mexico's coffee sector by spurring a dramatic increase in the number of organized small producers. Two decades of statist policies thus made it virtually impossible that the implementation of neoliberal reforms would automatically revive the prestatist status quo, a period when most peasant coffee producers were disorganized and hence at the mercy of a long chain of middlemen controlled by local oligarchs. The emergence of powerful organizations of small producers in the 1980s – especially the autonomous cooperative movement that INMECAFE ironically helped spawn – meant that the neoliberal reforms, rather than resurrecting the prestatist status quo, would result in new kinds of economic institutions.

Subnational Variation in Societal Forces. Under INMECAFE's supervision, a relatively uniform national scheme regulated Mexico's coffee sector in the 1970s and 1980s. At the end of the 1980s, neoliberal reforms destroyed this national-level framework, giving state governors opportunities to launch new regulatory initiatives at the subnational level. Because the configuration of societal forces varied across the coffee-producing states, governors faced different constraints on the range of reregulation strategies available to them when INMECAFE withdrew.

As seen in Tables 2.3 and 2.4, there was no coffee oligarchy in Guerrero, where production was carried out almost entirely by peasants.[34]

---

[33] Ejea and Hernández (1991); Hernández (1992).

[34] Despite their comparatively small numbers, the coffee producers in Guerrero were extremely well organized and concentrated in politically volatile areas of the state, factors that considerably amplified their power. See Chapter 4.

Table 2.3. *Stratification of Coffee Producers, by State (in Hectares)*

Size of Holding	Number of Coffee Producers			
	Oaxaca	Guerrero	Chiapas	Puebla
Less than 20 hectares	55,064	10,414	73,314	30,534
20–100 hectares	191	83	312	154
more than 100 hectares	36	0	116	11
Total producers	55,291	10,497	73,742	30,699

Note: Order of cases corresponds to order of presentation in the text. One hectare equals 2.47 acres.
Source: INMECAFE (1992).

Table 2.4. *Stratification of Coffee Holdings, by State (in Hectares)*

Size of Holding	Land Area in Coffee Production			
	Oaxaca	Guerrero	Chiapas	Puebla
Less than 20 hectares	155,759 (89.64)	48,327 (95.18)	188,415 (82.55)	51,522 (84.81)
20–100 hectares	8,615 (4.96)	2,447 (4.82)	14,650 (6.42)	7,010 (11.54)
more than 100 hectares	9,392 (5.40)	0 (0.00)	25,191 (11.04)	2,220 (3.65)
Total land for Coffee production	173,766 (100.00)	50,774 (100.00)	228,256 (100.01)	60,752 (100.00)

Notes: Figures do not necessarily reflect producers' total land holdings, but only the amount of land area used for coffee production. Figures in parentheses are the percentage of total land for coffee production. Because of rounding, percentages do not always add to 100. One hectare equals 2.47 acres.
Source: INMECAFE (1992).

By contrast, Chiapas, Oaxaca, and Puebla had dual production profiles in which large coffee estates coexisted with thousands of smallholders. Powerful coffee oligarchies operated in each of these three states. The strength of the oligarchs in Chiapas and Oaxaca can be seen in their control over land.[35] In Chiapas, 116 large farmers owned an average of 217 hectares of

---

[35] Control over production and agro-industrial infrastructure was also an important component of the power of the coffee oligarchs in Chiapas and Oaxaca.

Table 2.5. *Organizational Density in the Mexican Coffee Sector*

	Total Number of Producers	Number of Producers Affiliated with an Organization	Organized Producers (%)
Oaxaca	55,291	43,813	79.2
Guerrero	10,497	11,161	106.3
Chiapas	73,742	77,806	105.5
Puebla	30,699	14,170	46.2

Notes: The total number of producers is from INMECAFE's last census, which was completed in May 1992. The number of producers affiliated with an organization (for example, CNC, CNOC) is from the National Coffee Trust Fund's (FIDECAFE) census, which was completed in September 1994. In addition to the two-year lag between censuses, the fact that in Guerrero and Chiapas the number of producers affiliated with an organization exceeds the total number of producers probably reflects the strong incentives producer organizations had to inflate their ranks in the 1994 FIDECAFE count, because access to FIDECAFE and other federal government resources depended on organization size. Despite such incentives, the percentage of organized producers in Puebla was still far smaller than in the other states.
Sources: INMECAFE (1992); FIDECAFE (1994).

coffee and collectively controlled more than 25,000 hectares. In Oaxaca, a tight-knit group of 36 big farmers owned an average of 261 hectares of coffee and controlled more than 9,000 hectares. In Puebla, where a far smaller group, 11 large landholders, owned an average of 202 hectares and together controlled just over 2,000 hectares, the power of the coffee oligarchy was based more on its control of agro-industrial infrastructure than on direct land ownership (see Chapter 6).

Although all four states had large numbers of smallholders, the power of small producers varied. As summarized in Table 2.5, which shows the level of organizational density in the coffee sector in each state, small producers were extremely well organized and thus quite powerful in Chiapas, Guerrero, and Oaxaca, whereas they were far less organized and hence weak in Puebla.[36]

In Guerrero and Puebla the distribution of power between small producers and oligarchs strongly constrained the reregulation strategies open to governors when INMECAFE withdrew. As illustrated by Figure 2.1, the absence of a coffee oligarchy in Guerrero eliminated crony capitalism as a feasible strategy. In Puebla, by contrast, the weakness of small pro-

---

[36] Organizational density refers to the percentage of coffee farmers in each state who were affiliated with a producer organization such as CNOC or the CNC.

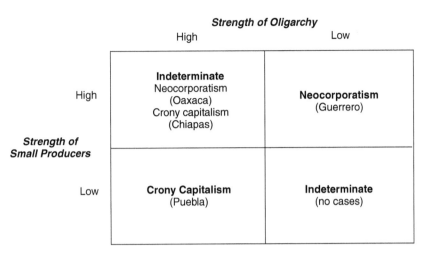

Figure 2.1. Societal Forces and Reregulation Strategies.

ducers eliminated neocorporatism as a viable strategy. Although this sub-national variation in socioeconomic structure helps explain why crony capitalism was not possible in Guerrero, and, conversely, why neocorporatism was not possible in Puebla, a focus on societal forces alone is not sufficient to account for reregulation initiatives. Reregulation projects resulted from the actions of governors, not from lobbying by coffee farmers. Hence, societal pressures do not explain why politicians sought to reregulate in the first place: If they had been passive instruments of organized societal interests, the governors of Guerrero and Puebla should have responded to INMECAFE's withdrawal by doing nothing. The absence of a "reregulation lobby" in the two cases strengthens the argument that the impulse to reregulate stemmed not from interest group pressure but from governors' institutionally defined career incentives.

The cases of Oaxaca and Chiapas, which saw different reregulation projects despite similar configurations of societal forces, further underscore why a focus on socioeconomic structures cannot by itself explain politicians' reregulation strategies. Figure 2.1 shows that the coexistence of powerful small producers' movements and powerful oligarchies in Oaxaca and Chiapas weakly constrained governors' reregulation options: They could have chosen neocorporatist or crony capitalist projects. To understand why the governor of Oaxaca pursued neocorporatist policies favoring smallholders, whereas the governor of Chiapas chose crony capitalist policies favoring oligarchs, we need to analyze their divergent policy repertoires.

Policy Repertoires: Populists and Neoliberals

The governors of Oaxaca and Chiapas when INMECAFE withdrew had sharply contrasting policy repertoires. The governor of Oaxaca had a *populist* repertoire, whereas the governor of Chiapas had a *neoliberal* repertoire. Because societal forces in the coffee sector weakly constrained the policy options available to these two governors, their policy repertoires played a decisive role in their choice of reregulation strategies.

The governor of Oaxaca at the end of the 1980s, Heladio Ramírez López (1986–92), was a relic of a bygone populist era. He had launched his political career in the early 1970s with support from close advisers to President Luis Echeverría Alvarez (1970–6), and his political identity and policy preferences were forged in the mold of the statist-populist policies dominant at that time.[37] Ramírez articulated his vision of the appropriate role for government in Oaxaca through the concepts of "Social Liberalism" and "Social Rule of Law."[38] According to the official document summarizing the "legislative framework" for Ramírez's administration, the Social Rule of Law sought to "overcome the limitations of classical, individualistic liberalism, which was characterized by state abstention, through dynamic state intervention that . . . promotes social justice and welfare." The document criticized perspectives that saw the government's role as limited to contract enforcement and protection of individual rights, because they were "imbued with a liberal, individualistic philosophy that paralyzes [the state's] activity and minimizes its role" (Gobierno del Estado de Oaxaca 1992a:18). Ramírez codified government responsibility for economic management by amending the state constitution to stipulate that "the state will plan, implement, coordinate, and orient local economic activity and carry out the regulation and promotion of activities corresponding to the public interest" (ibid.:45–6).

Given Ramírez's populist roots and policy orientation, it is not surprising he responded to the dismantling of INMECAFE by choosing the neocorporatist option over the crony capitalist one. The governor even

---

[37] Camp (1995:575). Ramírez's political biography is analyzed in detail in Chapter 3.
[38] The concept of "Social Liberalism" was in vogue at the national level after 1988. See Centeno (1997:205–10).

40

appointed a former director of INMECAFE, Fausto Cantú Peña, to supervise the reregulation of the coffee sector. During the mid-1970s, as a member of President Echeverría's populist government, Cantú had orchestrated INMECAFE's transformation into a giant public enterprise with more than seven thousand employees. Under Ramírez's guidance, Cantú founded a new state government agency, the State Coffee Council of Oaxaca, which he envisioned as a mini-INMECAFE that would resurrect on a subnational scale the regulatory framework he had built fifteen years earlier at the national level (Cantú Peña 1989).

In Chiapas, by contrast, the governor had a starkly different conception of the appropriate role for government. José Patrocinio González Garrido (1988–93) avidly embraced President Salinas's project of market-oriented reform and economic "modernization."[39] González's economic policies combined privatization of government-owned enterprises with promotion of external investment in tourism, urban consumer goods and services, and agricultural exports.[40]

In the rural sector, González's government sought to expand large-scale commercial agriculture, especially cultivation of tropical fruit. Export crops, such as banana, mango, melon, and citrus fruits, received special attention, as evidenced by the government's major project to upgrade the state's port facilities (Mota Marín 1994:338–9). Large agribusiness export firms benefited most from these improvements in infrastructure, which helped lower their transportation costs and reduce shipment delays.

In contrast to Ramírez in Oaxaca, who pumped resources into a new government agency (the State Coffee Council) and launched a massive campaign of public investment that targeted small coffee producers, González sought to increase the export potential of large-scale agribusiness, which neoliberal doctrine defined as the most efficient, competitive form of production. And neoliberalism, with its emphasis on increasing the export potential of big agribusiness in sectors where Mexico had comparative advantages, was interpreted by the governor of Chiapas as legitimating crony capitalist reregulation. To promote coffee exports, González created a small regulatory agency charged mainly with issuing export licenses. He appointed owners of major coffee exporting firms to

[39] On the complex meanings of modernization among Mexican political elites, see Centeno (1997:ch. 7).
[40] See the analysis of González's government in Chapter 5.

supervise the new agency.[41] In the hands of these elites, regulatory power served as a tool for attempting to block efforts by cooperatives of small producers to export their coffee directly instead of selling it at exploitively low prices to elite-controlled exporting firms.[42] The governor's response to the dismantling of INMECAFE, which was congruent with his neoliberal policy orientation, gave agrarian-industrial oligarchs in Chiapas an important opportunity to reassert their monopoly control over coffee exports.

Negotiating the Terms of Reregulation

Although Mexico's state governors moved decisively to control the policy domains vacated by INMECAFE, they often failed to achieve their vision of how reregulation should be carried out. In Chiapas, for example, a powerful small-producer movement blocked the governor's efforts to help the oligarchy. And in Oaxaca, despite the governor's plan to impose an exclusionary policy framework that favored smallholders affiliated with the PRI, small-producer organizations autonomous from the ruling party gained a dominant position within the new framework. As summarized in Figure 2.2, three key variables explain these different outcomes: the type of reregulation project; the response of small-producer organizations[43]; and the strength of those organizations.

The cases of Oaxaca and Guerrero highlight how the responses of producer organizations to governors' projects influenced the results of reregulation. Although neocorporatist projects were launched in both states, reregulation led to strikingly different institutional outcomes because of the distinct strategies of powerful producer movements. In Oaxaca the producer movement pursued an *engaged productivist* strategy, which combined a focus on economic development goals with efforts to modify the governor's project. Because this strategy emphasized nonpartisan economic objectives that did not pose a political threat to the state govern-

---

[41] Subcomité Especial de Producción y Comercialización del Café (1989a).
[42] Interviews with leaders of coffee producer organizations, Chiapas, Nov. 1995.
[43] As we shall see in the case chapters, producer organizations that pursued distinct strategies often coexisted in the four states, and, at times, the strategies of specific organizations changed. Hence, a note of caution is warranted concerning "the response" of small-producer organizations to reregulation projects, as this response was often complex and not necessarily monolithic. To manage this complexity, this study focuses on the dominant strategy in each case, that is, the strategy chosen by the most important producer organizations in each state.

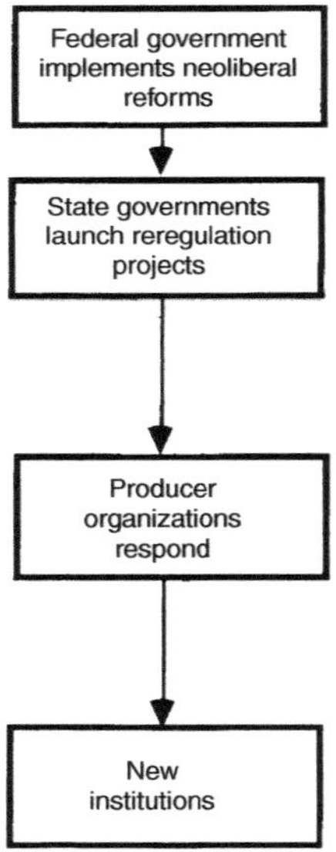

	Oaxaca	Guerrero	Chiapas	Puebla
Reregulation Project	Neocorporatist	Neocorporatist	Crony capitalist	Crony capitalist
Response of Small-Producer Organizations	**Engaged productivist strategy** (i.e., seek to modify project)	**Partisan strategy** (i.e., seek to defeat project)	Disengaged productivist strategy (i.e., ignore project)	Disengaged productivist strategy (i.e., ignore project)
Strength of Small-Producer Organizations	High	High	**High**	**Low**
New Institutions	Participatory policy framework	Exclusionary policy framework	Stalemate; federal intervention subsequently leads to participatory policy framework	Exclusionary policy framework

Federal government implements neoliberal reforms → State governments launch reregulation projects → Producer organizations respond → New institutions

Figure 2.2. The Politics of Reregulation in Oaxaca, Guerrero, Chiapas, and Puebla: Reregulation Project, the Response and Strength of Small-Producer Organizations, and Resulting Institutions.

43

ment, the governor was eventually willing to accommodate the producer organizations, and a participatory policy framework resulted. In Guerrero, by contrast, the powerful producer movement joined a broader struggle for political democracy in Mexico, thereby choosing a *partisan* strategy aimed at defeating the governor's project. Consequently, the possibilities for accommodation between the governor and the producer organizations were much weaker than in Oaxaca, and an exclusionary framework resulted.

The cases of Chiapas and Puebla show how variation in the strength of producer organizations affected reregulation processes. In both states producer organizations faced crony capitalist projects and chose *disengaged productivist* strategies, which ignored the governor's project and focused instead on autonomous, grassroots development initiatives. Despite these similar producer responses, reregulation led to distinct institutional outcomes because of the varied strengths of the producer movements in the two cases. In Chiapas reregulation resulted in a stalemate because a powerful producer movement was capable of stalling the governor's crony capitalist initiative through its refusal to participate in his scheme. This stalemate was subsequently broken by an alliance between federal government reformists and the producer movement, which led to a participatory framework. By contrast, because a weak producer movement in Puebla lacked the capacity either to achieve a stalemate or to forge an alliance with federal reformists, reregulation resulted in an exclusionary framework.

The following sections analyze how institutions for market governance were reconstructed in each of the four cases after INMECAFE was dismantled. The discussion focuses on the interactions between state governors and producer organizations as they competed for influence over the new institutions that replaced those destroyed by the neoliberal reforms.

Participatory Policy Frameworks: Oaxaca and Chiapas

The cases of Oaxaca and Chiapas illustrate two distinct paths from deregulation to participatory institutions for market governance. In Oaxaca, the lack of a dominant socioeconomic group in the coffee sector enabled the governor to pursue his populist policy agenda when INMECAFE withdrew. He took advantage of this opportunity by launching a neocorporatist reregulation project designed to benefit small producers affiliated with the PRI's official peasant confederation, the CNC. When the governor launched his project in early 1989, a handful of autonomous small-producer organizations were operating outside the CNC. A further objective of the neocorporatist project was to contain and weaken these autonomous groups by restricting representation within the new policy framework to CNC affiliates.

Ironically, the governor's project had the opposite effect: Instead of undermining the independent producer organizations, it helped strengthen them. The threat of exclusion from the new institutions for market governance gave the independent organizations a powerful incentive to join forces and mobilize. They soon formed a statewide confederation of autonomous producer organizations, the Statewide Coordinating Network of Coffee Producers of Oaxaca (CEPCO). By offering marketing support and technical assistance, CEPCO rapidly recruited thousands of small producers who had previously depended on INMECAFE for these services. By late 1989, CEPCO was the most powerful producer organization in Oaxaca, comprising more than half of the state's 55,000 small coffee farmers.

CEPCO pursued an engaged productivist strategy, which integrated a focus on economic development goals with efforts to gain inclusion in the emerging state-level policy framework. The organization successfully challenged the governor's neocorporatist project, winning formal representation in the State Coffee Council, the new state government agency responsible for policy in the coffee sector. The council subsequently served as an arena in which the government of Oaxaca and the producer organizations designed innovative, collaborative programs that made small coffee farmers more competitive in global markets.[44]

In Oaxaca the combination of institution building from above (i.e., the governor's neocorporatist project) with organized pressure from below (i.e., CEPCO's engaged productivist strategy) resulted in new institutions that enhanced the efficiency and quality of smallholder production. Through his efforts to strengthen peasant support for the ruling party by reregulating coffee, the governor of Oaxaca unwittingly supplied institutional raw materials that a powerful grassroots movement was able to rework into a participatory policy framework.

In Chiapas, by contrast, reregulation took a different course. There the governor's reregulation project posed a major obstacle to constructing a participatory policy framework, in its reliance on a crony capitalist

---

[44] See the analysis of the State Coffee Council in Chapter 3.

strategy. The crony capitalist project rested on the assumption that small farmers should cede responsibility for coffee processing and marketing to elite-owned agro-industrial firms. Because the principal goal of most small-producer organizations in Chiapas was precisely to gain control of these lucrative processing and marketing activities, the crony capitalist project gave small farmers weak incentives to choose an engaged productivist strategy. In contrast to Oaxaca's small-producer organizations, which encountered a neocorporatist project compatible with their core economic objective of managing the processing and marketing of coffee, the small-producer organizations in Chiapas confronted a reregulation project premised on denying these very aspirations. Consequently, they pursued a disengaged productivist strategy, ignoring the governor's crony capitalist initiative and directing their energies instead toward autonomous economic development projects.[45] By launching their own marketing cooperatives, the small-producer organizations denied the elite-owned agro-industrial firms sufficient quantities of raw coffee to consolidate the crony capitalist scheme. The politics of reregulation in Chiapas thus initially led to a stalemate.

The stalemate ended in 1994 as a consequence of the Zapatista peasant rebellion in eastern Chiapas.[46] The severe threat of ungovernability posed by the Zapatistas induced reformist federal officials to ally with the small coffee producers' movement against the state government and coffee oligarchy. This reformist alliance defeated the crony capitalist forces, laying the foundations for a participatory policy framework.

In both Oaxaca and Chiapas powerful grassroots producer movements played pivotal roles constructing participatory institutions for market governance. But in Chiapas the governor's crony capitalist project supplied weak incentives and poor institutional ingredients for a Oaxaca-style reworking from below. To forge a participatory policy framework, the producer movement in Chiapas first had to defeat the crony capitalist coalition of the state government and the coffee oligarchy. External allies proved necessary to achieve this goal.

---

[45] Attempting to defeat the crony capitalist project would have been extremely costly for the small producers, given the state government's coercive capacities and demonstrated willingness to repress peasants. On state government repression in Chiapas, see Harvey (1994) and Pólito and González Esponda (1996).

[46] On the Zapatista uprising, see Collier with Quaratiello (1994) and Harvey (1994, 1998).

Exclusionary Policy Frameworks: Guerrero and Puebla

The cases of Guerrero and Puebla show how the politics of reregulation can result in exclusionary policy frameworks detrimental to small producers. Like his counterpart in Oaxaca, the governor of Guerrero also launched a neocorporatist project in response to INMECAFE's dismantling. In Guerrero, as in Oaxaca, a powerful small-producer movement organized outside the PRI's official peasant confederation. However, Guerrero's independent producer movement had consolidated at the beginning of the 1980s, significantly earlier than the independent movement in Oaxaca, which formed in 1989 in direct response to the governor's reregulation project. The early consolidation of Guerrero's independent movement shaped its reaction to the governor's reregulation project in ways that hindered the construction of a participatory policy framework.

After hotly contested presidential elections in July 1988, the coffee producers' movement in Guerrero became increasingly involved in partisan politics. The most important producer organization threw its support behind the center-left Party of the Democratic Revolution (PRD), and many rank and file became militant members of this new opposition party.[47] When the governor launched his neocorporatist reregulation project the following year, the independent producer movement had already committed itself to the struggle for political democracy. In contrast to the newly formed statewide producer organization in Oaxaca, CEPCO, which carefully avoided partisan affiliations and focused instead on engaging and modifying the governor's neocorporatist project, Guerrero's independent organizations pursued a partisan strategy intended to advance political democratization and defeat the neocorporatist project. In Guerrero the producers' choice of a partisan strategy contributed to politicization and polarization of the coffee sector, which led to an exclusionary policy framework that yielded virtually no economic benefits for the farmers.

In Puebla, by contrast, small producers had few options. An engaged productivist strategy was not feasible, because Puebla's small-producer organizations, like their counterparts in Chiapas, faced a crony capitalist project. Furthermore, the extreme weakness of Puebla's producer

---

[47] On the PRD, see Bruhn (1997).

movement due to its small size and limited cohesion eliminated the possibility of mobilizing to defeat the governor's project. Because of these constraints, Puebla's producer organizations had little choice but to pursue a disengaged productivist strategy.

In contrast to their powerful counterparts in Chiapas, who also chose such a strategy, Puebla's small-producer organizations were not strong enough to achieve a stalemate. In Puebla, as in Chiapas, reformist federal officials eventually attempted to intervene against the crony capitalist forces. These efforts failed, however, because of the weakness of Puebla's small-producer organizations. The absence of a strong producer movement undercut the potential for an alliance between grassroots organizations and reformist federal officials. Whereas such an alliance defeated the crony capitalist coalition and forged a participatory policy framework in Chiapas, the crony capitalist forces in Puebla faced no significant opposition. The politics of reregulation thus resulted in an exclusionary policy framework that served the interests of the oligarchy.

Conclusion

The analysis of the Mexican coffee sector confirms the value of the framework for explaining the politics of reregulation that I introduced in Chapter 1. Rather than unleashing free-market forces, the deregulation of coffee triggered reregulation projects by subnational politicians looking to control policy areas abandoned by the federal government agency, INMECAFE. Producer organizations responded to these reregulation projects in different ways. The interactions between politicians and producer organizations, in turn, resulted in contrasting institutions for market governance across Mexico's coffee-producing states. As we have seen, a dual focus on politicians' reregulation projects and the subsequent bargaining between politicians and societal actors over the terms of reregulation explained these varied institutional outcomes.

By juxtaposing the four cases in order to pinpoint causal relationships among hypothesized explanatory variables, this chapter emphasized one aspect of the subnational comparative method: controlled comparisons across subnational political units. The next four chapters, each of which focuses on the politics of reregulation in a particular Mexican state, emphasize another major component of the subnational comparative method: ethnographic analysis based on key informant interviews and participant observation. The textured evidence in subsequent chapters provides an in-depth look at the complex process of reregulation as it unfolded in each of the four cases. By zooming in on the motives, strategies, and choices of the key actors, this within-case perspective highlights the causal mechanisms that actually generate the relationships among the variables that were analyzed in this chapter. Thus the following chapters strengthen our understanding of the politics of reregulation and provide further support for my argument.

PART II

The Cases

3

*Remaking Corporatism from Below:
A Participatory Policy Framework
in Oaxaca*

The politics of reregulation in Oaxaca began with a surprising appointment. In late 1988, as efforts to deregulate coffee were intensifying at the national level, the governor of Oaxaca invited Fausto Cantú Peña to coordinate his government's policy for the state's coffee sector. Cantú, who had directed INMECAFE during the mid-1970s, was a relic of a bygone period of nationalist-populist policies.[1] He had orchestrated INMECAFE's transformation from a small federal agency with limited capacities to a giant enterprise with more than 7,000 employees. To the neoliberal technocrats who dominated national economic policy during the late 1980s, Cantú represented the worst excesses of the statist policies of prior decades: bloated, corrupt bureaucracy; a leviathan, paternalistic state; and irrational, antimarket government intervention.

The policy environment in Oaxaca differed dramatically from the environment at the national level, however. Oaxaca's governor, Heladio Ramírez López (1986–92), welcomed individuals like Cantú, whose nationalist ideology and talent for state building were out of step with the national-level policy of neoliberalism and state shrinking. In Ramírez's administration, advisers with strong nationalist-populist credentials wielded powerful influence.

Cantú's vision for Oaxaca's coffee sector was to build a new set of centralized government institutions to regulate the marketing of coffee. These regulatory institutions would be accompanied by corporatist mechanisms of controlled interest representation to manage producers' demands. In short, he sought to create a mini-INMECAFE, resurrecting on a smaller,

---

[1] For Cantú's perspective on economic policy, see the interviews with him in Carbot (1989).

subnational scale the regulatory scheme he had designed at the national level fifteen years earlier.

When he first arrived in Oaxaca in 1988, Cantú could not have imagined that his neocorporatist reregulation project would ultimately result in a curious institutional amalgam that corresponded neither to the state-controlled policy arena he envisioned nor to the unregulated markets advocated by his neoliberal nemeses in Mexico City. Instead, his neocorporatist project would be transformed from below by a grassroots small-producer movement. This transformation resulted in a participatory policy framework that stimulated collaborative efforts by organizations of small producers and Oaxaca's government to improve the welfare of coffee farmers.

This chapter explains the formation of Oaxaca's participatory policy framework in terms of the variables presented in Chapter 1. It shows how this institutional outcome resulted from the intersection of Cantú's neocorporatist project with a powerful, autonomous producer movement that eschewed partisan politics and focused on gaining inclusion in the emerging, post-INMECAFE policy arena. Moreover, the chapter analyzes how subnational authoritarian elites, through their efforts to seize political opportunities created by national neoliberal reforms, unintentionally provided incentives and institutional raw materials that helped grassroots organizations build a participatory policy framework.

The first section of the chapter explores how an individual like Cantú, whose policy prescriptions were anathema to the neoliberal technocrats who dominated economic policy at the national level in the 1980s, came to play a key role in a subnational policy jurisdiction. I argue that a populist political regime emerged in Oaxaca in the late 1980s, which in many ways reproduced at the subnational level the statist policies that had prevailed at the national level in the 1970s. By building new regulatory institutions and frameworks of controlled interest-group representation, this subnational populist regime sought to move into policy areas abandoned by the federal government as a result of neoliberal reforms.

The next section traces the evolution of the organizational profile of Oaxaca's coffee sector, analyzing the grassroots producer organizations that emerged during the 1970s and 1980s. These organizations would form the backbone of a new, statewide federation that subsequently coalesced in opposition to Cantú's project. During the critical juncture of 1989–90, this federation transformed Cantú's neocorporatist scheme into a participatory policy framework.

54

The final section focuses on the dynamics of the participatory policy framework by analyzing the performance of Oaxaca's State Coffee Council. It highlights how collaboration between producer organizations and the state government redefined the roles of grassroots organizations and government in ways that helped improve the welfare of small coffee farmers.

Political Context of Reregulation: The Populist Regime in Oaxaca

Heladio Ramírez López was a curious choice as the PRI's candidate in Oaxaca's gubernatorial election of 1986. Ramírez's political career had taken off in the early 1970s with the support of close advisers to President Luis Echeverría Alvarez (1970–6), and his political vision and policy preferences had been forged in the mold of the statist-populist policies dominant at that time. His policy orientations were strongly at odds with the neoliberal, technocratic approach characterizing Miguel de la Madrid's (1982–8) presidency. This technocratic orientation was reflected in de la Madrid's marked preference for gubernatorial candidates with strong administrative credentials.[2] Ramírez, by contrast, was a career politician with modest administrative experience.

In addition to being out of step with national policy currents, Ramírez was strongly opposed by Oaxaca's private sector elite. Local elites blamed the populist policies of the 1970s for intense social unrest that had rocked Oaxaca throughout that decade, resulting in the removal of a conservative, pro-business governor.[3] They saw Ramírez's nomination as the harbinger of another round of instability and government confrontation with the private sector. Oaxaca's most important newspapers vocally expressed the local elites' fears by responding to the news of Ramírez's nomination with headlines proclaiming a "black night for Oaxaca" and denouncing the candidate as a "delirious leftist" (*Noticias*, April 1 and 2, 1986).

Ramírez's unlikely nomination highlights an important feature of Mexican politics under the old PRI-dominated regime. Despite the

---

[2] De la Madrid's preference for technocrats as governors is illustrated by his choice of gubernatorial candidates such as the following: Rodolfo Félix Valdés in Sonora; the ex-secretary of energy, mines and parastatal industry, Francisco Labastida Ochoa, in Sinaloa; and the ex-secretary of agrarian reform, José Luis Martínez Villicaña, in Michoacán (Yescas Martínez 1991:29).

[3] On the fall of Governor Manuel Zárate Aquino (1974–7), see Martínez Vásquez (1990:ch. 4).

temptation to infer homogeneity across political subunits from the extreme centralization of the Mexican political system, one cannot simply "read off" the logics of subnational regimes from that of the national regime. During the sixty years of PRI hegemony, state governments were frequently characterized by policy orientations and political dynamics distinct from those of the national government. This divergence between subnational and national politics, however, did not necessarily mean that the conventional scholarly wisdom about the highly centralized nature of Mexico's political system was completely unfounded.[4] Indeed, Ramírez's nomination, which was imposed from the center against the wishes of local elites, confirms this view by illustrating that subnational deviations from the national rule could, in fact, be deliberately orchestrated and supported by national-level elites.

What motivates national political elites to promote such deviations? Or, to phrase the question differently, why would the president have supported a candidate like Ramírez whose policy preferences did not reflect his own, when, according to the rules of Mexican federalism, the president almost always hand picked candidates for governor? Many students of Mexican politics have noted the national PRI regime's heterogeneity, describing it as a coalition of diverse personalistic factions (*camarillas*) and policy currents.[5] This heterogeneity was reflected in the distribution of ministry portfolios and administrative positions, which were an important ingredient of the glue that held together the ruling coalition. The ruling coalition's heterogeneity also acquired a territorial expression through the distribution of governorships and municipal presidencies, which often represented quotas of power to PRI factions.

Ramírez's nomination can be understood in part as such a quota of power. Ramírez had powerful allies in de la Madrid's administration, most notably the Secretary of Planning and Budgeting, Carlos Salinas de Gortari, and the Secretary of Agriculture, Eduardo Pesqueira Olea.[6] His nomination as the PRI's gubernatorial candidate in Oaxaca thus highlights the important role that allies at the "center" (that is, at the national level)

---

[4] On the centralization of the Mexican political system, see Reyna and Wienert (1977); Centeno (1997); and Weldon (1997).

[5] See, for example, Smith (1979); Purcell and Purcell (1980); and Centeno (1997). On policy currents within the PRI regime, see Fox (1993:36–9).

[6] These allies did not necessarily share Ramírez's political ideology. For example, Salinas de Gortari, whom Ramírez had met while the former was a young undergraduate at the National Autonomous University of Mexico (UNAM), favored neoliberal policies.

often played in shaping the political fortunes of aspiring governors. At the same time, however, it would be a mistake to understand subnational regimes in Mexico as exogenously determined products of factional bargaining at the national level. The case of Ramírez's nomination also reveals how internal political processes within a state could decisively shape the outcome of that bargaining.

Ramírez was not the only candidate for Oaxaca's governorship who had powerful elite allies at the center. Jorge Tamayo López Portillo, because he was a member of the family of de la Madrid's predecessor, President José López Portillo (1976–82), also had close ties to high-ranking federal government officials. In addition to these allies, Tamayo López Portillo had important assets that Ramírez lacked. First, Oaxaca's private-sector elite did not oppose his candidacy. Second, given de la Madrid's preference for technocratic governors, Tamayo López Portillo's engineering background presumably made him an especially attractive candidate. Tamayo López Portillo's failure to receive the nomination illustrates how local political dynamics could influence factional bargaining at the center over governorships.[7]

In 1986 Oaxaca faced an ongoing crisis of governability. This crisis was not just a local phenomenon. Political unrest in Oaxaca had thrust itself into both the national and international arenas. Dissident political organizations in the city of Juchitán had made their local struggle for democratic reforms an international issue by seizing embassies in Mexico City. Moreover, a powerful statewide movement seeking internal democratization of the teachers' union formed a central pillar of a growing national movement. Finally, rapidly increasing migration from Oaxaca to the United States was becoming an international problem just as the issue of economic integration between Mexico and the United States was moving onto the national political agenda. Hence local politics in Oaxaca during the mid-1980s was having increasing repercussions in Mexico City and beyond.[8]

---

[7] In 1986 the "technocratic option" for Oaxaca was also available to de la Madrid in the form of candidate José Antonio Carranza Palacios. However, Carranza Palacios, according to Yescas Martínez (1991:45), "was rejected because he lacked the political experience needed to govern the state of Oaxaca. . . . [He] had proven himself to be a good administrator, with good relations with business groups, but Oaxaca needed something more than that."

[8] For analyses of the political situation in Oaxaca in the mid-1980s, see Martínez Vásquez (1990) and Sorroza Polo (1994). On the case of Juchitán, see Rubin (1997). On the teachers' movement, see Cook (1997) and Foweraker (1993).

Because of the external ramifications of the governability crisis in Oaxaca, de la Madrid could neither accommodate the state's private sector elites, who opposed a return to past populist policies, nor impose a technocrat whose policy preferences mirrored his own. Recognizing that different states required different styles of governance, the president chose the populist Ramírez to restore stability in Oaxaca.

In sum, while reconfirming the important role that the national PRI regime played in state politics, the case of Ramírez's nomination also reveals how subnational political dynamics could constrain that role, resulting in regimes at the state level with logics distinct from that of the national regime. Thus this case underscores the importance of a multilevel analytic perspective that treats subnational regimes as complex products of internal and external factors, rather than reducing them to mere outgrowths of a hegemonic, all powerful center.

Leadership and Ideology

Because of the highly personalistic nature of political power at the state level in Mexico, we need to analyze the leadership styles and career trajectories of governors in order to understand the dynamics of subnational regimes.[9] Ramírez was a career politician who had worked his way up the PRI hierarchy by holding a variety of appointed and elected party positions. A review of his political biography reveals his interest in, and engagement with, rural, social sector issues. This intense focus on the needs of the rural poor, which reflected Ramírez's self-described "passion for the countryside," would become the hallmark of his tenure as Oaxaca's governor. Ramírez's career trajectory also confirms the common perception about state politics in Mexico that "the road to the state house always passes through Mexico City." Like most recent state governors, Ramírez had spent most of his previous political career in the nation's capital.

Ramírez first arrived in Mexico City to complete his high school studies.[10] He launched his political career in 1959 at the age of twenty,

[9] See Snyder (1999b) and Rodríguez (1997:ch. 2).
[10] The biographical information on Ramírez presented in this and the following paragraphs is from Camp (1995:575) and "Heladio Ramírez López: Político con futuro," *Expresión!* 22 (May 1976). See also the interview with Ramírez's father in "Personajes de Oaxaca: Don Antonio Ramírez López," *Expresión de Oaxaca!* 31 (Dec. 1976–Jan. 1977), p. 31.

when he founded the PRI's Youth Tribunal. Through the Tribunal, which, as one of his close advisers put it, quickly became a "forum for aspiring politicians," Ramírez made important contacts with other young PRIistas, including future president Carlos Salinas, who participated in the Tribunal during the mid-1960s as an undergraduate at the National Autonomous University of Mexico (UNAM).[11] During this period, Ramírez also won several oratory contests, demonstrating a remarkable talent for public speaking. Ramírez's passionate, moving speeches would subsequently become a distinguishing feature of his governorship.

Between 1966 and 1970 Ramírez served as the PRI's director of youth for the Federal District (i.e., Mexico City). Through his involvement with these party youth organizations in the 1960s, Ramírez integrated himself into a political faction – the "nationalist current" – headed by then secretary of the interior, Luis Echeverría Alvarez (Yescas Martínez 1991:30–1). When Echeverría became president in 1970, Ramírez quickly emerged as a rising political star. According to local political lore in Oaxaca, when Ramírez accompanied Echeverría on a presidential visit to Oaxaca in the mid-1970s, Echeverría remarked, "This young man [Ramírez] will be governor of Oaxaca one day."

In 1976, at the end of Echeverría's administration, Ramírez won his first elected office, becoming a federal deputy for his home district of Huajuapan de León. Between 1977 and 1981, he served as president of the PRI's Regional Committee for the state of Oaxaca and, in 1982, was elected to the federal senate, where he chaired the Commission of Indigenous and Migrant Worker Affairs until his election as governor in 1986.

In addition to these elected and appointed party posts, Ramírez played an important role in the PRI's National Peasant Confederation (CNC). In 1972 he was appointed Agrarian Delegate to the city of Puerto Vallarta, a position he held until 1977. And in 1981 Ramírez joined the CNC's national leadership, becoming a member of its National Executive Committe and holding the position of secretary of union affairs. His work during this period focused on organizing agricultural workers, one of the most marginalized segments of the rural population. This rural unionizing project, which he described at the time as "a vehicle to guarantee social peace" in the context of increasing penetration of capitalist class relations into the Mexican countryside, presaged what would later become the

---

[11] Interview, Oaxaca, Oaxaca, June 1995.

centerpiece of his rural policy as governor: organizing rural producers within the folds of the CNC (Ramírez López 1981:11).

In sum, Ramírez was a paradigmatic *político*, whose strong institutional base within the PRI and considerable experience in elected office set him apart from the so-called *técnicos*, whose main political resource was technical expertise.[12] During de la Madrid's administration, *político* governors became less common because of the president's preference for governors with technocratic backgrounds. Examples of such *técnico* governors include the governor of Sinaloa, Fernando Labastida Ochoa (1986–92); the governor of Sonora, Rodolfo Félix Valdés (1985–91); and the governor of Michoacán, Luis Martínez Villicaña (1986–8). Their career trajectories differed strikingly from Ramírez's. None had held elected office before becoming governor, and all had limited experience as PRI cadres.[13] In contrast to Ramírez, who had held several CNC posts, these *técnico* governors had played only minimal roles in PRI corporatist organizations. For example, Martínez Villicaña and Félix Valdés had served short terms as presidents of the Student Society of the National School of Engineering, and the former had briefly been secretary general of the College of Agricultural Engineers (Camp 1995:228, 451). These governors' political careers consisted mainly of administrative appointments in federal ministries that focused on issues such as public planning, finance, transportation, and communications (Camp:450–1, 228–9; 379–80).

As argued above, Ramírez's selection as the PRI's gubernatorial candidate in Oaxaca should be understood largely as a product of the political instability in Oaxaca and de la Madrid's recognition that a technocratic governor was not suitable for this problematic state.[14] Had the political situation in Oaxaca in 1986 been more stable, as in Sinaloa, Sonora, and Michoacán at the time, de la Madrid might very well have opted for another technocrat. However, in Oaxaca, a technocrat would not do, and, as Yescas Martínez (1991:47) put it, de la Madrid chose to "open the door to career politicians."

[12] On the *político/técnico* distinction, see Cornelius, Gentleman, and Smith (1989:10).
[13] Labastida Ochoa and Martínez Villicaña served brief stints at the PRI's policy think-tank, the Institute of Economic, Political, and Social Sciences (IEPES).
[14] The unsuitability of a technocratic governor for Oaxaca was evidenced by the legacy of instability and ungovernability left by Oaxaca's previous governor, Pedro Vázquez Colmenares (1980–6), a distinguished technocrat.

The Governor's Advisers.   Ramírez's choice of advisers reflected his ideological formation. His team of advisers included several professors from the UNAM's department of economics, which had a strong prostatist orientation.[15] Their policy perspectives were a far cry from those of the typically foreign-trained, neoliberal economists who advised the president. As one of Ramírez's advisers put it, "We were taboo for the neoliberals. They thought we were from a premodern epoch."[16]

In addition to academics who rejected the prevailing neoliberal orthodoxy, Ramírez's circle of advisers included prominent individuals who had held high-level federal government posts during Echeverría's administration. As noted above, Fausto Cantú Peña, whom Ramírez invited to supervise policy for the coffee sector, had served as INMECAFE's director under Echeverría. Augusto Gómez Villanueva, who advised Ramírez on rural policy issues, had directed the federal Department of Agrarian Affairs and Colonization during Echeverría's administration. They brought to Ramírez's government considerable hands-on experience administering populist policies.

Ideological Foundations: Social Liberalism and State Building.   These advisors' vision of the appropriate role for the public sector was articulated by the doctrine of Social Liberalism and the related concept of the "Social Rule of Law" (Estado Social de Derecho).[17] This doctrine justified government regulation to promote social and economic welfare. As stated in the official document summarizing the "legislative framework" for Ramírez's government, the Social Rule of Law sought to "overcome the limitations of classical, individualistic liberalism, which was characterized by state abstention, by means of dynamic state activity that . . . promotes social justice and welfare." The document criticized perspectives that saw the state's role as limited to contract enforcement and protection of

---

[15] For example, Armando Labra, who advised the governor on social policy, and David Colmenares Páramo, who served as secretary of the treasury had both been faculty members in the UNAM's department of economics.

[16] Interview, Oaxaca, Oaxaca, June 1995. Another prominent member of Ramírez's team, Enrique Astorga, specialized in analysis of rural labor markets. Astorga's contacts with the International Labor Organization were an important source of external funding for public works programs during Ramírez's administration.

[17] The concept of "Social Liberalism" was in vogue at the national level after President Salinas introduced it during his second State of the Nation address, on Nov. 1, 1989. See Cornelius, Craig, and Fox (1994b:fn. 1). See Villareal (1993) for a fuller elaboration.

individual rights, because such perspectives were "imbued with a liberal, individualistic philosophy that paralyzes [the state's] activity and minimizes its role." Ramírez's government is described as "permeated by the ideology of Social Liberalism" and characterized by an ongoing quest for "increasing state intervention" in order to "coordinate and harmonize [Oaxaca's] diverse interest groups" and "redistribute goods and services according to the necessities of each [of Oaxaca's] regions" (Gobierno del Estado de Oaxaca 1992a:18, 1992b:249).

Their efforts to reform the constitution of Oaxaca in order to codify government responsibility for economic management and development indicate that Ramírez and his advisers took this rhetoric seriously. The reform of Article 20 of the state constitution affirmed the public sector's role as "rector" of economic development and empowered it to take measures necessary to promote Oaxaca's economic and social development. This constitutional reform delegated broad responsibilities to the public sector, stipulating that "the state will plan, implement, coordinate, and orient local economic activity and carry out the regulation and promotion of those activities corresponding to the public interest" (Gobierno del Estado de Oaxaca 1992a:45–6).

In addition to the State Coffee Council, new public institutions for economic management created during Ramírez's tenure included a state-owned company to coordinate highway and airport construction (Caminos y Aeropistas de Oaxaca) as well as a government agency to regulate the lumber sector (Consejo Forestal y de la Fauna Silvestre del Estado de Oaxaca). Although such instances of state building can be counted on one hand, the surprising fact is that *any* new government regulatory agencies were formed, given the increasing national-level efforts during this period to reduce the public sector's economic role.

Financing Peripheral Populism

An important difference between Oaxaca's "peripheral populism" in the 1980s and Mexico's national populism in the 1970s is that the former was carried out in an overall context of shrinking public budgets and growing fiscal restraints.[18] How were subnational populist policies in Oaxaca reconciled with the national budget cutting mandated by neoliberal reforms?

[18] Between 1988 and 1992, for example, overall public spending as a percentage of gross national product fell from 28.7% to 18.0% (INEGI 1994:273).

Although its overall budget decreased due to neoliberal austerity measures, Mexico's federal government reallocated resources in the late 1980s
so that some states actually received *more* federal funds than they did
before the shift to neoliberalism. In Oaxaca, federal funds increased so
dramatically during the late 1980s that the state government was literally
awash in resources. During the second half of Ramírez's administration,
for example, Oaxaca's government actually received more federal money
than it could spend and was forced to return billions of pesos to the federal
government![19] In 1989, the government of Oaxaca refunded 3 billion of
the 21 billion pesos authorized by the federal government for social development projects, because it lacked the administrative capacity to spend
the money.

Between 1986 and 1991, public spending by the government of Oaxaca
increased 56.9 percent in real terms (Gobierno del Estado de Oaxaca
1992c:56). Federal investment in Oaxaca grew at the remarkable rate of
60 percent annually between 1988 and 1991, and by 1992 total federal
investment in Oaxaca had expanded to six times its 1986 level.[20] These
federal resources fueled the construction of highly visible public works,
which proliferated notably after the contested presidential elections of
1988. Preferred projects included medical clinics, roads, and drinking
water systems as well as remodeling of municipal government offices and
schools.

The fiscal surplus that sustained this social spending can be explained
by several factors. First, Ramírez was extremely adept at lobbying federal
government agencies. The extensive personal contacts with key federal
officials that Ramírez had cultivated through three decades of political
work in Mexico City and his negotiating skills partially account for his
success at the budgetary game. Much of the explanation for this success,
however, involves Ramírez's close friendship with Carlos Salinas since the
early 1960s. According to one of Ramírez's top advisers, Salinas's personal
confidence in the governor's capabilities afforded him crucial leverage in
his negotiations with the federal bureaucrats who controlled the planning
and budgeting process.[21] Ramírez's greatest success lobbying for federal

[19] Interviews, Mexico City, May 1995. See *Extra de Oaxaca*, Jan. 8, 1990: "Faltaron por ejercer
3 mil MDP del pronasol, dice SPP," p. 4A.
[20] Gobierno del Estado de Oaxaca (1992c:19). During the period 1982–92, average real
growth in federal *participaciones* (transfers) in Oaxaca exceeded that of any other state (Díaz
Cayeros 1995:95).
[21] Interview, Oaxaca, Oaxaca, Dec. 1994.

resources was undoubtedly the special status Oaxaca achieved in the National Solidarity Program (PRONASOL). Oaxaca became a showcase for PRONASOL, receiving more funds from the program than any other state.[22]

In addition to Oaxaca's expanded share of the federal budget, a major increase in World Bank lending to Mexico for antipoverty and environmental projects also explains the ability of Ramírez's government to sustain populist spending in the face of national fiscal austerity. For the five-year period 1986–90, only 8.6 percent of the World Bank's U.S. $9.9 billion lending commitments to Mexico was allocated to poverty-targeted loans. During 1991–5, although total lending fell slightly to $8.4 billion, the share allocated to antipoverty lending rose to 27.9 percent (Fox and Aranda 1996:xi–xx). Oaxaca was one of the main beneficiaries of this shift in lending practices. The World Bank's social sector strategy for Mexico, which included large loans for basic health, education, and community infrastructure, specifically targeted Oaxaca.[23] The World Bank's special interest in Oaxaca was publicized through a visit by its president, Barber Conable, to the state in January 1990. After Conable's visit, Ramírez announced with great fanfare the launching of a World Bank–funded, 1.5 billion peso social development initiative to be implemented during the three remaining years of his term.[24]

Managing Partisan Opposition: A Penchant for Negotiation

Ramírez's regime was characterized by relative tolerance of partisan opposition groups. As one of the governor's top advisers put it, Ramírez's paramount goal was to "avoid a rupture between the opposition and his government."[25] Ramírez's handling of postelectoral conflicts after municipal elections in 1986 and again in 1989 illustrates his preference for managing political opposition through negotiation. When Ramírez entered office on December 1, 1986, postelectoral conflicts stemming from elec-

---

[22] Consejo Consultivo del Programa Nacional de Solidaridad 1994:Table A6. PRONASOL was a massive federal government social welfare program launched by President Salinas. See Cornelius, Craig, and Fox (1994).

[23] Three other states were also targeted: Hidalgo, Chiapas, and Guerrero (Fox and Aranda 1996:xi–xx).

[24] Fausto Ramírez Aguilar, "COPLADE en acción," *Extra de Oaxaca*, Jan. 18, 1990, p. 7A.

[25] Interview, Oaxaca, Oaxaca, June 1995. As we shall see in the next chapter, Ramírez's flexibility and penchant for negotiated solutions to partisan conflicts contrasted sharply with the intolerance of his counterpart in Guerrero, José Francisco Ruiz Massieu.

tions held the previous August raged in 73 of Oaxaca's 570 municipalities. The new governor moved swiftly to resolve these conflicts.

His flexible approach to managing the postelectoral conflicts is exemplified by the case of the Authentic Democratic Front of Tlacolula (FUDT), one of the first groups to mobilize to challenge the election results. When three hundred of the Front's followers arrived at the state house and occupied the city of Oaxaca's main plaza, Ramírez addressed the group, inviting them to a dialogue. The governor heard their demands and promised to intervene on their behalf. Unsatisfied with the governor's vague promise, the demonstraters pressured for more concrete measures. Ramírez acceded, signing an agreement with the organization to hold a plebiscite in the muncipality three days later. Much to the surprise and dismay of local PRI elites in Tlacolula, who felt the governor had betrayed them, the FUDT's candidates won the plebiscite and took office the same day (Díaz Montes 1992).

During Ramírez's first month in office, postelectoral conflicts were similarly resolved through plebiscites in three other cases, with opposition groups winning in two instances. A total of ten of the seventy-three municipal conflicts were ultimately resolved through plebicites, and opposition parties or dissident PRI factions won in six cases. Twenty-nine conflicts were resolved through political pacts that formed muncipal councils integrating members of the disputing parties. Thirty-two conflicts were settled by incorporating one or two opposition members directly into the local government (Díaz Montes 1992:60–5.)

Ramírez made political stability his first priority. He thus preferred political pacts and negotiation over the potentially more volatile method of holding new elections,[26] even when negotiation meant including opposition groups in municipal governments and alienating local PRI elites (Díaz Montes 1992:69).[27] In sum, during the 1986 postelectoral conflicts, Ramírez honed a multipronged, flexible strategy that emphasized frank, direct negotiations with political opposition groups.

---

[26] Only two of the postelectoral conflicts were resolved through new elections (Díaz Montes 1992:60).

[27] Indeed, as Díaz Montes (1992:69) points out, Ramírez often proved "more committed to political stability than to respect for the law," since in some cases pacted settlements were formally illegal because the state legislature had previously decreed the holding of new elections. And in several cases, the legislature was pressured to approve municipal councils, that had been "illegally" named by the governor, since, technically, the legislature should have approved the councils beforehand.

After contested municipal elections in 1989, when the center-left Party of the Democratic Revolution (PRD) clearly established itself as the second political force in Oaxaca, Ramírez again employed this multi-pronged strategy to deal with postelectoral conflicts.[28] In the case of the Coalition of Workers, Peasants, and Students of the Isthmus (COCEI), which operated across several municipalites of the Isthmus region and formed a core part of the PRD's support base in Oaxaca, Ramírez recognized its electoral victory. However, he conditioned his acceptance of COCEI's triumph on its distancing itself from radical *Cardenismo* and succeeded, with the help of generous PRONASOL resources, in inducing the COCEI to adopt a more moderate posture.[29]

In sixteen municipalities which, according to Sorroza Polo, were "totally lost for the PRI," Ramírez unconditionally recognized opposition victories. In other cases, where PRI and opposition forces were more or less equal, or where Ramírez deemed it necessary to maintain a degree of PRI control, he managed the postelectoral conflicts through political pacts.

As we shall soon see, Ramírez's flexible, at times conciliatory, style of managing partisan opposition played a critical role preventing growing pressures for democratization from politicizing Oaxaca's coffee sector. Combined with the nonpartisan, engaged productivist strategy adopted by the independent coffee producer organizations, Ramírez's flexibility helped pave the way for a participatory policy framework.

Internal Bases of Power

The composition of Ramírez's internal support coalition is suggested by the response of a prominent member of Oaxaca's private sector elite when asked to characterize the governor's term in office: "He [Ramírez] governed for the poor and marginalized the rich."[30] As noted previously, Ramírez's relations with Oaxaca's private sector were strained even before he entered office. Rather than accommodate the local elite, he sought instead to build a support coalition rooted in Oaxaca's social sector.

---

[28] The PRD was a national center-left opposition party formed in Oct. 1988 by the most important parties that had supported Cuauhtémoc Cárdenas's unsuccessful bid for the presidency earlier that year. On the PRD, see Bruhn (1997).

[29] Sorroza Polo (1994:301). Fox and Moguel (1995) suggest that Ramírez's decision to recognize COCEI's victory in 1989 was the reluctant result of sustained prodding by the federal government. On COCEI, see Rubin (1997).

[30] Interview, Oaxaca, Oaxaca, June 1995.

The principal tools Ramírez used to forge and sustain this coalition were the PRI's official corporatist organizations: the CNC, in which he had held top national leadership positions, and the Confederation of Mexican Workers (CTM). These coalition-building tools had been blunted, however. Internal inertia and corruption together with external competition from new, independent organizations that had proliferated across Oaxaca since the early 1970s had weakened the longstanding monopoly of these official corporatist unions. Ramírez sought to rejuvenate these declining corporatist mechanisms of controlled interest group representation, especially the CNC.

Organizing for Production?: Neocorporatism in the Countryside. Ramírez's government focused on promoting peasant unions, a task the governor had mastered during his tenure as the CNC's secretary of union affairs in the early 1980s. Thus Oaxaca experienced a veritable explosion of official rural organizations. The overall organizational scheme was structured around branches of production and based on a three-tiered hierarchy: First-level organizations, such as *ejidos* and agrarian communities, were incorporated into second-level Unions of Ejidos; Unions of Ejidos, in turn, were grouped into third-level, statewide Rural Collective Interest Associations (ARICs).[31] ARICs performed a dual function, serving both as collective marketing boards and as sectoral cupulas that monopolized interest intermediation for each agricultural production branch. Between 1986 and 1992, nine ARICs were created, and the total number of Unions of Ejidos increased tenfold, from nine to ninety.[32]

This organizing campaign, dubbed "the agricultural revolution through peasant organization," was touted by Ramírez's government as a rural development strategy that would yield substantial increases in agricultural productivity (Gobierno del Estado de Oaxaca 1992b:49). Not surprisingly, given Ramírez's political formation, this strategy of promoting second- and third-level organizations around production branches had been introduced nationwide in the mid-1970s during Echeverría's presidency (Fox and Gordillo 1989:142–3). Despite the colorful rhetoric of promoting economic development that surrounded Oaxaca's rural organizing

---

[31] Gobierno del Estado de Oaxaca (1992b:55–9). *Ejidos* are collective production units established as part of Mexico's postrevolutionary agrarian reform.
[32] There had been no ARICs in Oaxaca prevously. See Gobierno del Estado de Oaxaca (1992b:56).

campaign,[33] this project, like Echeverría's before it, was a top-down effort to revitalize corporatist mechanisms of government-controlled interest representation.

Ramírez's government revived an earlier practice established during Echeverría's administration of forcibly incorporating rural communities into the new second- and third-level organizations. The ARICs and Unions of Ejidos in Oaxaca fostered many of the same abuses of power that had characterized the earlier, Echeverría-era projects.[34] These new organizations were usually characterized by mismanagement of resources and often by outright fraud and corruption. According to one federal government official who worked in Oaxaca during Ramírez's administration, many of the Unions of Ejidos were literally created overnight and served mainly as "legal shells" to secure funds for corrupt CNC leaders. From his frequent dealings with the coffee sector ARIC, he concluded that its leadership's main objective was "to steal money" by obtaining fraudulent bank loans.[35]

In another revival of a pernicious practice from the Echeverría period, the notoriously corrupt National Rural Credit Bank (BANRURAL) played an active role through its local subsidiary promoting ARICs, since it could unload huge loans easily by concentrating producers into large-scale agro-industrial and marketing projects. Such oversized loans also helped conceal corruption by BANRURAL and ARIC officials.

These new government-sponsored organizations did not merely line the pockets of corrupt officials, however; they also served as tools for attempting to block the expansion of producer organizations not affiliated with the PRI. When these independent organizations sought to form their own Unions of Ejidos in order to take advantage of special financing opportunities available to such unions, they often found they had been preempted by a CNC-affiliated union. For example, the independent Union of Indigenous Communities of the Northern Isthmus (UCIZONI) discovered that it could not form its own Union of Ejidos, because many

[33] A vivid example of such rhetoric is Ramírez's proclamation: "Organization makes possible the miracle of transforming the weak into the strong and the *campesinos* can achieve what they never could have individually" (Gobierno del Estado de Oaxaca 1989a:26).
[34] According to Fox (1993:58), "the size and technical sophistication of these projects made bureaucratic control easier, creating many opportunities for political and economic abuse of power."
[35] Interview, Dec. 1995.

of the *ejidos* to which its members belonged had already been incorporated into a CNC union (Aranda Bezaury 1992:91). An independent group of INMECAFE's Economic Units for Production and Marketing (UEPCs)[36] in the Mazateca region encountered a similar obstacle. When they tried to break free from the official "Uni-Nuu" cooperative, a CNC-affiliated organization that formed the backbone of the coffee sector ARIC, the UEPCs were denied permission to form their own Union of Ejidos by the delegate of the federal Ministry of Agrarian Reform.[37]

In sum, despite rhetorical claims of igniting an "agricultural revolution," Ramírez's organizing campaign was more an effort to reassert government control over rural interest groups in the face of a growing threat from independent producer organizations. The campaign's success in this respect was limited, especially in the coffee sector, where, as we shall see, independent organizations expanded considerably during Ramírez's tenure. In the end, perhaps the campaign's most concrete achievement was to create fresh opportunities for illicit enrichment by CNC and BANRURAL officials.

Because of his overall focus on reviving mechanisms for controlling rural interest representation, it is not surprising that Ramírez responded to INMECAFE's withdrawal by launching a neocorporatist reregulation project to occupy the policy areas vacated by the federal agency. As illustrated by the rural organizing campaign, Ramírez's populist regime sought to leave no political space unfilled. This imperative was especially strong in the coffee sector, because coffee was the state's most important agricultural activity, making a crucial contribution to the livelihood of approximately 300,000 of Oaxaca's 3 million citizens, and because independent grassroots organizations had made their greatest advances in that sector.

Hence, for Ramírez, the challenge posed by INMECAFE's withdrawal was clear: Build a new set of institutions that would encapsulate small coffee producers and stop the spread of independent organizations. To achieve this objective, Fausto Cantú, the architect of national coffee sector policy under Ramírez's political mentor, President Echeverría, was the natural choice.

---

[36] On the UEPCs, which operated as credit and technical assistance associations that obliged small coffee farmers to sell their harvest to INMECAFE, see Chapter 2.

[37] Interview, Oaxaca, Oaxaca, Dec. 1994.

Reregulation Project and Producer Response: Neocorporatism from Above, Engaged Productivism from Below

When Cantú arrived in Oaxaca in late 1988, the vast majority of Oaxaca's small coffee producers were affiliated with the CNC.[38] Although several autonomous producer organizations had formed outside the CNC, they were dispersed geographically and had established minimal linkages among themselves. Taken together, these independent organizations numbered at most 5,000 producers, less than 10 percent of the total number of producers in Oaxaca. From Cantú's perspective, Oaxaca must have seemed a propitious context for his neocorporatist project to exclude independent organizations and restrict the representation of small producers to officially sponsored CNC groups.

Within just two years, however, the organizational profile of Oaxaca's coffee sector would be transformed dramatically, making Cantú's exclusionary project unfeasible. The independent producer organizations joined together to form a new, statewide *coordinadora*, or coordinating network, that encompassed 20,000, or almost 40 percent, of Oaxaca's 55,000 small coffee producers (Moguel and Aranda 1992:187). This new organization – the Statewide Coordinating Network of Coffee Producers of Oaxaca (CEPCO) – quickly became Oaxaca's most powerful producer organization in terms of both size and mobilizational capacity. CEPCO's most notable early accomplishment was to challenge successfully the Ramírez government's neocorporatist project, forcing Cantú's ouster and transforming the post-INMECAFE policy arena in Oaxaca from an exclusionary to a participatory one.

What explains the sudden formation of an independent movement with such a broad base of support? The movement's rapid emergence is especially puzzling because it occurred in the context of a political regime that actively pursued a rural organizing campaign intended to prevent the spread of autonomous organizations. The following factors explain CEPCO's rapid formation. First, preexisting independent organizations had crucial mobilizational experience that enabled them to serve as "organizational pillars" that helped accelerate the construction of a new, statewide confederation. When these organizations joined to form CEPCO, they received critical support from allies in federal government

---

[38] In most cases this affiliation was "automatic" by virtue of their membership in INMECAFE's UEPC's, which entailed obligatory CNC membership.

agencies. In several instances, INMECAFE's field staff actually helped CEPCO recruit newly available producers let loose by the dismantling of the state-owned company's network of UEPCs. This support from INMECAFE workers and CEPCO's strategy of actively recruiting UEPC members help explain the dramatic, rapid expansion of the new organization's ranks. Furthermore, mid- and upper-level officials of federal social development agencies (especially PRONASOL) provided important financial support to CEPCO, which helped the fledgling organization consolidate.

Finally, the state government's neocorporatist project itself played an important role in CEPCO's birth by providing new incentives for the independent organizations to join forces and mobilize to gain inclusion in the emerging policy framework. As one of CEPCO's leaders put it, Cantú's project ironically provided the "detonator" for a wave of intense mobilization that shattered the CNC's hegemony in Oaxaca's coffee sector.[39]

CEPCO's engaged productivist strategy – which focused on challenging and seeking to modify the state government's initiative for the coffee sector while avoiding affiliations with a political opposition party – contributed significantly to the formation of a participatory policy framework. In contrast to coffee producer organizations in Chiapas and Puebla, which pursued a disengaged productivist strategy that ignored the governor's reregulation project and focused instead on autonomous economic development goals, CEPCO challenged the project and demanded inclusion in the policy framework. However, unlike producer organizations in Guerrero, CEPCO opposed the state government's reregulation project in *nonpartisan* terms, voicing its discontent through interest group rather than electoral politics.

This nonpartisan strategy together with CEPCO's size and strength convinced a reluctant Governor Ramírez to accept the independent organizations as legitimate actors in the post-INMECAFE policy arena. The fact that CEPCO had not allied with the partisan opposition made it easier for the governor to acquiesce to the organization's demand for inclusion in the policy arena. Moreover, the very real threat that CEPCO would

---

[39] Hence, the neocorporatist project exemplifies the potentially double-edged character of efforts to establish government control over interest intermediation: Such efforts may unintentionally provide resources to the very groups that they intend to exclude and disorganize.

renounce its productivist position and embrace a partisan strategy if it were *not* included significantly raised the costs to Ramírez's government of inflexibility. As one participant observed, Ramírez saw that it was better to have CEPCO inside the policy framework, where he could at least potentially control it, rather than "constantly mobilizing and making noise on the outside."[40]

Organizational Pillars: Independent Regional Producer Organizations

In the late 1970s and early 1980s, a number of independent organizations of small coffee producers formed across Oaxaca. Until 1989 these organizations were dispersed and made few efforts to coordinate joint activities. This dispersion was due in part to Oaxaca's rugged mountainous terrain, which posed natural barriers to interregional communication. Ethnic divisions reinforced these natural barriers: Oaxaca's population is divided into seventeen ethnic groups with distinct languages and customs.[41] In 1988 the most important independent coffee-producer organizations were spread across four regions populated by at least seven ethnic groups.[42]

In addition to these geographical and cultural barriers, the diverse developmental trajectories of the organizations further impeded collective action. Most had formed around local issues not directly related to coffee production, such as improving access to food or securing better rural roads. For example, the Union of Indigenous Communities "One Hundred Years of Solitude" (UCI "Cien Años"), which represented approximately 500 producers from the coastal region, had formed in the early 1980s as an organization of Community Food Councils.[43] UCI "Cien Años" expanded into coffee production in the mid-1980s.[44] Similarly, the United Villages of the Corner cooperative, which by 1990 represented 343 Zapotec coffee growers from the Sierra Juárez, had originally formed as

---

[40] Interview, Chilpancingo, Guerrero, Dec. 1995.

[41] On Oaxaca's ethnic diversity, see Barabas and Bartolomé (1986). The state's linguistic diversity is so rich that members of the same ethnic group often speak mutually unintelligible dialects.

[42] The four regions were the Isthmus, the Mazateca, the Coast, and the Sierra Juárez. Among the ethnic groups were Chinanteco, Mazateco, Mixe, Mixteco, Triqui, Zapoteco, and Zoque (Aranda Bezaury 1992:111).

[43] The Community Food Councils were part of the national Mexican Food System (SAM) launched by President López Portillo in 1980. See Fox (1993).

[44] Interviews, Pochutla, Oaxaca, Dec. 1994.

part of a local struggle to secure rural roads and bus service for isolated indigenous communities.[45]

By contrast, the 1,200-member Union of Indigenous Communities of the Isthmus (UCIRI), which was founded in the early 1980s by Jesuit priests, had focused on organic (pesticide-free) coffee production since its inception. UCIRI's clerical leadership instilled its Zapotec and Mixe rank and file with a Jesuit work ethic that emphasized the moral obligation of the membership to grow high-quality organic coffee. From the start, UCIRI successfully tapped into European organic coffee markets with the help of Church-affiliated, agro-ecological organizations.[46] The Isthmus region was also home to another major independent organization, UCIZONI. UCIZONI, which represented more than 600 coffee producers, did not share UCIRI's religious orientation, and, despite their geographical proximity, the two organizations had little formal contact.

In sum, by 1988, several independent, yet isolated, producer organizations had formed across Oaxaca. Indeed, these organizations might very well have remained dispersed had not Cantú's exclusionary project provided a common point of reference that helped them discover a shared interest in gaining inclusion in the emerging post-INMECAFE policy framework.

Scaling Up: Birth of a Statewide Coordinating Network (CEPCO)

In February 1989 Governor Ramírez organized a forum to unveil legislation that Cantú had drafted proposing a Law for the Promotion and Integral Development of Coffee Production in the State of Oaxaca.[47] The forum, which was held in the town of Santiago Astata, proved a pivotal event in both the emergence of statewide opposition to Ramírez's neocorporatist project and the subsequent formation of a participatory policy framework.

Although the meeting was officially called the First State-Wide Forum for Study, Analysis, and Training about Coffee Production, its purpose was less to stimulate analysis and study than to demonstrate the coffee sector's support for the governor's project. According to several participants, the

[45] Interview, Oaxaca, Oaxaca, June 1995.
[46] Similar agro-ecological organizations also formed in Chiapas and, on a smaller scale, in Puebla.
[47] See Cantú (1989). The proposed law had recently (Dec. 15, 1988) been sent for review – and almost certain approval – by the state legislature.

forum was intended as a political show staged mainly for invited representatives of various federal government agencies. One participant described the forum as "precooked," pointing out that the official book, which supposedly *summarized* the conference's conclusions, had been prepared beforehand.[48] Not surprisingly, the forty-three organizations listed in the forum's program as representing small producers included only official organizations affiliated with the CNC. Independent organizations, such as UCIZONI, UCI "Cien Años," and United Villages of the Corner, were not invited.[49]

The forum at Astata did not turn out as Ramírez and Cantú had planned. Although they had not been invited, leaders of independent organizations showed up anyway. Many had been tipped off about the event by a high-ranking official of a federal government social development agency, who believed that the post-INMECAFE policy arena should include independent organizations and thus urged them to attend the forum. Several of these uninvited leaders gained the floor and voiced their opposition to the new legislation. Their criticisms focused especially on the composition of the proposed State Coffee Council, which, in their view, "implied the exclusion of broad sectors of producers from the council's management and decision-making processes" (quoted in Moguel and Aranda 1992:180). They also criticized the legislation's proposal that the Coffee Council control export quotas and financing, which they saw as a threat to their organizations' primary economic objective: achieving autonomous control by small producers over the marketing and exporting of their coffee.[50]

In addition to the immediate effect of fracturing the illusion of consensus the state government had tried to project, the independent organizations' presence at Astata would soon have more serious consequences for Ramírez's neocorporatist project. At the forum, many of these independent organizations met for the first time and discovered their common opposition to the governor's plan. Their shared status as illegitimate organizations in the eyes of the government helped foster a sense of collective

---

[48] Interviews, Oaxaca, Oaxaca, Dec. 1994.
[49] Moguel and Aranda 1992:179; Fausto Ramírez Aguilar, "Astata y la caficultura," *Extra de Oaxaca*, Feb. 2, 1989, p. 7A; Fausto Ramírez Aguilar, "Los subjetivos acuerdos de Astata," *Extra de Oaxaca*, Feb. 4, 1989, p. 7A.
[50] The Astata Forum was held five months prior to the rupture of the International Coffee Organization's (ICO) international quota system, after which control of export quotas became a moot issue.

identity. These initial contacts soon served as the basis for launching a statewide campaign against the governor's project.

The Astata conference also contributed to the forging of new links between these organizations and other actors who would become important allies in the subsequent struggle against the governor's neocorporatist initiative. INMECAFE field staff from across Oaxaca attended the conference. Some INMECAFE workers sought to end the traditional practice that had compelled the communities with which they worked to accept leaders imposed by outside CNC officials who were often insensitive to local needs. At Astata, many of these democratically inclined INMECAFE workers, who sought to ensure that the producers could choose their own leaders, first learned about the independent organizations. They immediately saw these organizations as attractive alternatives to the authoritarian, usually corrupt, CNC unions.[51] These field-workers would soon help recruit producers affiliated with INMECAFE's network of UEPC's into the process of constructing a new, statewide organization. Their links and legitimacy with UEPC communities were important resources that helped the nascent CEPCO rapidly expand its ranks. And when their jobs with INMECAFE disappeared as its dismantling proceeded, many of these field-workers became technical advisers to CEPCO or one of its constituent regional organizations.[52]

At the Astata Forum the seeds were planted for the birth of a new, statewide producer organization opposed to the governor's reregulation project. Instead of demonstrating producer unity behind their project, as Ramírez and Cantú had planned, the forum became the catalyst and point of departure for an opposition movement that would force its modification.

After Astata. In the weeks following the Astata Forum, the independent producer organizations embarked on an intense campaign of grassroots mobilization. They organized "alternative forums" in coffee-producing communities to discuss the state government's proposed legislation. These forums were attended by many producers who had not previously been affiliated with an independent organization (e.g., members of

---

[51] Interviews, Oaxaca, Oaxaca, Dec. 1994 and May 1995.
[52] One might speculate that in early 1989 these INMECAFE workers had "read the writing on the wall" and were actually looking for new career opportunities in the face of the impending dismantling of INMECAFE.

INMECAFE's UEPCs), and, hence, they served to recruit new members. Modifying the governor's proposed legislation soon became the rallying point for thousands of small producers. By launching his neocorporatist project, Ramírez had thus unintentionally given the independent organizations both a stimulus to join forces and a useful tool with which to expand their bases of support.

The independent organizations also began to draft an alternative to Cantú's legislation. This alternative rejected Cantú's proposal to give the State Coffee Council control of export quotas and financing, a plan that the independent organizations saw as an attempt to undermine their efforts to appropriate the coffee production process.[53] Control of export quotas had long been a source of corruption for INMECAFE's staff as well as an important instrument for sustaining the CNC's monopoly in the coffee sector. Government-controlled financing, in addition to providing more opportunities for corruption, had forced producers to sell to INMECAFE, which offered preharvest loans that obliged producers to repay the credits "in kind" with their crops. As a document opposing the State Coffee Council's control of financing bluntly put it, "[Cantú's proposal] would create a financial instrument – to control the money – that would be directed by a single individual who would not be chosen by the producers" (CEPCO 1989).

The independent organizations also proposed modifications to shift control of the State Coffee Council's executive committee from government agencies to the producers. As envisioned by Cantú, the executive committee would have included just two representatives from producer organizations – the secretary general of the CNC's Agrarian Leagues and the president of the CNPP's State Federation of Small Property Owners – both members of the official, corporatist apparatus.[54] The rest of the committee would comprise state and federal government officials, with the governor serving as the committee's president.[55]

---

[53] Government control of export quotas and financing were part of the proposed "Fund to Guaranty and Defend Coffee Production." According to the original proposal, the Fund, which would serve as the Coffee Council's "marketing and financing arm," would "administer the quotas corresponding to the production of coffee in Oaxaca" and would "manage and secure financial credits" for the sector. See Cantú Peña (1989).

[54] The CNPP was the PRI's National Confederation of Smallholders.

[55] According to Cantú's proposal, the executive committee would include the governor; three secretaries of state government agencies (Finance; Planning; and Rural Development); the director of the committee (a position that Cantú himself would occupy); and representatives of several federal government agencies (the Ministry of Agriculture; the Ministry of

The independent organizations proposed instead that the council's executive committee be expanded to include four representatives of small producer organizations, ten "at-large" representatives of producers drawn from each of the state's coffee regions, and two seats for private sector industrialists and exporters. This expanded committee would give a majority of votes to the producers' representatives.

Finally, the independent organizations sought to reduce the power of the executive committee's director – a post certain to be held by Cantú. They proposed instead an executive council, which would consist of a general director, INMECAFE's delegate to Oaxaca, the state government's secretary of rural development, and the four representatives of small-producer organizations who would be incorporated into the expanded executive committee (CEPCO 1989; Moguel and Aranda 1992:181).

After several months of grassroots consultation and mobilization, the independent organizations decided that the issues raised in their alternative forums should be discussed at a general meeting in the city of Oaxaca. This meeting, which became known as the First Forum of Consultation,[56] was held on June 2, 1989, in the auditorium of the National Union of Education Workers (SNTE). The meeting's location is significant because it reveals the close ties and mutual support between independent coffee organizations and Oaxaca's teachers' movement, which had been struggling for a decade to win internal union democratization.[57] The teachers' movement had been a powerful political force in Oaxaca since the late 1970s, and Ramírez had spent much energy trying to subdue it. His efforts to coopt some of the movement's leaders had indeed weakened it (Sorroza Polo 1994:300). Nevertheless, the prospect of a new coalition uniting teachers and coffee producers alarmed Ramírez.[58] Threatening to ally with the teachers was thus a valuable tactic for the coffee organizations because it raised the potential costs to Ramírez of ignoring their demands.

The independent organizations' forum was attended by a large contingent of representatives from INMECAFE's UEPCs, a fact that reflected the success of recruitment efforts in the five months since the official

---

Agrarian Reform; INMECAFE; and the National Rural Credit Bank (BANRURAL). Cantú Peña (1989:13).

[56] The full name was The First Forum of Consultation Regarding the Problematic of Coffee in Oaxaca.

[57] On Oaxaca's teachers' movement, see Cook (1996).

[58] This point was made by a former leader of the CNC's State Union of Coffee Producers. Interview, Mexico City, April 1995.

forum at Astata. The independent forum concluded with a strong condemnation of the governor's project, which was criticized as a scheme designed by bureaucrats and middlemen against the interests of "authentic producers."[59]

This productivist discourse, which cast the independent organizations as defenders of authentic producers, made it easier to build a broad coalition. Indeed, the goal of modifying the governor's project transcended the official-vs.-independent divide. Productivist factions of the CNC (especially the State Union of Coffee Producers) opposed parts of the reregulation project, such as Cantú's plan for a quasi-public company – Oaxaca Pro-Export – that would monopolize coffee exports.[60] These productivist CNC factions saw this plan as a scheme to enrich a small group of bureaucrats and private sector elites at the expense of CNC rank and file. On several occasions leaders of CNC factions participated in the independent organizations' meetings, and the two groups joined forces in a tacit alliance against Cantú's proposed legislation.[61]

On June 15, two weeks after the first forum, the independent organizations held a larger meeting in the city of Oaxaca that included 335 delegates from 105 UEPCs (CEPCO 1989). At this second forum, the independent organizations decided to formalize their relationship by establishing CEPCO.

The second forum was also attended by leaders of the recently created National Coordinating Network of Coffee Producers' Organizations (CNOC), who offered solidarity and key advice to Oaxaca's independent organizations. The two organizing processes, CEPCO's at the state level and CNOC's at the national level, were mutually reinforcing as valuable exchanges of information, experiences, and enthusiasm occurred between the two new organizations. In an effort to strengthen this dynamic of mutual support, CNOC chose Oaxaca as the site for its first national meeting. The meeting, which was held in early July in the town of Lachiviza, brought together representatives of twenty-five independent coffee-producer organizations from six states.

For CEPCO's members, CNOC's national meeting in Oaxaca was an energizing experience that linked their local struggle to a larger, national

---

[59] Luis Castellanos, "Cafeticultores condenan la iniciativa de ley de cafeticultura." *Extra de Oaxaca* (June 2, 1989), p. 5A.

[60] On Oaxaca Pro-Export, see Gobierno del Estado de Oaxaca (1989b).

[61] Interviews, Oaxaca, Oaxaca, May 1995 and Mexico City, April 1995.

movement. In the years to come, CNOC would provide much more than just inspiration and a sense of larger purpose. The national organization gave CEPCO and other regional organizations like it critical leverage in the policy process by pressuring the central offices of federal government agencies in Mexico City. CNOC's direct access to the central staffs of federal agencies opened important new bargaining channels for subnational producer organizations like CEPCO.[62]

CEPCO Consolidates. During the rest of 1989, while continuing to oppose the governor's neocorporatist project, CEPCO expanded its focus to economic development projects. The new organization began to channel rank-and-file demands for government assistance to help improve productive infrastructure, obtaining a 500 million peso PRONASOL grant to purchase 2,000 manual depulping machines.

CEPCO also began to operate as a marketing cooperative through which producers could sell coffee at a higher price than offered by either INMECAFE or private buyers. This new marketing role was partially forced on CEPCO by INMECAFE's drastic reduction of coffee purchases. For the harvest of 1989–90, INMECAFE declared that it would purchase a maximum of 25 percent of Oaxaca's production and that it would only buy coffee that was almost fully processed (*pergamino seco*). This sharp reduction of INMECAFE's purchasing quota left thousands of small producers with few options but to sell their harvests at exploitively low prices to local middlemen. The crash of global coffee prices after the rupture of the International Coffee Organization's (ICO) quota system in July 1989 exacerbated this difficult situation.[63]

Ironically, economic crisis helped CEPCO grow and consolidate. The intense uncertainty faced by Oaxaca's small producers created new opportunities for independent organizations to expand their ranks by incorporating those who had previously depended on INMECAFE. CEPCO soon began to substitute for INMECAFE in various ways, taking charge of credit management, harvesting, processing, and national and international marketing.[64]

---

[62] See Hernández (1992:90–2) on this aspect of CNOC.

[63] As analyzed in Chapter 2, the collapse of the ICO's global quota system resulted in a severe oversupply of coffee and a precipitous drop in global coffee prices that lasted until 1994. During this period, the price of Mexican coffee plunged to its lowest level in 15 years.

[64] In 1990 CEPCO's organizations were able to offer a price of 3,200 pesos per kilo, 436 pesos above INMECAFE's price of 2,764 pesos (Moguel and Aranda 1992:184).

These efforts to take control of the production process were supported by middle- and high-level federal government officials who channeled resources to CEPCO via PRONASOL. In late 1989 the organization received a 2 million peso loan through the newly formed INI-PRONA-SOL Program for Coffee Harvesting and Marketing.[65] This loan enabled CEPCO to purchase coffee from its members at competitive prices. The same federal official who had previously informed the independent organizations about the Astata Forum played a pivotal role in securing this loan.[66] Prior to the presidential elections in 1988, this official had led a successful campaign to garner tacit endorsements from Oaxaca's independent organizations for the PRI's candidate, Carlos Salinas de Gortari, by securing their signatures on neutral-sounding newspaper advertisements.[67] Hence CEPCO was beginning to reap the rewards of the decision by many of its major constituent organizations not to oppose Salinas's candidacy during the previous year's presidential elections.

In less than a year CEPCO had evolved from a loose social movement into a full-blown *campesino* (peasant) enterprise uniting some 20,000 small producers. This remarkable transformation, which was supported in crucial ways by reformist federal government officials, ensured that CEPCO would not fade away after the struggle to modify Ramírez's neocorporatist project had been won. On the contrary, as we shall see, CEPCO would endure and become a major player in the post-INMECAFE policy arena.

The Electoral Conjuncture That Wasn't: CEPCO's Nonpartisan Strategy

As analyzed in the next chapter, hotly contested municipal elections in the state of Guerrero in late 1989 became a focal point for partisan mobiliza-

---

[65] Gracida, Guzmán, and Moreno (1990). INI was the federal government's National Indigenous Institute. On the INI-PRONASOL program, see INI-SOLIDARIDAD (1994).
[66] Interviews, Oaxaca, Oaxaca, Dec. 1994 and June 1995.
[67] See, for example, "A la opinión publica," *La Jornada*, July 2, 1988, p. 25. The independent coffee producer organizations from Oaxaca that signed the document included UCI "Cien Años" and the Independent Organization "United Villages of the Corner of the Sierra Juárez." See also the open letter to Salinas de Gortari from "autonomous, self-managed, peasant organizations from the state of Oaxaca" that affirmed support for Salinas's emphasis on respecting these organizations' autonomy from traditional, ruling party confederations and on transferring productive functions and resources from the public sector to the producers. In addition to the two organizations mentioned above, which signed the July 2 document, this open letter was also signed by UCIZONI, which, together with UCI "Cien Años" and "United Villages," would play a central role in CEPCO's formation (*La Jornada*, June 30, 1988).

tion in support of the PRD by the rank and file of independent coffee-producer organizations. These elections and the prolonged postelectoral conflicts that followed were major factors contributing to an exclusionary institutional outcome to the politics of reregulation. In Guerrero, the turbulent struggle for competitive electoral politics narrowed the margins for inclusionary interest-group politics.

In Oaxaca municipal elections in August 1989 were also strongly contested. Postelectoral conflicts erupted in some forty municipalities, and the PRD clearly established itself as the second political force in the state.[68] The strongest support for the PRD was concentrated in major coffee-producing regions, most notably the Isthmus and Mixteca,[69] where CEPCO had established itself as an important force. Given this concentration of PRD votes in CEPCO's strongholds, we might have expected a Guerrero-style politicization resulting in an exclusionary policy framework. No such politicization occurred in Oaxaca, however. Instead, bargaining over the shape of the post-INMECAFE policy arena was insulated from electoral and partisan conflicts. What explains this separation of interest group from partisan politics in Oaxaca? Why did postelectoral conflicts have such different effects on institution-building in the coffee sectors of Guerrero and Oaxaca?

CEPCO's nonpartisan, engaged productivist strategy helps explain the absence of politicization in Oaxaca. During the elections of 1989, CEPCO carefully separated its activities from the struggle for competitive elections and political democracy. The organization focused strictly on economic development projects and the narrowly defined, nonpartisan objective of gaining admission into the coffee sector policy arena.

CEPCO's postelectoral behavior illustrates its nonpartisan strategy. The organization's most significant postelectoral mobilization was its seizure of INMECAFE's offices in the city of Oaxaca in September 1989.[70] This mobilization, which was launched only days after twenty-five town halls around the state had been forcibly occupied by partisan opposition groups,[71] focused on the economic objective of securing 5 billion pesos of overdue payments from INMECAFE. All small coffee farmers, regardless of their partisan affiliation, stood to benefit from the disbursement of these

---

[68] Chávez and Yescas (1989); Bailón (1995:218).
[69] See Chávez and Yescas (1989) on the "Mixteca de Cárdenas."
[70] "Nuevo problema para INMECAFE," *Extra de Oaxaca*, Sept. 19, 1989, p. 3A.
[71] "¡25 palacios ya están tomados!" *Extra de Oaxaca*, Sept. 15, 1989, p. 1A.

overdue funds. Indeed, CEPCO coordinated its activities jointly with the CNC, whose rank and file also participated in the mobilization.

As we shall see in the next chapter, rather than occupying INMECAFE's offices to protest against overdue funds, Guerrero's independent producer organizations focused their postelectoral mobilizations on seizing town halls to protest against electoral fraud by the PRI. Hence, they directly threatened Guerrero's state government. By contrast, CEPCO's postelectoral mobilization was more an opportunity than a threat for Oaxaca's government. The seizure of INMECAFE's offices allowed Ramírez to cast himself as the small producers' ally against a recalcitrant, insensitive federal agency that failed to understand their desperation. He interceded on behalf of the producers with the federal secretary of agriculture and INMECAFE's director, taking credit for INMECAFE's subsequent decision to release the overdue funds.[72]

What explains CEPCO's choice of a nonpartisan strategy? How was CEPCO able to sustain this strategy given the decision by important segments of its rank and file to support the PRD? As noted above, some of CEPCO's constituent organizations had already placed their bets with a nonpartisan strategy during the previous year's presidential elections by signing neutral sounding newspaper advertisements expressing tacit support for Salinas (although not for the PRI per se). At the time of the municipal elections in 1989, they were finally starting to reap the rewards of that strategy in the form of generous support from PRONASOL (e.g., the 2 million peso loan that CEPCO received in 1989). The risk of losing these rewards weakened the incentives to shift tactics and ally with an opposition party.

Ideal incentives reinforced these material incentives. The dominant productivist ideology of the national, independent small farmers' movement emphasized mobilizing around issues of production by building nonpartisan, pluralistic organizations. In the coffee sector, this ideology was championed by CNOC, which, as noted, played a key supportive and advisory role to CEPCO.

This combination of material and ideal incentives helps explain why CEPCO's leadership preferred a nonpartisan strategy. However, rural producer organizations in contemporary Mexico often faced strong pressures to define a partisan identity both from outside and above (i.e., from the

[72] "HRL intercederá ante Toledano y De la Vega por cafeticultores," *Extra de Oaxaca*, Sept. 21, 1989, p. 3A.

PRI regime) and from inside and below (i.e., from their rank and file).[73] As analyzed in Chapter 4, in Guerrero part of the leadership of the most important independent producer organization also supported CNOC's productivist ideology and attempted to maintain a nonpartisan stance. Because of the rank and file's decision to support the PRD, however, this stance proved unsustainable.

In 1989 core segments of CEPCO's rank and file in the Mixteca and Isthmus regions strongly backed the PRD.[74] By 1994, according to estimates by both CEPCO's leadership and government officials, more than 70 percent of the organization's rank and file supported the PRD. How was CEPCO's leadership able to avoid a "partisan pull" from below that undermined similar efforts by their counterparts in Guerrero to sustain a nonpartisan strategy?

Several important features of CEPCO's internal organizational structure help explain its ability to reconcile a nonpartisan strategy with the fact that significant portions of its rank and file supported the PRD. First, as a statewide federated association, CEPCO drew its membership from a broad territorial base. This broad territorial scope helped CEPCO ride above local political conflicts. CEPCO's widespread presence across many municipalities helped it keep its distance from political disputes in particular municipalities even when its members were directly involved in these conflicts. By contrast, the support base of Guerrero's independent producer organizations was concentrated in a handful of municipalities. When those municipalities became postelectoral trouble spots in late 1989, the producer organizations were quickly drawn into the ensuing conflicts because their narrow territorial scope made it difficult to dissociate themselves from local struggles in which their rank and file were involved.

Second, CEPCO's horizontal, nonhierarchical internal structure, which allowed affiliated organizations to retain autonomy, enabled it simultaneously to represent these affiliates and disclaim responsibility for their actions. Hence, particular affiliates could identify closely with opposition parties without jeopardizing CEPCO's overall nonpartisan position.

---

[73] On the dilemmas faced by Mexico's independent small producer organizations, see Fox and Gordillo (1989) and Fox (1994a).

[74] Although data linking coffee producers to PRD votes is difficult (if not impossible) to find, this assertion is based on the PRD's strong electoral performance in important coffee-producing zones (e.g., the Mixteca) combined with anecdotal evidence obtained through interviews with producers and government officials in Oaxaca.

Finally, in at least one important instance, an organizational division of labor at the local level helped insulate the partisan and nonpartisan activities of producers. In the case of the CEPCO-affiliate UCIZONI, the vast majority of its 600 coffee producers were also members of COCEI, perhaps the most important base of organized PRD support in Oaxaca in 1989. This dual membership allowed the producers to maintain a double identity: They conducted interest-group politics through UCIZONI and channeled electoral protest through COCEI. As one UCIZONI member put it, "When we block highways to contest electoral fraud and support the PRD, we do so as COCEI."[75]

CEPCO's broad territorial scope, nonhierarchical internal organization, and local divisions of labor between partisan and interest group functions helped it sustain a nonpartisan strategy. However, these internal factors by themselves do not fully explain CEPCO's ability to maintain a nonpartisan strategy. Under the old PRI regime, the strategies of Mexican producer organizations were shaped in important ways by *external* factors, such as pressures from government officials to define a political identity (Fox 1994a). As we shall see in the next chapter, such pressures were extremely strong in Guerrero. In Oaxaca, by contrast, they were far weaker.

From the beginning of his term, Ramírez demonstrated a willingness to tolerate independent producer organizations. In contrast to his counterpart in Guerrero, José Francisco Ruiz Massieu, Ramírez did not automatically dismiss such organizations as fronts for opposition parties. Indeed, the governor of Oaxaca worked hard to prevent producer organizations from establishing close ties with opposition parties by offering positive incentives (e.g., PRONASOL resources) not to engage in electoral politics. Ramírez's relative tolerance of independent producer organizations can be explained in part by his preference for negotiated, inclusionary solutions to political problems. This tolerance is also explained by several distinctive features of Oaxaca's political system that mitigated the threat posed by opposition parties.[76]

---

[75] Interview, Oaxaca, Oaxaca, June 1995.

[76] This is not to say that opposition parties posed no political threat to Oaxaca's government – in the local elections of 1986, for example, postelectoral conflicts resulted in over 40 deaths (Chávez and Yescas 1989). Hence, the threat of ingovernability was real for Ramírez.

Oaxaca has an extraordinarily atomized municipal structure that comprises 24 percent of Mexico's municipalities (570 of 2,392). This atomization diluted the impact of opposition victories. In any other Mexican state, opposition victories in more than 30 municipalities, as occurred in Oaxaca's local elections in 1989, would have posed a serious threat to the incumbent regime. In Oaxaca, however, the total number of muncipalities captured by the opposition was only a tiny fraction of the state's 570 municipalities, less than 1 percent.

In addition to the effects of atomization, Oaxaca's many "communitary" municipalities further diluted the threat posed by opposition parties. In such municipalities, the designation of local authorities took place outside the electoral arena through traditional, indigenous community assemblies, whose decisions were perfunctorily ratified by the PRI on election day.[77] Consequently, the PRI was virtually guaranteed control of these communitary municipalities, which, in 1989, comprised more than 450 of Oaxaca's 570 municipalities. Hence, only one-quarter of the state's municipalities were actually vulnerable to a victory by an opposition party – as suggested by the fact that in 219 municipalities the PRI received 100 percent of the vote in the 1989 elections.[78]

Furthermore, by 1989, Ramírez had accumulated considerable experience dealing with opposition victories in municipal elections, having honed tactics for managing partisan opposition during the postelectoral conflicts of 1986. He was therefore less threatened by the prospect of opposition victories than was his counterpart in Guerrero, who had entered office in 1987 and for whom the local elections of 1989 were his first.[79]

In sum, Oaxaca's atomized, predominantly communitary municipal structure and Ramírez's confidence based on prior experience that he could cope with opposition victories helped reduce the threat posed by organizations like CEPCO that refused to support the PRI. CEPCO's productivist strategy further mitigated this threat. CEPCO thus faced weak pressures from above to define a political identity, which, in turn, made it easier for the organization to sustain a productivist strategy.

---

[77] On communitary municipalities, see Bailón (1995:205–7).

[78] Díaz Montes (1992). This system has been under strain recently as local elites have increasingly begun to play political parties off against one another.

[79] Furthermore, as we shall see in the next chapter, the local elections in Guerrero followed hotly contested presidential elections in 1988 during which Guerrero was a principal center of PRD support.

Designing an Institution: Formation of the State Coffee Council

In October 1989 the state legislature finally sent the governor's proposed coffee sector legislation for review by its Agriculture, Forest, and Mines Committee. This action shifted the attention of independent producer organizations to the legislative review process. CEPCO soon launched a campaign to gather petitions expressing opposition to the legislation. The campaign yielded more than 20,000 signatures, which were soon delivered to the legislature. Of course, influencing the legislature was not the main objective, since it was little more than the governor's rubber stamp. As one of CEPCO's leaders explained, "The point [of the petition campaign] was not to impress the legislators. It was to make the governor take note of our strength."[80]

CEPCO's leaders also attended the legislative committee's meetings and participated actively in its debates. In early December CEPCO finally secured formal recognition from the state government, when its leaders were officially invited to participate in a legislative forum to analyze and modify the governor's proposal. When asked about this forum, one of CEPCO's leaders recalled: "We felt like honorary legislators!"[81]

The modified legislation was finally approved on February 6, 1990, fourteen months after Ramírez had first sent it to the legislature. A comparison between the final legislation and Cantú's original proposal reveals the significant achievements of the producer movement.[82] First, Cantú's proposal that the State Coffee Council control marketing and financing through a Fund for the Defense and Guaranty of Coffee Production was watered down considerably.[83] Although the final legislation did stipulate the formation of such a fund, participation in it was strictly voluntary. Few producers chose to participate, and the fund was never established.

Regarding the structure of representation in the council, the final legislation expanded the executive committee to include four additional seats for nongovernmental organizations, one of which was specifically designated for CEPCO's president. Cantú's original proposal had granted just two executive committee seats to producer organizations (to the PRI's rural corporatist confederations, the CNC and the CNPP). By contrast,

---

[80] Interview, Mexico City, March 1995.   [81] Interview, Mexico City, March 1995.

[82] Compare Cantú Peña (1989) with Gobierno del Estado de Oaxaca (1990).

[83] The issue of who would control export quotas was now moot, due to the prior rupture of the International Coffee Organization's quota system in July 1989.

six seats would have been assigned to government officials under the original proposal. The modification to the structure of the executive committee, which established an even distribution of seats between governmental and nongovernmental representatives, reflected CEPCO's demand that the council include greater representation of producers.[84] Although CEPCO's proposal that the council include ten at-large representatives from coffee regions was rejected, the final legislation did leave the door open for producers to increase their weight in the council through a provision that any legally constituted producer organization could subsequently join with the council's approval.[85] Furthermore, the important power to convoke extraordinary council meetings, which in Cantú's original proposal had been restricted to the council's president (the governor), was expanded to include the "coffee producers represented in the council" (Gobierno del Estado de Oaxaca: 1990).

The final legislation did not adopt CEPCO's proposal to limit the discretion of the coffee council's director by establishing an executive council that included four representatives from producer organizations. However, fears that the director would monopolize power and block producer participation were assuaged by the governor's decision to dismiss Cantú. The new director, a local coffee producer himself, soon demonstrated a firm commitment to include all producer organizations in the council. His frank, consensus-seeking style and honest reputation would play a critical role in the council's subsequent consolidation and success.

Thus CEPCO had accomplished a remarkable goal. In little more than a year, the producer organization had transformed itself from an officially unrecognized, excluded actor into a legitimate, autonomous force in a new State Coffee Council it had helped design.

Institutional Outcome: A Participatory Policy Framework

The thousands of small producers who struggled for inclusion in Oaxaca's new institutions for coffee sector governance obviously valued the ability

---

[84] The additional seats also satisfied the demand (made jointly by CEPCO and productivist CNC factions) that the council include a total of four representatives of small producer organizations. The final legislation included seats for CEPCO, CNC, CNPP, and ARIC. The CNC and CNPP had already been included in the original proposal. Two of the four new seats were for the industrialists and the exporters.

[85] Indeed, several new organizations would eventually gain seats on the council, including two former CEPCO affiliates that later left the organization.

to participate in policy decisions that affected their lives. However, Oaxaca's participatory policy framework gave them much more than a voice: The new State Coffee Council played an important developmental role that improved the economic welfare of small coffee farmers.

Participation by producer organizations enabled the council to carry out this positive role by helping it secure crucial collective goods for the coffee sector, such as a large share of the government's budget as well as development projects that responded to the producers' needs and yielded significant advances in productivity and quality. The involvement by the producer organizations in the council also served as the basis for a new strategy of development that targeted public resources to support and augment the organizations' existing capacities. Rather than competing with grassroots organizations and duplicating the important activities (e.g., marketing) that they performed, as had INMECAFE, the coffee council sought instead to complement the producer organizations by mixing their social capital with its government capital through developmental joint ventures.[86]

These partnerships between producer organizations and government combined the organizations' local knowledge, hands-on experience, and infrastructure with the government's financial resources and technical capacity. In the context of tight public-sector budgets imposed by national neoliberal policies, these government–producer partnerships proved effective, low-cost tools for promoting economic development.

Provision of Collective Goods

Oaxaca's State Coffee Council achieved a high degree of centrality in the interactions between producer organizations and other government agencies. The council functioned as an almost exclusive window through which producer organizations channeled demands and negotiated policies and projects. The council also served as a forum where the diverse interest groups in Oaxaca's coffee sector mobilized consensus on public policy issues. This consensus combined with the council's centrality to strengthen the coffee sector's influence in the larger public policy arena: By channeling demands collectively through the council, Oaxaca's producer organizations presented a united lobbying front to the multiple state and federal agencies in charge of rural policy and programs. The ability to form a

---

[86] On social capital, see Putnam (1993) and Evans (1996a, b).

unified front yielded especially large returns during the annual governmental budgeting process.

Moreover, the council operated as a kind of policy antechamber, where the coffee sector put its own house in order by deciding its needs and how public resources for the sector should be spent. Once consensus and clarity were reached on these issues, the council's technical staff worked together with the staffs of the producer organizations to draft proposals for programs and projects chosen by the organizations. Consequently, the council's director was able to lobby government officials in charge of planning and budgeting equipped not only with the unified support of the producer organizations but also with solid, crisp policy proposals in hand. The steady annual growth of the council's budget reflects the success of these lobbying efforts.[87]

After the State Planning Commission of Oaxaca (COPLADE) had established the coffee sector's annual budget, the council met to decide how the programmed funds would be distributed across the menu of projects previously chosen by the producer organizations. At this stage leaders of the producer organizations also decided how projects would be distributed among the organizations. This latter phase of the planning process was always quite contentious, since the shared goal of securing as much money as possible for the sector as a whole, which had previously united the organizations, was now supplanted by each organization's individual goal of commanding the largest possible share of the overall project pie. This situation created strong pressures for an economically inefficient, pork-barrel pattern of resource allocation characterized by unnecessary duplication of projects, especially in regions cohabitated by rival organizations.

At this stage of the policy process, the coffee council's staff and director supplied an important collective good by performing a disciplinary role that defused the potential for a pork-barrel pattern of project allocation. The council's *microbodega* (or miniwarehouse) program[88] exemplifies how this disciplinary role helped prevent the inefficient use of scarce public resources. The council's staff prepared a list of all localities where competing organizations (typically a CEPCO affiliate and a CNC affiliate) had made overlapping requests for *microbodegas*. The council's director then contacted the leaders of the rival organizations, informing them that it was

---

[87] For example, between 1993 and 1994, the council's total budget increased sixfold, from 22,441,340 pesos to 120,586,760 pesos. See Consejo Estatal del Café del Estado de Oaxaca (1994a).

[88] *Microbodegas* are small warehouses for storing harvested crops.

not possible to build more than one bodega in their communities and that they therefore would either have to agree to share a single, expanded bodega or receive no bodegas. The council would fund construction of a partition to divide the expanded bodega into separate compartments. Faced with these options, most disputing organizations soon agreed that part of a big bodega was better than none. Thus the council's director prevented unnecessary project duplication and, displaying his talent for inducing consensus, devised a solution that compelled rival organizations to learn to live together.[89]

The council also supplied an important collective good by helping insulate the planning and resource allocation processes from conjunctural political pressures, which often strongly influenced public planning in Oaxaca. When asked to compare the coffee sector with other sectors, one top state-government planning official candidly responded that public resources were typically allocated in a haphazard, case-by-case fashion and that the organizations that "shouted the loudest" usually benefited most. In the coffee sector, by contrast, he noted that the coordination and consensus achieved by producer organizations through the council helped insulate government planners from the volatility of short-run political pressures, a process that resulted in long-term integrated programs that addressed real developmental needs rather than conjunctural political issues.[90]

The council's program for controlling pests and plagues exemplifies both its provision of collective goods and its strategy of establishing developmental partnerships with producer organizations. In 1993 the council founded a Regional Committee for Plant Sanitation. The principal challenge confronting this committee's small staff of agronomists was a growing infestation of Oaxaca's coffee fields by the *broca* beetle.[91] By 1994 the *broca* plague had affected an estimated 45,000 of Oaxaca's 174,000 hectares of coffee, jeopardizing the livelihoods of roughly 10,000 producers across the state.[92] If unchecked, the plague threatened to damage the state's entire production.

---

[89] Based on observations, Dec. 1994, and Consejo Estatal del Café del Estado de Oaxaca (1994b).

[90] Interview, Oaxaca, Oaxaca, June 1995.

[91] The *broca* beetle boars into the coffee cherry destroying the bean. In addition to *broca*, *roya* (coffee rust) was also a problem in Oaxaca.

[92] Escalante Durán, Ruiz Vega, and Rojo Soberanes 1994. The *broca* was first detected in Oaxaca in 1989, when it was estimated to have affected 28,000 of the state's 174,000 total hectares of coffee.

Because of the magnitude of the *broca* plague and the modest resources available to the Plant Sanitation Committee, the committee could have done little to control the infestation problem by itself. In the context of these resource constraints, a top-down, INMECAFE-style solution that relied on standardized, mass-produced technical packages distributed directly to producers was not possible. Fortunately, the committee had other options. In the wake of INMECAFE's withdrawal and the elimination of most government-provided technical assistance, many of the producer organizations had, of necessity, hired their own technical advisers.[93] Hence, by 1993 the most important producer organizations had acquired formidable in-house technical expertise which, as the committee's staff recognized, could be deployed to combat the *broca* plague.

In the design and implementation of the anti-*broca* campaign, the Plant Sanitation Committee focused its energies where it could achieve the most value-added: training the producer organizations' own technical staff in the best techniques for combating the plague as well as coordinating and disseminating results of academic research to monitor and improve plague control.[94] Furthermore, the committee drew the organizations' technical advisers as well as their rank and file into the research process by promoting their participation in data collection. Eliciting the involvement of producer organizations in the anti-*broca* campaign made sense because of the important local knowledge their members could provide regarding climatic and biological conditions.

Local variation in factors such as altitude and humidity has an important impact on the severity of *broca* plagues. Such variation also influences the effectiveness of different strategies for combating *broca*. For example, university researchers discovered that the *Beauveria bassiana* mushroom, which poisons *broca* beetles when applied to the soil around coffee plants, worked most effectively in areas of high humidity.[95] The detailed

[93] Indeed, many of these advisers were prior INMECAFE employees who had lost their jobs when the state-owned company was dismantled.

[94] For example, the Plant Sanitation Committee disseminated the findings of a team of university researchers from the Autonomous Technological Institute of Oaxaca (ITAO), which identified an important local source of the *Beauveria bassiana* mushroom, an especially effective agent for fighting *broca*. The committee also published a bi-monthly newsletter. One issue was devoted almost entirely to the results of government-supported research on strategies for controlling *broca*.

[95] In conditions of high humidity, when ingested by a *broca* beetle, the mushroom spores reproduced on the cadaver of the poisoned beetle and infected other beetles (Córdoba Gamez 1994).

knowledge producers could provide about local production conditions helped ensure the adoption of the most appropriate strategy for fighting the *broca* plague.

The public sector thus fashioned a new role for itself in Oaxaca. In contrast to the old INMECAFE model of massive top-down intervention, the coffee council's Plant Sanitation Committee functioned more like a public-service consulting firm, training the organizations' own staffs in the best techniques for managing the *broca* problem. Moreover, the committee promoted the development of better technologies for plague control by linking academic researchers with producer organizations. And by drawing producers into the fight against the *broca* plague, the council's plant sanitation program helped transform them from passive recipients of mass-produced technical packages into active agents with important roles in protecting their own livelihoods.

Joint Ventures between Government and Producers

The coffee council developed an innovative strategy to improve the welfare of Oaxaca's small coffee producers by complementing the existing capabilities of their organizations and incorporating them into the planning and implementation of development projects. This government–producer collaboration yielded targeted, low-cost programs that responded to producers' needs and promised significant advances in productivity and quality.

The *microbodega* project exemplifies this strategy of forming government–producer joint ventures. The project's goal was to construct bodegas in 73 communities in order to benefit more than 10,000 small coffee producers.[96] The bodegas, which were each designed to hold up to 400 bags of semiprocessed, *pergamino* coffee, would improve quality by providing regulated humidity and protecting recently harvested beans from natural adversities.

The official project planning document emphasized how lack of adequate short-term storage facilities seriously hindered the ability of Oaxaca's small producers to compete in export markets. This document further justified the *microbodega* project as an effective way for the public sector to complement and strengthen the marketing and processing infrastructure already owned by producer organizations. According to the document, "The organizations will have considerable savings with regard to transport costs, since they will no longer have to purchase coffee directly in each

---

[96] Each bodega would measure 8 by 5 meters.

community, but rather at the [*microbodega*] collection centers, which will be strategically located in each coffee-producing zone so that collection will occur in large quantities rather than with small jeeps traveling community by community."[97] The document also explained how the *microbodegas* would benefit the producer organizations by helping guarantee a reliable supply of primary materials for their agro-industrial infrastructure. Indeed, the document explicitly acknowledged the producer organizations as the source of the initial project proposal.

The implementation of the *microbodega* project further illustrates government–producer collaboration. In the spirit of "coresponsibility" between the public sector and the beneficiaries of government programs, the council's staff restricted its role to designing the bodegas, administering project funds, and providing technical supervision.[98] The rank and file of producer organizations supplied construction materials and labor.

The *microbodega* project was a collaborative, low-cost program designed to help plug an important leak in the production process identified by Oaxaca's small-producer organizations: inadequate short-term storage facilities. The project promised to boost their ability to compete in global markets by reducing transportation and processing costs and by improving quality.

Another important collaborative project was the construction of nearly three thousand small-scale wet-processing plants across 165 communities. These processing plants, which consisted of a small tank for washing and fermenting depulped coffee beans as well as concrete patios for drying them, were easy to build and inexpensive. In contrast to the microbodegas, each of which benefited approximately 135 producers, the wet-processing plants were "family-sized" agro-industry designed for just one or two producers and their families. Like the *microbodegas*, however, the wet-processing facilities were cheap, highly effective solutions to problems of productivity and quality.

The council's justification for the processing plant project resembled that for the *microbodega* project: promoting the ability of small-producer organizations to compete in export markets by improving coffee quality and reducing production costs. The official document summarizing the project articulated the council's goal of buttressing and augmenting the

---

[97] Consejo Estatal del Café del Estado de Oaxaca (1995a).
[98] The idea of coresponsibility was a central component of the national PRONASOL program.

producer organizations' existing capacities: "Given the organizations' experience in harvesting, processing, and marketing, this project seeks to expand their ability to operate in the external market, since good processing guarantees good quality, which boosts market competitiveness."[99] The project's ultimate goal was to increase Oaxaca's overall production of export-quality coffee by 15 percent.[100]

The small-scale processing plants appealed to producers because the new infrastructure would enable them to increase the value of their product. This family-sized agro-industry promised significant gains in the price small producers could command for their crops, since the wet-processing stage has a critical effect on coffee quality. Unprocessed coffee cherries start to decompose within twenty-four hours after picking, and, because of Oaxaca's rugged, mountainous terrain, small farmers often had difficulty getting freshly picked cherries to a wet-processing plant within this time limit. In many cases, producers owned small, hand-cranked depulpers, yet lacked tanks to ferment and wash the depulped beans, washing them instead in crude, unsanitary plastic basins. Another important barrier to improving quality was the lack of concrete patios for drying washed beans, a situation frequently resolved by drying coffee in the dirt. The official project document bluntly summarized the consequences of these various deficiencies in wet-processing infrastructure: "bad taste in the cup."[101]

In addition to improving quality, the wet-processing plants promised large efficiency gains for producer organizations, since their truck fleets would no longer have to transport unprocessed coffee – with its dead weight of pulp – from the communities to centralized processing factories. Because on-site wet-processing reduced total weight by a factor of approximately 4, these efficiency gains were considerable.[102] Furthermore, producers could use the coffee pulp as compost and organic fertilizer. Hence, it made little sense to transport the pulp out of their communities. Finally, the family-sized processing plants avoided the massive environmental contamination caused by runoff from centralized, large-scale factories.

---

[99] Consejo Estatal del Café del Estado de Oaxaca (1995b).

[100] From 75% to 90%.

[101] Consejo Estatal del Café del Estado de Oaxaca (1995b). According to the document, approximately 50,000 of Oaxaca's small and medium producers lacked sufficient infrastructure to guarantee the quality of their product.

[102] Two hundred forty-five kilograms of coffee cherry produces 57.5 kilograms of dry *pergamino* (the result of wet processing). The *pergamino* must then be dry processed to produce green coffee (*café oro*).

The wet-processing plant and *microbodega* programs exemplify how Oaxaca's participatory policy framework supported projects solicited by grassroots organizations and implemented through government–producer partnerships. In these partnerships the public sector made strategic contributions of technical expertise and money to help close gaps in the production process through which quality and competitiveness were lost. By identifying these gaps, the producer organizations provided the crucial information that guided the public sector's targeted interventions. Furthermore, the organizations played the central role in project implementation.

Conclusion: Participatory Policy Frameworks from Neocorporatism

The case of Oaxaca shows how politicians in pursuit of power can unintentionally supply institutional raw materials that grassroots movements may be able to transform into participatory policy frameworks. The governor of Oaxaca launched a neocorporatist reregulation project that gave organizations of small coffee producers powerful incentives to join forces and mobilize against it. By pursuing an engaged productivist strategy that focused on economic rather than partisan issues, the small-producer movement succeeded in remaking exclusionary corporatist institutions into a participatory policy framework that helped improve their welfare. The case of Oaxaca thus raises the intriguing possibility that in places with powerful grassroots organizations capable of transforming old corporatist institutions into participatory policy frameworks, an authoritarian corporatist heritage may in fact offer important institutional advantages for achieving economic development after neoliberal reforms. Hence, the task in contemporary Mexico and the many other developing countries with such corporatist heritages may be to make corporatism work by making it inclusive and participatory, rather than to get rid of it.[103] This possibility is explored further in the concluding chapter.

---

[103] Others (e.g., Kaufman 1988; Berins Collier 1992) have argued that corporatist institutions served as an important resource that helped Mexico's federal government implement neoliberal reforms. The present analysis goes beyond such arguments by showing how corporatist arrangements at the subnational level may provide an institutional foundation for competitive reinsertion into global markets after the implementation of neoliberal reforms.

If the case of Oaxaca suggests an intriguing affinity between neocorpo-ratist reregulation projects and participatory policy frameworks, the case of Guerrero, which is analyzed in the next chapter, shows how pressures for democratization can weaken that affinity. Because the politics of rereg-ulation in Mexico occurred in a context of growing political instability and escalating demands for democratization across the country, the reregula-tion projects launched by state governors were often intended as tools for managing these pressures. Consequently, the way that producer organiza-tions responded to the projects – especially whether they chose partisan or nonpartisan strategies – had a decisive impact on the institutional outcomes of reregulation. In Oaxaca producer organizations mobilized against the governor's project by pursuing an engaged productivist strategy that insulated their struggle from partisan politics. This strategy helped explain why the politics of reregulation led to a participatory outcome. In Guerrero, by contrast, organizations of small coffee produc-ers responded to a neocorporatist project by joining the broader struggle for political democracy in Mexico. As we shall see, this decision to be democrats first and producers second contributed to an exclusionary outcome that denied Guerrero's small producers the important economic benefits enjoyed by their counterparts in Oaxaca.

4

When Corporatism and Democracy Collide: An Exclusionary Policy Framework in Guerrero

In the state of Guerrero, as in Oaxaca, the reregulation of coffee occurred in the context of a powerful small-producer movement. Indeed, Guerrero's producer movement was actually stronger in important respects than its counterpart in Oaxaca. In the mid-1980s, when the independent organizations of small coffee farmers in Oaxaca represented at most 10 percent of the state's producers, the organizations in Guerrero had recruited the majority of producers. By 1989, when INMECAFE began to withdraw, Guerrero's most important independent organization had already scaled up by joining a statewide association of rural producers.[1] Finally, in Guerrero's coffee sector, agrarian elites had virtually been wiped out by radical land reforms during the 1920s and 1930s.[2]

As analyzed in the previous chapter, the powerful grassroots producer movement in Oaxaca was able to forge a participatory policy framework by challenging the state government's reregulation project. Because a powerful movement also emerged in Guerrero, a similar, participatory outcome would seem to have been possible. Moreover, the governor of Guerrero, like his counterpart in Oaxaca, launched a neocorporatist reregulation project. In Oaxaca, the neocorporatist project provided key incentives and institutional raw materials for a reworking from below by

---

[1] In Oaxaca, by contrast, the independent producer movement did not establish a coordinated, statewide presence until *after* INMECAFE had started to exit. Although the overall economic importance of coffee in Guerrero, where it was the fourth leading agricultural product, was significantly less than in Oaxaca, where coffee was the most important crop, the organizational strength of the coffee producer movement in Guerrero made it a major political force.

[2] See Jacobs (1982); Salazar Adame et al. (1987); and Bartra (1996a).

producer organizations. Similar incentives and raw materials should also have been present in Guerrero.

Despite these important similarities between Oaxaca and Guerrero, the new institutions that replaced INMECAFE in the two states differed dramatically. In Guerrero, INMECAFE's withdrawal led not to a participatory policy framework, as in Oaxaca, but rather to an exclusionary policy framework that denied producers a role in the policy process and failed to improve their welfare. What explains the contrasting outcomes in these two cases? Why did the combination of a powerful grassroots movements with a neocorporatist reregulation project lead to such different policy frameworks?

The following analysis highlights the importance of considering both the strength and the strategies of producer organizations in order to explain the new institutions that emerge after neoliberalism. In Oaxaca the producer organizations chose an engaged productivist strategy and sought to modify the governor's neocorporatist project without allying with a political opposition party. In Guerrero, by contrast, producers chose a *partisan* strategy that tied their opposition to the governor's neocorporatist project to a larger struggle for democracy that was unfolding across Mexico in the late 1980s and early 1990s. This strategy contributed to a polarization of Guerrero's coffee sector and helps explain why the politics of reregulation resulted in an exclusionary outcome.

A focus on the strategies of producer organizations compels us to widen the scope of analysis to the overall political context in each state. To explain these strategies and their impact on the politics of reregulation, we need to look beyond the coffee sector by analyzing factors such as the kind of subnational political regime that launched the reregulation project and the structure of party competition at the state level.[3] The case of Guerrero highlights especially how the type of political regime behind the reregulation project shaped the perceptions of producer organizations about the costs and payoffs of different strategies. Although the governor of Guerrero when INMECAFE withdrew, José Francisco Ruiz Massieu (1987–93), like Ramírez in Oaxaca, launched a neocorporatist reregulation project, his modernizing authoritarian regime was quite distinct from the populist regime in Oaxaca. Key differences in the leadership styles and power bases of the two regimes led to important variation both in how the neocorpo-

---

[3] On subnational political regimes in Latin America, see O'Donnell (1993); Fox (1994b;c); and Snyder (1999b).

ratist projects were implemented and in how political elites reacted to opposition to their projects. As we shall see, this variation, in turn, helps explain why the producer organizations in Oaxaca chose an engaged productivist strategy, whereas the producer organizations in Guerrero chose a partisan strategy.

The first part of the chapter analyzes the populist regime of governor Alejandro Cervantes Delgado (1981–7) and highlights how it contributed to the emergence of a powerful small producer movement. The next section turns to the regime transition of 1987, when the populist regime was replaced by a modernizing one. The analysis shows how the dynamics of the modernizing regime help explain why a neocorporatist project was launched in the coffee sector.

The focus then shifts to the strategies of producer organizations. I explain how Guerrero's most important organization of small coffee producers became embroiled in partisan postelectoral conflicts that swept the state between 1988 and 1991. I also explore the important question of whether the producers' choice of a partisan strategy was an inevitable consequence of powerful structural constraints or a tactical error in a context where other strategies were available. The final section analyzes the exclusionary policy framework that resulted from the politicization of the coffee sector after INMECAFE withdrew.

Prelude to Reregulation: The Populist Regime in Guerrero

The regime of Alejandro Cervantes Delgado in Guerrero (1981–7), like that of Ramírez in Oaxaca, exemplifies what I called peripheral populism in the previous chapter. Even more than Ramírez, Cervantes emphasized inclusion and negotiation. Moreover, his tenure, which coincided with the neoliberal reforms launched at the national level by President de la Madrid, saw a remarkable expansion of the public sector in Guerrero, as evidenced by the creation of twenty-eight new state government enterprises.[4]

In contrast to his counterpart in Oaxaca, however, Cervantes did not build a set of new regulatory institutions in the coffee sector. Because INMECAFE had not yet begun to withdraw when his term ended, Cervantes did not have an opportunity to launch a reregulation

---

[4] Estrada Castañón (1994a:51). The total number of state government enterprises grew from 8 to 36.

project.[5] Although the opportunity to reregulate did not arise until after Cervantes left office, his populist regime nevertheless had an important, if indirect, impact on the politics of reregulation because a strong, independent movement of small coffee producers formed during his administration. This producer movement, which was tolerated and at times actually supported by Cervantes's government, displaced the official, PRI-sponsored CNC as Guerrero's most important coffee producer organization, and, by the mid-1980s, 90 percent of Guerrero's 10,000 coffee producers were affiliated with independent organizations (FIDECAFE 1994).

The climate of tolerance characterizing the Cervantes administration not only made it easier for these organizations to expand rapidly but also shaped their expectations about how government should behave. The hostile environment subsequently created by Cervantes's successor, Ruiz Massieu, violated these expectations and triggered strong opposition from the producer organizations. Cervantes's populist regime thus warrants a close analysis in order to understand both the organizational profile of Guerrero's coffee sector and the response by grassroots organizations to the neocorporatist reregulation project subsequently launched by Ruiz Massieu.

A Presidential Mission: Restoring Political Stability

President José López Portillo (1976–82) chose Cervantes as governor of Guerrero based on his confidence that Cervantes could restore political stability after a tumultuous decade of rural guerilla movements and intense militarization.[6] Cervantes's mission was to engineer a gradual political opening that would consolidate the order achieved through the repressive, hard-line tactics of his predecessor, Rubén Figueroa Figueroa (1975–81).[7]

---

[5] Because of national budget cuts, INMECAFE did reduce its purchasing levels during the last years of Cervantes's administration, thus enabling grassroots marketing cooperatives, as well as private-sector buyers, to increase their market shares. In the 1980–1 harvest, INMECAFE purchased approximately 80% of Guerrero's production. By the 1983–4 harvest, however, it purchased less than 50%. See Aguirre Benítez (1995:249).

[6] In the late 1960s, two rural guerrilla movements organized in Guerrero (one led by Lucio Cabañas, the other by Genaro Vázquez). These movements developed from civic conflicts during the early 1960s. See Bartra (1996a); Rubio Zaldívar (1994); and Sotelo Pérez (1991).

[7] Although noted most for its intolerance and repression, Figueroa's administration did focus some attention on economic development and poverty-relief programs. See López Hernández (1994:16–17).

As we shall see, independent producer organizations were one of the main beneficiaries of Cervantes's quest for political stability.

Leadership and Ideology. Cervantes's ideological formation reflected the nationalist revolutionary values of the old PRI. As a youth, he had supported the Marxist labor leader, Vicente Lombardo Toledano. Cervantes subsequently studied and taught at the UNAM's department of economics, a bastion of nationalist-statist ideology.[8]

Cervantes had substantial experience in public administration at both the federal and state levels, and he had twice held elected office before becoming governor, serving as federal deputy (1973–6) and senator (1976–80) from Guerrero.[9] The extensive contacts with federal bureaucrats involved in fiscal planning that Cervantes had cultivated through years of experience in these areas served him well as governor by helping him secure resources for his state. At the UNAM, he had been professor of public finance, which further strengthened his understanding of the federal government's fiscal process and contributed to his subsequent success manipulating this process to his state's advantage.

Like Ramírez, Cervantes sought frequent, direct contact with citizens. He was the first governor to visit virtually all of Guerrero's communities, and he made special efforts to travel to villages so that he could meet with peasants. Cervantes often consulted taxi drivers about his performance, which reflected his conviction that humble, ordinary citizens were the most important barometer of his popularity and success. Moreover, many of his top advisers had leftist backgrounds: Some had played prominent roles in the national student movement of 1968, while others had been militants in opposition parties (Calderón Mólgora 1994:77).

In contrast to his predecessor, Figueroa, who had an aggressive, confrontational style, Cervantes cultivated a gentile, tolerant image. Political conflict in Guerrero decreased dramatically during his administration, and, in the few major conflicts that did emerge, Cervantes played a

---

[8] As noted in Chapter 3, many of Governor Ramírez's close advisers had been faculty members in the UNAM's department of economics.

[9] Cervantes had held positions in the federal Ministry of Industry and Commerce, the Ministry of Finance, and the Ministry of Government Properties. In Guerrero's state government, he had been director of treasury and economy (1963–5), and director of the office of fiscal policy (1953–6) (Camp 1995:148).

conciliatory role.[10] For example, when violent disputes erupted between employees and owners of a local bus company, Cervantes mediated the conflict and helped the two sides reach a compromise.[11]

Cervantes's government was also the first in Guerrero to recognize victories by opposition parties. In local elections during 1983, the Communist Party of Mexico's (PCM) candidate for municipal president of Alcozauca was officially acknowledged as the winner. In the local elections of 1986, opposition parties won forty municipal council seats across the state, as well as six seats in the state legislature (Gama Santillán 1992:98).

Plan Guerrero: An Experiment in Participatory Planning. Cervantes created an innovative system of participatory public planning based on "permanent dialogue" and reciprocal accountability between government and citizens.[12] The backbone of this public planning system consisted of a network of regional and municipal planning committees established across the state.

Cervantes's government launched novel community development programs that elicited citizen involvement through contributions of labor and construction materials. These programs, which focused on building rural schools and recreation centers, often had colorful names (e.g., "Tit for Tat") and earned widespread popularity.[13] According to López Hernández (1994:19), such programs drew rural citizens into government-designed activities, a process that contributed to "growing acceptance of the government's legitimacy."

These participatory public-works programs should be understood, in part, as products of the ideological commitments of Cervantes's advisers. A further impetus for these programs involved the fiscal constraints imposed by the national economic crisis of 1982 and President de la Madrid's neoliberal policies. In the context of these budgetary constraints,

---

[10] As one observer noted, a clear indicator of Cervantes's accomplishments with regard to restoring political stability is that, unlike many of his predecessors, he finished his term by delivering his last State of the State address without police and army guards (Martínez Nateras 1992:134).
[11] López Hernández (1994:19). See also López Hernández (1988:47).
[12] Gobierno Constitucional del Estado de Guerrero (1983:20–1). The official planning document explicitly prioritized the state's role as the guarantor of social and economic development. For a detailed analysis of Plan Guerrero, see López Hernández (1988:56–63).
[13] See Sánchez Andraka (1987) for a journalistic account of these programs.

increased community participation in government-sponsored development projects offered a way to reduce the public sector's financial burden.[14] As one top official in Cervantes's administration explained, "The crisis of 1982 was really a blessing in disguise, because it stimulated us to find new ways to promote social welfare that redefined the relationship between state and society."[15]

In contrast to Ramírez in Oaxaca, Cervantes did not enjoy a close relationship with the president.[16] He had been appointed at the very end of López Portillo's term, and his populist career trajectory and policy orientation were incongruent with de la Madrid's neoliberalism. Given his "out-of-phase" status and the national context of growing fiscal austerity during the early 1980s, how was Cervantes able to finance his populist agenda?

The guerilla movements and endemic violence that erupted in Guerrero in the early 1970s commanded much national and international attention. Consequently, Guerrero was seen as a "special case" by federal officials. According to one of Cervantes's top aides, the governor skillfully used the threat of a new round of instability to secure federal resources for his development programs, politely explaining to recalcitrant federal bureaucrats that he could not be responsible for "the consequences" if they refused his request for funds.[17]

Like Ramírez in Oaxaca, Cervantes also benefited from an extensive network of contacts established through many years of work in Mexico City. Furthermore, he and several of his advisers (most notably his secretary of agriculture, who had formerly worked in the federal Ministry of Budget and Planning, the SPP) had previously held posts in the key federal ministries responsible for fiscal planning and administration. In addition to valuable personal contacts, they thus had first-hand experience with the federal budgetary process, which helped them secure resources

---

[14] A similar logic would animate the federal government's massive, antipoverty program, PRONASOL, which was launched by the Salinas administration in 1989.

[15] Interview, Cuernavaca, Morelos, July 1995.

[16] Cervantes did not have access to the kind of massive external funding that helped fuel Ramírez's populist agenda in Oaxaca, because the World Bank did not launch its major antipoverty initiative for Mexico until 1990. Moreover, PRONASOL was not created until two years after Cervantes had left office.

[17] Interview, Mexico City, May 1995. Federal funding to Guerrero began to decline in 1985–6, however, due to the overall economic crisis. See López Hernández (1988:63–7) on the annual process of intergovernmental bargaining over fiscal issues between Cervantes's government and the federal bureaucracy.

for their programs despite the overall trend toward shrinking budgets and tightening fiscal constraints.[18]

Political Opening in the Countryside

Cervantes's government helped rural producer organizations that showed a genuine commitment to improving the welfare of their members, regardless of whether they were affiliated with the officially santioned CNC. This nonpartisan approach in part reflected the convictions of reformist officials in Cervantes's administration that public resources should be distributed according to nonpolitical criteria. Other members of Cervantes's government, by contrast, saw their support for independent producer organizations as a way to control such groups by providing positive incentives to eschew partisan and, more importantly, armed resistance.

Independent organizations in a variety of agricultural sectors actively participated in government-sponsored development programs, such as Credit on Your Word.[19] Through these programs, autonomous organizations of hibiscus, sesame, lumber, and coffee producers acquired valuable experience in the administration of credit and collective marketing.[20] The most important independent coffee producer organization during this period was the Union of Ejidos Alfredo V. Bonfil, which had been founded in 1979 by eighteen *ejidos* from the municipality of Atoyac in the Costa Grande region north of Acapulco. By 1984, with the support of the state government, the Union Alfredo V. Bonfil had expanded to forty-five *ejidos* from across the Costa Grande and had extended its reach south to the La Montaña region bordering Oaxaca. By the mid-1980s, the union represented 90 percent of Guerrero's 10,000 coffee-producing families (Cobo and Paz Paredes 1991:55).

The Union Alfredo V. Bonfil initially focused on pressuring federal government agencies – especially INMECAFE and BANRURAL – for

---

[18] This observation is based on interviews with high-ranking officials of Cervantes's administration in Mexico City, April–May 1995; Cuernavaca, Morelos, July 1995; Chilpancingo, Guerrero, Dec. 1995.

[19] This credit program would subsequently be adopted in a modified form at the national level by PRONASOL, forming the backbone of its national coffee sector program in the early 1990s.

[20] Cobo and Paz Paredes 1991:55–6. Twenty-four new Unions of Ejidos and 129 new producer organizations formed during Cervantes's tenure (López Hernández 1988:72).

higher purchasing prices and cheaper, more flexible credit.[21] In 1982, as a result of intense mobilization, the union secured a retroactive increase in INMECAFE's purchasing price. From BANRURAL, the union won an expansion of credit and more lenient debt repayment terms. In 1982 and 1983, the union started to coordinate with independent coffee producer organizations in Chiapas, Oaxaca, and Veracruz. Together, these organizations initially focused on winning increases in the price that INMECAFE paid for their coffee. By 1984, however, as part of a broader transformation in the ideology and strategy of Mexico's peasant movement, the coffee producer organizations began to shift their efforts to achieving self-management of the production process. Through rural development programs like Credit on Your Word and Integrated Development of Coffee-Producing Zones, Cervantes's government was an important ally in the Union Alfredo V. Bonfil's struggle to take control of the production process. In 1984, for example, state government assistance helped the union build wet-processing facilities and buy coffee depulpers. And the Credit on Your Word program gave the union new incentives to start collectively managing credit for its members.

These improvements to the union's agro-industrial infrastructure resulted in a dramatic increase in the amount of coffee it sold. In the 1984–5 harvest, the union sold 5,346 *quintales*, benefiting approximately 500 producers.[22] By 1987 this figure had risen to 13,000 *quintales*, benefiting more than 1,600 producers. The new infrastructure also led to large increases in the amount of export-grade coffee, resulting in substantial gains in earnings. By the 1986–7 harvest, the new marketing channels opened by the union had begun to force both INMECAFE and private elite buyers to raise their prices. Hence union members were able to sell their surplus coffee (i.e., coffee the union did not purchase) at higher prices.

The resources provided by Cervantes's government, together with the new skills acquired through the union's efforts to take control of the production process, transformed and strengthened the organization. The complexities of managing credit, operating agro-industrial plants, and exporting

---

[21] This and the following paragaphs draw on Paz Paredes and Cobo (1992:125–8). The debt problem with BANRURAL was linked to the large reduction in overall levels of public credit during this period. See Aguirre Benítez (1995:249).

[22] One *quintal* equals 100 pounds.

coffee led to a major upgrading of the union's technical and administrative capacities. At the community level, the task of collectively managing credit and wet-processing machinery resulted in the formation of local Collective Work Groups (GTC).[23] These GTC's promoted grassroots participation and helped strengthen the union's membership base.

Peasant organizations across Guerrero took advantage of the climate of tolerance and support for nonpartisan, productivist organizations created by Cervantes's government. In addition to the Union Alfredo V. Bonfil, organizations of sesame, hibiscus, and lumber producers also expanded and consolidated. These diverse organizational experiences culminated in the formation of a statewide, federated association of independent producer organizations – the Alliance of Autonomous Campesino Organizations of Guerrero. The Alliance was established in April 1987, just as Cervantes's term ended.[24]

In sum, Cervantes's populist regime left a legacy of mature, autonomous producer organizations accustomed to the tolerance and support of the state government. These organizations had embraced nonpartisan, productivist strategies and abstained from open involvement in political and electoral issues. Guerrero's new governor would soon destroy this legacy.

Political Context of Reregulation: From Populism to "Modernization"

The transfer of power from Cervantes to Ruiz Massieu on April 1, 1987 marked the transition from a populist to a modernizing authoritarian regime. In contrast to Cervantes, a seasoned politician nearing the end of his career when he became governor, Ruiz Massieu was a rising young star. Because of his youth (he was elected governor at the age of forty) and ambition, Ruiz Massieu looked forward to securing a top national-level position after finishing his term.[25] He knew that a key prerequisite for sustaining the momentum of his promising career trajectory was a successful

---

[23] GTC's were also created for corn and honey production (Paz Paredes and Cobo 1992:127).

[24] As one of the participants explained, the founding of the Alliance was in many ways a defensive step taken in anticipation of the possibility of problems with the new governor, Ruiz Massieu. Interview, Atoyac, Guerrero, Dec. 1995.

[25] The 1988 election as Mexico's president of his brother-in-law Carlos Salinas de Gortari surely strengthened such expectations. Ruiz Massieu had forged close political ties with Salinas during his undergraduate studies at the UNAM's School of Law in the late 1960s (Camp 1995:641).

term as governor, the principal measure of which would be his ability to (1) maintain political stability and (2) deliver his quota of votes to the PRI. Ruiz Massieu's economic strategy, which destroyed the participatory community development programs launched by his predecessor and focused on attracting external investment to Guerrero's tourist enclaves, would greatly complicate these two tasks.

Leadership and Ideology

Ruiz Massieu's career trajectory contrasts sharply with those of both Cervantes and Ramírez. He was a *técnico* (technocrat) who had never held elected office. Indeed, Ruiz Massieu's principal professional achievements had not even been in politics: He was a well-regarded scholar of public administration and democratic theory.

Ruiz Massieu began his political career in the early 1970s with low-level administrative posts in the Mexican Social Security Institute (IMSS).[26] In 1972 he was appointed director of orientation and legal services for the National Worker Housing Institute (INFONAVIT). The only post he had held in Guerrero was a brief stint (1980–1) as secretary general of government during the last year of Rubén Figueroa's administration. In 1983 Ruiz Massieu was appointed undersecretary of planning for the federal Ministry of Health and Welfare (SSA), a position he held until becoming governor.

Ruiz Massieu had held no major party positions. He served briefly as undersecretary general of regional coordination for the PRI's policy think-tank, the Institute of Economic, Political, and Social Sciences (IEPES) (1981–2) and was subsequently appointed to the Institute's Advisory Board (1983–6). Nor had Ruiz Massieu served in any of the PRI's corporatist confederations.

In contrast to Cervantes and Ramírez, Ruiz Massieu was very much in step with the neoliberal doctrine dominant at the national level. He saw Mexico's ongoing economic crisis as a consequence of the populist policies of the 1970s (Estrada 1994b:104). For Ruiz Massieu, the solution to this crisis was "economic modernization," which required drastically shrinking the public sector. According to Estrada (1994a:142), "The first

[26] This and the following paragraph draw on Estrada (1994a:141); Camp (1995:632–3); and interviews with various state and federal government officials who worked in Guerrero during the 1980s and early 1990s.

stage of Ruiz Massieu's administration was characterized by the almost orthodox application of the *fondomonetarista* [International Monetary Fund] measures promoted at the national level." During his first two years as governor, in what he called the "reining in of the public sector," Ruiz Massieu cut the number of state government enterprises by half, from thirty-six to seventeen, and fired hundreds of public employees.[27] His government introduced computerized systems in all areas of public administration in order to make further personnel cuts.[28] Ruiz Massieu also eliminated the system of participatory planning and rural development programs created under Cervantes.[29]

Tourist Enclaves as Growth Poles. Ruiz Massieu's economic development strategy focused on attracting private investment (both foreign and domestic) to the three tourist enclaves that formed Guerrero's "Triangle of the Sun": Acapulco, Taxco, and Ixtapa-Zihuatanejo. Rather than implementing a large number of small-scale development projects, such as rural schools and community centers, as had Cervantes, Ruiz Massieu concentrated public investment in a handful of grandiose megaprojects intended to attract large amounts of foreign capital. These megaprojects included a luxury condominium and shopping complex in Acapulco (Punta Diamante) and a new superhighway from Cuernavaca, in the adjacent state of Morelos, to Acapulco. The extremely high tolls charged by the private sector consortium that managed the superhighway precluded the bulk of Guerrero's population from using it. As one peasant leader bluntly remarked, "[Ruiz Massieu] only cared about Acapulco. He didn't give a damn about the rest of Guerrero!"[30]

During Ruiz Massieu's administration, the partnerships between government and poor communities that had characterized Cervantes's populist regime were replaced by joint ventures between government and large private firms. Because of the huge scale of the investment required by Ruiz

---

[27] Ruiz Massieu stated that his goal was to reduce the total number of state employees by approximately two-thirds (Estrada 1994a:142; López Hernández 1988:75).

[28] Estrada (1994a:142–3); López Hernández (1988:75).

[29] López Hernández (1988:76–7). One area of the public sector that received increased investment under Ruiz Massieu was the repressive apparatus. Public security forces were given larger budgets and supplied with modern equipment, and police personnel received up to 300% increases in salaries between 1987 and 1990, which was portrayed as a necessary step to combat narcotics traficking (Estrada 1994a:144).

[30] Interview, Mexico City, May 1995.

Massieu's megaprojects, few local businesses had the resources to participate. Hence, national and, more often, foreign enterprises benefited most
from these projects. Close advisers to the governor, as well as the governor himself, reportedly received kickbacks from these firms and owned
large shares of their stock.

The scarce attention that Ruiz Massieu's government devoted to rural
development focused on a handful of sectors attractive to foreign multinational corporations. For example, the Filo Mayor highway project was
intended to make it easier for national and foreign firms to exploit Guerrero's vast forest and lumber resources. Transnational agribusinesses,
which had invested heavily in Guerrero's melon industry, were the principal beneficiaries of a project to renovate and expand irrigation facilities
in the Tierra Caliente region. Traditional crops, such as corn, sesame, and
coffee, were neglected.

The Regime's Weak Base of Power

Ruiz Massieu entered office with virtually no local base of support. The
leadership of the PRI machine in Guerrero had not even considered him
as a candidate for the governorship. His nomination was a fluke that
resulted because his mentor, Secretary of Health and Welfare Guillermo
Soberón Acevedo, declined the nomination himself and proposed Ruiz
Massieu instead.[31] With the exception of a one-year stint in Guerrero's
state government in the early 1980s, Ruiz Massieu had spent his entire
adult life in Mexico City. Like the many other Mexican governors who
achieved office through presidential designation and whose prior careers
had centered in Mexico City, Ruiz Massieu was seen as an outsider by
the local political establishment. Thus he faced a dilemma: On the
one hand, he had to build a support base in Guerrero in order to achieve
the basic tasks expected of all PRI governors – that is, maintaining political stability and securing his quota of votes for the party. On the other
hand, his economic policies were unlikely to help generate the local
support he needed because they mainly benefited business interests outside
Guerrero.

To manage this dilemma, Ruiz Massieu pursued a two-pronged strategy that combined strong support for the PRI's corporatist confederations

---

[31] Estrada (1994a:141). Ruiz Massieu's family ties to then Secretary of Planning and
Budgeting Carlos Salinas probably played a role in his nomination for governor well.

(especially the CNC) with repression of opposition parties and independent organizations not affiliated with the ruling party. In a stark reversal of the image of tolerance and sophistication this respected scholar of public law had cultivated before taking office, Ruiz Massieu was quick to unleash government security forces against groups ranging from urban squatters to supporters of opposition parties. The lofty rhetoric of "the politics of ideas and facts," which had marked his inaugural speech, was soon replaced by threatening declarations such as the following: "Those who come looking for a fight will get blood and problems, because the government of Guerrero is strong and ready to fight."[32] During Ruiz Massieu's tenure, violence against members of political opposition groups reached new heights, a trend that was reflected in the large number of assassinations of PRD supporters.[33]

In addition to repressing opposition groups, Ruiz Massieu, like his more tolerant counterpart in Oaxaca, Ramírez, also sought to channel economic benefits to the PRI's corporatist confederations. Their monopoly over rural interest representation had been weakened severely by the proliferation of autonomous producer organizations under Cervantes. In an effort to revive and strengthen the corporatist framework, Ruiz Massieu's government pumped resources into the CNC, which received generous distributions of subsidized credit and fertilizer. As illustrated by his treatment of the Union of Ejidos Alfredo V. Bonfil (analyzed below), Ruiz Massieu employed a combination of coercion and cooptation against independent *campesino* organizations in an effort to force them to affiliate with the CNC.

Ruiz Massieu also sought to make CNC-affiliated organizations the sole recipients of all government infrastructure transferred to producers in the

---

[32] This threat was made just after the strongly contested presidential elections of 1988. Quoted in Estrada (1994a:143). For the governor's inaugural address see Ruiz Massieu (1987).

[33] According to a report by the Pro Juárez Center, a human rights nongovernmental organization, between 1989 and 1995, 222 murders occurred in Guerrero. Of a total of 538 reported cases of human rights violations in Guerrero during this period, 187 were reported by PRD members. According to the center, "Repression has been focused primarily against members and sympathizers of the PRD in the context of electoral and post-electoral processes." See Triunfo Elizalde, "Han ocurrido 222 homicidios en Guerrero en 6 años," *La Jornada*, July 8, 1995. See also José Gil Olmos, "Ha sido principalmente contra el PRD la violencia política del gobierno de Figueroa," *La Jornada*, July 13, 1995. "Normal" rural violence (stemming from blood feuds (*venganzas*) and drunken brawls, for example), rather than politically motivated assassinations, probably accounts for a portion of the deaths.

process of dismantling state and federal government enterprises. This strategy conflicted with the approach pursued by INMECAFE's leadership, who aimed to transfer the state-owned company's infrastructure to the groups most likely both to pay for it and to use it productively.[34] As we shall see, in Guerrero the governor won.

Neocorporatist Reregulation in the Context of a Modernizing Regime

Although Ruiz Massieu in Guerrero and Ramírez in Oaxaca both saw the withdrawal of INMECAFE as an opportunity to rejuvenate the CNC by launching neocorporatist reregulation projects, their projects differed in important respects. These differences reflect the distinct subnational political regimes behind the reregulation projects. Because of his neoliberal policy repertoire, Ruiz Massieu focused far less on constructing new government agencies than did Ramírez. Consequently, he did not surround himself with advisers of a nationalist-populist persuasion: State-builders like Fausto Cantú Peña were not welcome in Guerrero.[35] And when Ruiz Massieu finally did propose a new state government agency to fill the policy areas abandoned by INMECAFE, the agency never received funding. Hence Guerrero's producer organizations lacked an equivalent to the focal point for coordinating an engaged productivist strategy that Cantú's proposal for a State Coffee Council provided their counterparts in Oaxaca. Moreover, Ruiz Massieu's modernizing regime was much more prone to violence than Ramírez's populist regime, which preferred negotiated, peaceful solutions to political conflicts. Thus the costs to producer organizations of opposing the neocorporatist project were far greater in Guerrero than in Oaxaca. Because of these characteristics of Ruiz Massieu's modernizing regime, the producer organizations in Guerrero had weak incentives to choose an engaged productivist strategy.

The Governor Enters "with His Sword Drawn." Ruiz Massieu's treatment of Guerrero's most important independent organization of small coffee producers, the Union of Ejidos Alfredo V. Bonfil, illustrates his

---

[34] INMECAFE (1990a). CNC affiliates were usually not the best candidates according to these criteria.

[35] As analyzed in Chapter 3, Cantú Peña was the populist former director of INMECAFE who Governor Ramírez invited to implement a neocorporatist project in Oaxaca's coffee sector.

neocorporatist tactics. Soon after entering office, his government launched a campaign to pressure and blackmail the union's leadership into affiliating with the CNC. With a combination of bribes and threats, CNC infiltrators, who were given personnel, vehicles, and money by Ruiz Massieu's government, attempted to coopt the union's rank and file. As one union leader put it, "the governor entered office with his sword drawn."[36]

The struggle to defend the union's autonomy focused on internal elections to renew its leadership in August 1987.[37] The CNC infiltrators sought to buy votes in exchange for credentials offering benefits such as free medical assistance and life insurance payments. They informed the union's rank and file that the governor had already decided the CNC's candidate would be the union's new president and threatened that all government support would end if the membership voted against him.

In the weeks before the election, CNC cadres attempted to bribe delegates from the union's constituent *ejidos*. Just five days before the elections, eleven of the twenty-two delegates were invited to attend a "training course" at a luxurious hotel in the neighboring state of Morelos. Ruiz Massieu met personally with the delegates and strongly "recommended" that they vote for the CNC slate if they wanted their *ejidos* to continue receiving government assistance.[38] As an additional inducement, each delegate was offered a wad of money as a "cash scholarship" for their children.

The elections resulted in the victory of the CNC's slate, which won the votes of twelve of the twenty-two community delegates. The defeated "democratic current," consisting of the ten delegates who had voted against the CNC slate as well as leaders from seventeen other *ejidos* not formally represented by delegates, soon withdrew from their hijacked union and took steps to establish a new independent organization. Ruiz Massieu's government sought to block this effort by refusing to give legal recognition to the new organization, a move that denied it access to BANRURAL credits for the approaching coffee harvest (Paz Paredes and Cobo 1992:128).

With the help of an extensive network of Community Food Councils that provided trucks, offices, and grassroots contacts, the independent

[36] Interview, Atoyac, Guerrero, Dec. 1995.
[37] The following analysis draws on Cobo and Paz Paredes (1991:60–3). See also UNORCA (1987:191–3).
[38] Ruiz Massieu's attendance at the event highlights his strong personal concern with coopting and breaking the independent union.

producers surmounted these obstacles.[39] On November 9, only three months after the CNC takeover, the producers who had withdrawn from the Union Alfredo V. Bonfil held a meeting in the town of Atoyac attended by approximately one thousand supporters. This meeting resulted in the formation of a new organization, the Coalition of Ejidos of the Costa Grande. The same day, the coalition demonstrated its capacity for mobilization by seizing INMECAFE's offices in Atoyac and making a successful demand for federal funds to support marketing and technical training programs. The coalition expanded rapidly by drawing on the pre-existing network of Community Food Councils to build support in nearly fifty communities across the Costa Grande region.[40] As one of the coalition's leaders explained, Ruiz Massieu's assault on the Union Alfredo V. Bonfil had turned out to be a blessing in disguise, because it resulted in the formation of a new organization with an even broader base of support.[41]

As we shall see, Ruiz Massieu's attack against Guerrero's independent producer movement left a legacy of hostility and mistrust that would have a crucial impact on the politics of reregulation.

The Governor Prevents a Pacted Withdrawal by INMECAFE. Between 1989 and 1991, the national leadership of INMECAFE pursued a strategy of transferring its agro-industrial infrastructure to grassroots producer organizations in order to help them take control of the production process. This strategy of "pacted withdrawal" had the most success in Oaxaca, where CEPCO had both the technical and organizational capacity to operate INMECAFE's infrastructure efficiently (especially its large-scale dry-processing plants).[42] As analyzed in the previous chapter, the support

---

[39] On the role of the Community Food Councils in Oaxaca and Guerrero, see Fox (1993).

[40] By 1988 the coalition numbered approximately 1,500 coffee producers, or 43.4% of the 3,456 producers in the coffee-producing zone of Atoyac (Fierro 1994:62). Although coffee producers formed the organization's backbone, producers of corn, honey, bananas, and coconut oil also played key roles.

[41] Interview, Atoyac, Guerrero, Dec. 1995. By contrast, the Union of Ejidos Alfredo V. Bonfil, now under CNC control, soon encountered difficulties. Although it received substantial government support, internal corruption and inefficiency led to rapid accumulation of debts, eliciting on numerous occasions threats of a credit embargo from BANRURAL. According to Cobo and Paz Paredes (1991:63), rank-and-file participation in the union evaporated, since the new leadership convoked neither community nor general assemblies and completely centralized the decision-making process.

[42] On the pacted strategy of dismantling state-owned companies in rural Mexico, see de la Fuente and Mackinlay (1994).

that CEPCO received from federal officials with INMECAFE and PRONASOL played a critical role in the success of its challenge to the state government's neocorporatist project.

In Guerrero, by contrast, Ruiz Massieu blocked the efforts of reformist federal government officials to support the Coalition of the Costa Grande.[43] In 1990, for example, the governor prevented the coalition's attempt to purchase INMECAFE's offices and dry-processing plant in Atoyac.[44] Although INMECAFE's director supported the sale and had even invited President Salinas to the ceremony at which the facilities were to be transferred to the coalition, Ruiz Massieu nevertheless sought to force INMECAFE to sell the infrastructure to the Union of Ejidos Alfredo V. Bonfil (now under CNC control), even though it could not offer a bid comparable to the coalition's.[45]

After months of delay, an agreement was finally reached. The accord stipulated that the state government, the Union Alfredo V. Bonfil, and the Coalition of the Costa Grande would jointly purchase INMECAFE's equipment. As a result of footdragging by the CNC, however, the agreement soon collapsed. In the end the coalition was forced to build new offices and processing machinery, and the CNC became the sole owner of INMECAFE's equipment. As of late 1995, this equipment had yet to be put to use.

Thus Ruiz Massieu's intervention in favor of the CNC deprived Guerrero's independent producer movement of critical external support from reformist federal officials. In contrast to their counterparts in Oaxaca, Guerrero's small producers faced the neocorporatist project alone.

Producer Response: Partisanship Prevails

To understand why Guerrero's producer organizations chose a partisan strategy that aimed to defeat the governor's neocorporatist project, we

[43] Ruiz Massieu's efforts to prevent reformist federal officials from aiding the coalition were helped by the coalition's prior refusal to support Salinas's presidential campaign in the summer of 1988, which strained its relations with reformist federal elites. As one leader of the coalition put it, the decision not to sign the neutral-sounding newspaper endorsement of Salinas in 1988 "cost me my relationship with Carlos Rojas" [Rojas was the national director of PRONASOL]. Interview, Atoyac, Guerrero, Dec. 1995.

[44] The remainder of this paragraph is based on interviews with members of the coalition in Atoyac, Guerrero, Dec. 1995. See also Cobo and Paz Paredes (1991:68).

[45] According to one member of the coalition, his organization had its "check in hand."

need to explore the intense political polarization that occurred in Guerrero during the conjuncture of 1988–91.

Presidential elections in July 1988 were a prelude to a prolonged confrontation between Ruiz Massieu's government and partisan opposition groups that would erupt after local elections in late 1989. According to official figures, Carlos Salinas triumphed in Guerrero with 60.53 percent of the vote, and Cuauhtémoc Cárdenas finished second with 35.8 percent (Calderón Mólgora 1994:94). Cárdenas's National Democratic Front (FDN) claimed its candidate had won 60 percent of the vote in Guerrero and that Salinas had captured just 30 percent.[46] The FDN immediately accused government officials of electoral fraud.[47]

Protests soon erupted in eight of Guerrero's 75 municipalities, including three of the five most important coffee-producing municipalities – Atoyac de Alvarez, Coyuca de Benítez, and Tecpan de Galeana – all located in the Costa Grande region.[48] The protestors demanded official recognition that Cárdenas had won the elections, and they sought the immediate removal of PRI municipal presidents suspected of having engineered local electoral fraud. In Coyuca de Benítez, supporters of the pro-Cárdenas "Coyuca Democratic Front" (FDC) seized the town hall and held it two months, until they were forcibly dislodged by the military.[49]

Even according to official electoral returns, Guerrero was one of the states where Cárdenas received the most support.[50] Among states that had traditionally registered the largest shares of votes for the PRI, which were southern, predominantly rural states, the ruling party's vote fell most

[46] Estrada (1994a:113); Calderón Mólgora (1994:122). As Estrada points out (p. 114), the official figures are called into question by the fact that they record the election of 1988, clearly one of the most contested and mobilizing political events in Guerrero's recent history, as having had less turnout than any other presidential election since 1964. Also, in contrast to the four previous presidential elections, the official results report the total number of votes cast in Guerrero for presidential candidates as less than those cast for plurality federal deputies.

[47] Half-destroyed ballots in favor of Cárdenas found in rivers and canyons across Guerrero lent support to this accusation.

[48] Estrada (1994a:113–14); Calderón Mólgora (1994:122). Protests also erupted in Petatlán, which had a small group of approximately 125 coffee producers. Malinaltepec and San Luis Acatlán are the other two major coffee municipalities in Guerrero. They are located in the Costa Chica region south of Acapulco.

[49] For a detailed account of events in Coyuca, see Calderón Mólgora (1994:134–42).

[50] According to the official data, Cárdenas received larger shares of the vote in only five other states: Michoacán (63.76%), Morelos (57.65%), the State of Mexico (51.33%), the Federal District (48.21%), and Nayarit (36.64%). See Estrada (1994a:113).

dramatically in Guerrero.[51] Thus Ruiz Massieu had clearly failed to deliver his quota of votes for his president and party – a failure this aspiring national leader was determined not to repeat in the local elections set for December 1989.

Local Elections of 1989

Local elections on December 3, 1989 marked the debut in Guerrero of the Party of the Democratic Revolution (PRD), which had been formed at the national level in October 1988 by the main opposition parties that had supported Cárdenas's unsuccessful bid for the presidency.[52] A climate of escalating violence preceded the elections. PRD leaders received numerous death threats, and the president of the PRI's State Executive Committee repeatedly denounced the PRD as the "party of violence and blood" (Estrada 1994a:145–6; Calderón Mólgora 1994:126–7). In April 1989 confrontations near Acapulco between PRI and PRD supporters left more than forty wounded. Soon after, the PRD threatened that, if necessary, it would seize town halls and block highways to defend its electoral victories.[53]

In the Costa Grande, PRD supporters destroyed PRI electoral propaganda in Atoyac and seized the offices of the Municipal Electoral Committee in Petatlán. As election day approached, Ruiz Massieu announced he was putting the army on alert to preserve "order and social tranquility" (Calderón Mólgora 1994:126). Five days before the elections, the State Electoral Committee distributed an ominous, intimidating pamphlet that described the severe punishment awaiting those who chose to employ traditional partisan opposition tactics, such as seizing town halls, blocking highways, and disrupting inaugural ceremonies.[54]

---

[51] The appeal of *Cardenismo* in Guerrero can be explained in part by the citizens' fond memories of Cuauhtémoc Cárdenas's father, President Lázaro Cárdenas, who carried out agrarian reform in Guerrero in the 1930s and subsequently directed the Rio Balsas Commission, a multistate economic development program in the 1960s that included Guerrero. Moreover, the Costa Grande and Tierra Caliente regions, where the FDN had the strongest showings in Guerrero, border on and have important cultural and economic links to Michoacán, Cuauhtémoc Cárdenas's home state and base of support.

[52] In Guerrero the PRD was formally established in early 1989 (Estrada 1994a:114).

[53] According to Balderas (1989:8), the PRD's campaign emphasized a "negative" electoral strategy focused on denouncing actual or imagined electoral fraud, rather than elaborating positive political alternatives.

[54] According to this pamphlet, which was entitled "Law to Punish Electoral Violence," participating in the occupation of a building could be punished by up to nine years in prison;

Internal ruptures inside the PRI heightened this tense, preelectoral atmosphere. These ruptures stemmed from disputes over the rules of the party's process for selecting candidates. After the PRD's strong performance in the national elections of July 1988, Ruiz Massieu announced that the PRI's internal nomination process in Guerrero would be reformed to end the traditional practice of top-down imposition of candidates by party elites. To promote the selection of candidates with genuine local support, Ruiz Massieu created a network of local Committees for Organization and Oversight of Internal Elections (COVEI).[55] And to limit the potential for this reform to cause tensions inside the PRI, all candidates who chose to compete for the party's nomination were obliged to sign a "pact of honor" in the governor's presence that affirmed their commitment to respect the results of the internal selection process.[56]

Despite these precautions, the new selection process ignited numerous conflicts among PRI factions. Throughout the summer of 1989, internal party struggles raged, typically pitting new groups encouraged by the governor's reforms and led by "natural leaders" with grassroots support against old-guard factions backed by the PRI's entrenched state leadership. This infighting led many local groups to withdraw from the PRI and join an opposition party, usually the PRD.

From the perspective of opposition parties, these rifts within the PRI seemed to open new possibilities for electoral triumph, a perception that encouraged preelectoral mobilization. From the standpoint of the PRI leadership, these divisions heightened their insecurity by intensifying the threat posed by the PRD. Factional conflict inside the ruling party thus

and blocking the election or installation of public officials constituted an act of "rebellion," which was punishable by 15 years in prison. Calderón Mólgora (1994:127).

[55] Ruiz Massieu also modified the state's electoral law in February 1989 and again in May 1989. The first reform, which increased the number of state legislators elected by plurality votes from 14 to 24, was designed to limit the weight of proportional representation (PR) seats, which were increasingly captured by opposition parties and the total number of which remained unchanged (Payan Torres 1990:81–2). The second reform was designed to punish coalitions and send the message to opposition parties, as Payan Torres (p. 82) put it, "Don't unite and you'll end up better off."

[56] It is questionable whether Ruiz Massieu himself genuinely sought to break with the traditional PRI practice of top-down selection of candidates. According to one observer, rather than transforming the internal candidate selection process into the "laboratory of electoral transparency" Ruiz Massieu had promised, "From the beginning, the governor and the party [leadership] helped and provided all kinds of resources to their preferred candidates, in order to guarantee that they won the internal election. In some municipalities, the state president of the PRI, who was himself chosen by Governor Ruiz Massieu, simply imposed candidates" (quoted in Calderón Mólgora 1994:124).

contributed to the overall atmosphere of violence and instability that characterized the period leading up to the local elections.[57]

Postelectoral Conflicts.   Although the PRD initially claimed victory in 16 of Guerrero's 75 municipalities, the preliminary official returns showed PRD triumphs in just three municipalities. For its part, the PRI initially claimed victory in 71 municipalities (Estrada 1994a:114–15).[58]

The first postelectoral violence erupted in the key coffee-producing municipality of Tecpan de Galeana in the Costa Grande region. Approximately 250 PRD militants gathered at the offices of the Municipal Electoral Committee to protest the suspected theft of ballot boxes by the PRI's candidate. They soon clashed with police, which resulted in many injuries on both sides. By December 5, two days after the elections, protests against electoral fraud had occurred in approximately 20 municipalities. The state government's violent response to the protests exacerbated the tense situation. Antiriot police forcibly expelled more than 100 PRD supporters from the town hall of Chichihualco. The secretary general of the state government declared this expulsion a lesson for others engaged in or contemplating similar protests. According to Payan Torres (1990:90), the government's policy was to "repress first, negotiate later."

In Atoyac, the stronghold of the independent coffee producer movement, 300 antiriot and state judicial police battled 400 PRD militants in front of the offices of the Municipal Electoral Committee. This conflict resulted in 36 injured (four gravely) and three disappearances. Both the rank and file and leaders of the Coalition of Ejidos of the Costa Grande participated in the confrontation.[59] The same day, in the adjacent coffee-producing municipality of Coyuca de Benítez, PRD supporters destroyed the PRI's local headquarters and attacked the offices of the Municipal Electoral Committee (Calderón Mólgora 1994:129, 141). On December 18, these militants seized Coyuca's town hall and installed the PRD's candidate as municipal president.

---

[57] According to a poll taken one week before the elections, in three of the state's most important cities (Acapulco, Chilpancingo, and Iguala) an average of 56% of those polled did not believe the vote would be respected. In Atoyac, this figure was 58% (Payan Torres 1990:119; 83–7).

[58] According to Velázquez Alzua (n.d.:109–10), the PRD clearly won in 8 municipalities and received vote shares close to those received by the PRI in another 26. Velázquez's analysis is based on data from individual ballot boxes.

[59] Interviews, Atoyac, Guerrero, Dec. 1995. The incident occurred on Dec. 10, 1989.

At the end of December, official election results were finally announced. According to these figures, the PRI had won 56 municipalities, and the PRD had captured nine (including one major coffee-producing municipality, Tecpan de Galeana). The official figures did not recognize the PRD's claim to have won Guerrero's two most important coffee-producing municipalities (Atoyac and Coyuca).[60] In those municipalities and approximately twenty others, postelectoral conflicts continued unresolved into the new year.

Violence resurged just before January 1, 1990, the day the new municipal governments were set to take office. In Coyuca de Benítez, PRD and PRI supporters clashed, leaving four dead and five wounded. On the eve of the inaugurations, a journalist described the tense situation in Atoyac as follows: "[PRD supporters] are coming down from their mountain villages and gathering in the church of this municipal capital. Most are armed with sticks and machetes" (quoted in Calderón Mólgora 1994:130). For its part, the state government announced that it was mobilizing 3,700 police to provide security on inauguration day.

At the end of February, violent confrontations occurred between police and PRD militants who attempted to shut down the airports of the key tourist resorts, Acapulco and Zihuatanejo. According to the PRD's state leadership, this conflict resulted in 50 wounded, 11 missing, and 22 imprisoned partisans. Soon after, more than 200 PRD militants, including the party's state leadership, were indicted by Guerrero's attorney general.

Three months after the elections, 20 town halls were still occupied by PRD militants, who in most cases had installed "parallel governments" that began to collect taxes, issue permits and licenses, and organize police forces. In such municipalities, the officially recognized PRI governments were often compelled to operate out of private homes.[61]

In early March, Rubén Figueroa Alcocer, the son of the hardline former governor, was appointed president of the PRI's executive committee in

---

[60] Balderas 1989:9–10. Additionally, the official figures recognized just one PRD victory in the contest for 24 plurality seats in the state legislature (District XII in the Tierra Caliente region). By contrast, the PRI won 22 seats. The PRD was given 2 of the 12 proportional representation seats (the PRI controlled 4). See Melgar (1990:290). The magnitude of election-day irregularities makes it difficult to know which party really won where. On these irregularities, see Payan Torres (1990:89–90).

[61] Although these officially sanctioned municipal governments maintained control of the uniformed police corps and received funds from the state government, they were often unable to administer municipal services, because the necessary documents and forms were in the hands of the PRD supporters who controlled the town halls.

Guerrero. Figueroa moved quickly to end the postelectoral conflicts by ordering police to expel PRD supporters from eight town halls.[62] At the same time, he also initiated negotiations with the PRD's state leadership, which soon led to a pact between the two parties and the state government. This pact granted proportional representation to the PRD in a number of municipal governments and successfully resolved most of the postelectoral conflicts.[63]

Problems persisted in seven municipalities (including Atoyac and Coyuca de Benítez) where local PRD militants rejected the pact signed by the state leadership of their party (Estrada 1994a:150–1). In Coyuca PRD supporters armed with rifles and machetes announced they would defend the town hall "at all costs" and would not accept bargains made on their behalf by party elites (Calderón Mólgora 1994:133).

Postelectoral conflict in Atoyac proved the most intractable of all. Even in Coyuca, an agreement was eventually reached and a compromise municipal government installed. In Atoyac, however, a tense political situation persisted through 1991. Because the bulk of Guerrero's coffee production as well as its most important independent producer organization were located in Atoyac, this case warrants closer analysis.

Postelectoral Conflict and the Coffee Sector: The Case of Atoyac. The PRI's candidate for municipal president of Atoyac in 1989 was Pedro Magaña, treasurer of the CNC-controlled Union of Ejidos Alfredo V. Bonfil.[64] Because of the hostility between the official Union Alfredo V. Bonfil and the independent Coalition of the Costa Grande, the bulk of the latter's rank and file joined a broad civic front that supported the PRD's candidate. In the face of this decision by the rank and file to support the PRD, some of the coalition's leadership attempted to protect its economic

---

[62] These police operations resulted in several deaths and scores of wounded and arrested. According to a top aide to the governor, these expulsions were a necessary retaliation for the PRD's failed attempt to seize the airports of Acapulco and Zihuatanejo (Calderón Mólgora 1994:133). For a positive assessment of Ruiz Massieu's management of the electoral conflict, see "Si Ruiz Massieu viviera, estaríamos celebrando la reforma," *La Jornada*, Sept. 29, 1995.

[63] According to Calderón Mólgora's calculations (1994:159–60), the postelectoral violence of 1989–90 in Guerrero resulted in 20 dead (15 PRDistas; 2 PRIistas; 3 police), 137 wounded (110 PRDistas; 13 PRIistas; 14 police), and 92 arrested (all PRDistas).

[64] This section draws on Cobo and Paz Paredes (1991:65) and on my interviews with participants in these events.

development projects from PRI reprisals by maintaining a nonpartisan, productivist position. However, this position soon proved unsustainable, because a widespread popular protest erupted against electoral fraud when Magaña's victory was announced.

In March 1990, after occupying Atoyac's town hall for three months, the pro-PRD civic front, which included hundreds of the Coalition of the Costa Grande's rank and file as well as the majority of its leadership, finally reached an agreement with Ruiz Massieu to form a plural municipal council.[65] A moderate *priista*, Jaime Coria, was appointed president of the council, and a prominent member of the coalition was chosen *síndico* (vice-president of the municipal council). The eight remaining council seats were distributed as follows: three for the PRI, three for the PRD, and two for the coalition.[66] Thus the new municipal council was a significant victory for the PRD and its allies from the coalition. A reactionary alliance of local and state-level PRI hardliners soon reversed this victory, however.

Despite the governor's increasing willingness by March 1990 to negotiate with partisan opposition groups in order to end the ongoing governability crisis in Guerrero, the local PRI faction led by Magaña vigorously opposed the pact that the governor had brokered for Atoyac. This faction refused to accept prominent members of the Coalition of the Costa Grande in a pacted municipal government. Moreover, the local *priistas* had powerful allies at the state level, most notably Figueroa Alcocer, the new president of the PRI's State Executive Committee. These local and state-level PRI hardliners joined forces and mobilized against the compromise municipal government, demanding that the governor respect the original election results in favor of Magaña.

The PRI hardliners launched their counterattack in May 1991. Figueroa forced the dismissal of the compromise municipal president and installed a new president backed by the local PRI faction.[67] PRD and coalition militants responded by forming a Municipal Front of Democratic

---

[65] The terms of this pact resembled those signed at the same time in other municipalities across the state.

[66] Interviews, Atoyac, Guerrero, Dec. 1995.

[67] Laura Sánchez Granados, "Figueroa Alcocer, tras la represión en Atoyac: PRD," *La Jornada*, July 1, 1991; "Figueroa: el caso Atoyac, solucionado," *El Sol de Acapulco*, June 21, 1991; Manuel Nava, "Violento desalojo de la presidencia municipal de Atoyac, Guerrero; 18 perredistas detenidos," *El Financiero*, June 19, 1991, p. 29.

Citizens and then seizing the town hall. State judicial police forcibly expelled them several weeks later, which resulted in another tense situation of ungovernability and instability.[68]

The continuing conflict between the CNC-controlled Union Alfredo V. Bonfil and the independent Coalition of the Costa Grande, which had begun in 1987 as a struggle over which organization would represent the region's coffee producers, had shifted to the broader issue of controlling local government. This shift of its struggle against the CNC to the electoral arena brought the Coalition of the Costa Grande into conflict with a new opponent – hardline, state-level PRI elites led by Figueroa Alcocer. The attack this hardline bloc launched against the coalition in 1991 prolonged and intensified the politicization of the coffee sector, thereby closing off whatever limited opportunities Ruiz Massieu's neocorporatist project may have offered for constructing a participatory policy framework through a Oaxaca-style remaking from below. Figueroa's election as governor in 1993 ensured that this politicization would persist.

Polarization in Guerrero: Was It the Producers' Fault?

As we have seen, Guerrero's most important grassroots coffee producer organization, the Coalition of the Costa Grande, pursued a partisan strategy during 1988–91. The coalition's rank and file actively supported the PRD and joined postelectoral protests to defend the ballot box. Moreover, some of the coalition's leaders held office alongside their PRD allies in the pacted municipal government formed in Atoyac in March 1990. In contrast to its counterpart in Oaxaca, CEPCO, which during this period focused on gaining admission into new, state-level institutions for policy-making in the coffee sector, the Coalition of the Costa Grande focused on democratizing and participating in local government.

In Oaxaca CEPCO's engaged productivist strategy, which carefully separated the struggle to modify the state government's neocorporatist reregulation project from partisan and electoral conflicts, played a key role in the formation of a participatory policy framework. In Guerrero, by contrast, the Coalition of the Costa Grande's partisan strategy deflected attention from the task of building new regulatory institutions to replace

---

[68] José Antonio Rivera Rosales, "Sorpresivo desalojo policíaco en Atoyac," *El Sol de Acapulco*, June 19, 1991; Manuel Nava, "Violento desalojo de la presidencia municipal de Atoyac, Guerrero; 18 perredistas detenidos," *El Financiero*, June 19, 1991, p. 29.

INMECAFE. Furthermore, the partisan strategy drew the coalition into conflict with hardline PRI elites at both the state and local levels, a confrontation that heightened the coffee sector's politicization and contributed to the construction of an exclusionary policy framework.

Because similar neocorporatist projects resulted in dramatically different policy frameworks in Oaxaca and Guerrero, we might infer that the divergent strategies of producer organizations by themselves explain these varied outcomes: Had Guerrero's independent producers, like their counterparts in Oaxaca, chosen an engaged productivist instead of a partisan strategy, a participatory policy framework would also have resulted in Guerrero. We might then conclude that the exclusionary outcome in Guerrero was the producers' "fault," because they chose the "wrong" strategy.

It would be a mistake to jump to this conclusion, however. Bargaining over the new institutions that replaced those destroyed by Mexico's neoliberal reforms occurred in the context of broader processes of political regime change both subnationally and nationally. This environment had an important impact on how the actors who participated in reregulation processes perceived the costs and payoffs of different strategies. To understand the strategies adopted by producer organizations thus requires that we look beyond the type of reregulation project these actors faced by considering the larger political context in which they operated.

At the end of the 1980s, the political contexts in Oaxaca and Guerrero differed in important respects. First, the two states had distinct types of subnational political regimes. Ramírez's populist regime in Oaxaca tolerated and eventually sought to negotiate with independent producer organizations, whereas Ruiz Massieu's modernizing regime in Guerrero repeatedly attacked such groups. Moreover, in contrast to Ramírez, Ruiz Massieu launched a neocorporatist project that emphasized rejuvenating the CNC far more than building new government regulatory institutions. These factors significantly weakened the Coalition of the Costa Grande's incentives for choosing an engaged productivist strategy.

Furthermore, in Guerrero a hardline bloc of traditional elites, which was determined to resist political liberalization at all costs, held significant power at the state level. In Oaxaca, by contrast, traditional elites had been greatly weakened both by social upheavals in the 1970s and by Ramírez's populist regime. Although Guerrero's coffee producers may not have anticipated this outcome, their partisan strategy forced them into a costly confrontation with the hardline bloc. This confrontation heightened the coffee sector's already intense polarization and further narrowed the possibilities for achieving a participatory institutional outcome.

To assess how these various factors shaped the strategy of Guerrero's producer organizations, it is helpful to address two questions. First, if the Coalition of the Costa Grande had chosen an engaged productivist strategy, would the resulting policy framework have been different? Second, was such a strategy possible?

The evidence suggests that if the coalition had chosen a productivist strategy, it could have reduced the intensity of political polarization in the coffee sector. First, such a strategy might have avoided the confrontation between the coalition and the hardline PRI bloc led by Figueroa. This confrontation was a key cause of the sector's politicization when INMECAFE withdrew, and Figueroa's subsequent election as governor in 1993 prolonged the polarization. Second, a productivist strategy might have allowed the coalition to take advantage of Ruiz Massieu's willingness to negotiate with it in March 1990. At that time the governor agreed to a political pact that gave a share of Atoyac's municipal government offices to the coalition. Moreover, by mid-1990 Ruiz Massieu was becoming somewhat more tolerant of independent producer organizations and was increasingly disposed to differentiate nonpartisan, productivist groups from opposition political parties. For example, in March 1990, after the bulk of the postelectoral conflicts had finally been resolved, a rapprochement occurred between Ruiz Massieu and the independent Alliance of Autonomous Campesino Organizations of Guerrero, with which the coalition was affiliated. After three years without any assistance from Ruiz Massieu's government, the Alliance signed seven "concertation" agreements with the state government that guaranteed generous state and federal funding for a range of rural development projects.[69] Hence the political space for semipluralist interest-group politics seems to have been expanding. If the coalition had embraced a productivist strategy in the spring of 1990, it might have turned this political opening to its advantage. By pursuing a partisan strategy that drew it into conflict with hardline traditional elites, however, the coalition may have missed this opportunity.

---

[69] Calderón Mólgora (1994:87). See also Alianza de Organizaciones Campesinas Autónomas de Guerrero, Comisión Coordinadora (March 1990), which sketches the Alliance's proposal for PRONASOL and state government funding for economic development projects.

Although a productivist strategy might have helped reduce polarization in the coffee sector, it nevertheless seems unlikely that Guerrero's small producers could have achieved a participatory policy framework similar to Oaxaca's. Ruiz Massieu's modernizing regime had a neoliberal orientation that resulted in a reregulation project focused more on rejuvenating frameworks of controlled interest representation than on constructing new institutions for market governance.[70] Consequently, Guerrero's small-producer organizations lacked the kind of new government regulatory institutions that their counterparts in Oaxaca were able to transform into a participatory policy framework. Because of this constraint, a decrease both in government repression and the coffee sector's polarization is perhaps the most Guerrero's small producers could have achieved if they had chosen an engaged productivist strategy.

Was an engaged productivist strategy possible in Guerrero in 1989 and 1990? Several factors suggest that such a strategy would have been very difficult to sustain. First, Ruiz Massieu's hostile takeover of the Union of Ejidos Alfredo V. Bonfil in 1987 had left a strong legacy of enmity and mistrust between him and the coalition. These sentiments were intensified in 1989 by the nomination as the PRI's candidate for the municipal presidency of Atoyac of a CNC leader (Pedro Magaña) who had played a key role in the takeover of the Union Alfredo V. Bonfil.

Second, the Costa Grande region's strong tradition of civic engagement and popular resistance reduced the likelihood that the coalitions' rank and file could have stood by idly while their friends and neighbors protested against electoral fraud. Coffee producers are citizens, too, and the citizens of the Costa Grande had a long history of mobilizing in support of democratic reform movements. In the 1960s, statewide prodemocracy movements led by Lucio Cabañas and Genaro Vázquez Rojas had their core bases of support in the Costa Grande region.[71] Thus it is not surprising that the coalition's rank and file enthusiastically joined the broad civic front that organized in Atoyac to protest against electoral fraud in 1989.

Finally, Guerrero's municipal structure posed additional barriers to a productivist strategy. As analyzed in Chapter 3, CEPCO's broad

---

[70] As noted, Ruiz Massieu had invited no equivalent of Cantú Peña to Guerrero.
[71] In fact, Cabañas was from Atoyac. Both his and Vázquez's movement subsequently developed into revolutionary, armed guerrilla organizations. Also, the Costa Grande was one of the most highly mobilized areas of Guerrero during the Mexican Revolution. See Bartra (1996a).

territorial scope and Oaxaca's atomized municipal structure helped the organization ride above local political conflicts by extending CEPCO's reach far beyond those municipalities that experienced postelectoral disputes. In Guerrero, by contrast, the average municipality was approximately eight times larger than in Oaxaca, and the coalition's membership was concentrated in just three municipalities (Atoyac, Coyuca de Benítez, and Tecpan). Because postelectoral conflicts involving its rank and file erupted in all three municipalities, it would have been very difficult for the coalition to distance itself from the ensuing partisan confrontations.

In Guerrero the volatility of the transition to competitive electoral politics narrowed the margins for pursuing a productivist strategy. In this context, insulating interest-group politics from the electoral arena was extremely difficult, if not impossible. Moreover, because Ruiz Massieu's neocorporatist project deemphasized state building, it supplied poor institutional raw materials for constructing a participatory policy framework. Even if Guerrero's most important producer organization *had* been able to sustain a productivist strategy, it appears unlikely that a participatory policy framework would have resulted.

Institutional Outcome: An Exclusionary Policy Framework

Between 1989 and 1992, grassroots organizations of coffee producers and the state government in Guerrero focused on partisan politics. Neither the Coalition of the Costa Grande nor Ruiz Massieu's government proposed any new institutions to replace INMECAFE.[72] The coalition had weak incentives to propose such institutions, because the governor would surely have tried to impose CNC control over them. In any case the organization's attention was absorbed by the more pressing problem of defending itself and the municipal government of Atoyac against attacks from hard-line PRI elites.

As for Ruiz Massieu, he preferred to destroy rather than build institutions for market governance. Moreover, he had weak incentives to construct such institutions in the coffee sector because officially sanctioned organizations comprised only a small minority of producers. If new institutions were built, the Coalition of the Costa Grande was likely to try to

[72] As analyzed above, Ruiz Massieu's main proactive intervention in the coffee sector during this period was to disrupt efforts by reformist INMECAFE officials to transfer the state-owned company's infrastructure to independent organizations.

126

dominate them. And if the coalition were forcibly excluded, these institutions might give it a convenient target on which to focus opposition.[73] Thus, when asked why Ruiz Massieu did not try to build new institutions for market governance in the wake of the withdrawal of INMECAFE, a member of the coalition explained, "He didn't want to give us an arena to shout in."[74]

In May 1992, after the conflicts stemming from the local elections of 1989 had finally subsided, Ruiz Massieu did issue an executive decree that created a state government agency to take over some functions previously performed by INMECAFE. As its name suggests, however, this Technical Services Agency for Coffee Producers was intended to play an extremely modest role limited to technical assistance and research.[75] The new agency was not authorized to carry out the kinds of broader tasks performed by the State Coffee Council of Oaxaca, (e.g., medium- and long-term planning, designing proposals for development projects, supervising and monitoring project implementation). Moreover, the agency never received funding and, hence, did not even accomplish the minimal activities assigned to it.

In April 1993 Ruiz Massieu finished his term as governor and was succeeded by Rubén Figueroa Alcocer. Because of his previous conflicts with the Coalition of the Costa Grande and his close links to hard-line traditional elites, Figueroa, perhaps even more than Ruiz Massieu, had little interest in building new institutions for coffee sector governance.

By 1993 Guerrero's independent producer organizations started to demand a State Coffee Council. Through their participation in the national organization, CNOC, Guerrero's producers learned about the benefits their counterparts in Oaxaca had received from the coffee council. Guerrero's producers also learned that councils had already been constructed in Mexico's other major coffee-producing states. Hence, Figueroa's government came under increasing pressure to create a state government agency to coordinate policy for the coffee sector.[76]

During this period the organizational profile of Guerrero's coffee sector changed in ways that made it easier for Figueroa's government to accede to these demands. Since 1991 the center of gravity of the independent

---

[73] As seen in Chapter 3, the new institutions proposed by Cantú in Oaxaca had such an effect.
[74] Interview, Atoyac, Guerrero, Dec. 1995. [75] Interviews, Atoyac, Guerrero, Dec. 1995.
[76] See Carlos García, "Se formó la coordinadora estatal de organizaciones cafetaleras," *El Sur*, May 23, 1994.

producer movement had shifted southward, from the Costa Grande to the Costa Chica region that borders Oaxaca. The Coalition of the Costa Grande had experienced internal conflicts and fragmentation, which stemmed largely from leadership mismanagement of credit union funds and bank loans. This factionalism divided and weakened the coalition.[77] At the same time, another organization of small coffee producers – the Union of Ejidos and Communities "Light of the Mountain," which was based in the Costa Chica and La Montaña regions – considerably expanded its influence and supplanted the coalition as Guerrero's principal independent organization.

Light of the Mountain's dramatic expansion in the early 1990s can be explained in part by the disengaged productivist strategy that it had pursued during the electoral conjuncture of 1988–91.[78] In contrast to the Coalition of the Costa Grande, Light of the Mountain had abstained from the postelectoral conflicts of 1988 and 1989. Indeed, no such conflicts occurred in the municipality from which the union drew most of its support – San Luis Acatlán. In the local elections of 1989, PRI hegemony was largely unchallenged in San Luis Acatlán, where the official party won 72 percent of the vote and the PRD received only 19 percent.[79] As we have seen, in other municipalities, such as Atoyac, the dynamics of the transition to competitive electoral politics narrowed the margins for grassroots organizations to pursue nonpartisan, productivist strategies. By contrast, in San Luis Acatlán, this transition had barely begun in 1989, a situation that made it easier for Light of the Mountain to pursue a productivist strategy.[80]

Light of the Mountain's earlier decision in 1987 *not* to join the Alliance of Autonomous Campesino Organizations of Guerrero also helped it sustain a productivist strategy. The Alliance's affiliates, which included the Coalition of the Costa Grande, had alienated close advisers to President Salinas by refusing to endorse preelection newspaper advertisements in support of Salinas's campaign in 1988. These advisers subsequently became top officials of PRONASOL, and they punished organizations that

---

[77] Interviews, Atoyac, Guerrero, Dec. 1995.

[78] Light of the Mountain's success highlights how the political context in Guerrero in the late 1980s tended to reward nonpartisan organizations.

[79] According to Velázquez Alzua (n.d.:145), in San Luis Acatlán "[The PRD] was still far behind the PRI in 1989."

[80] Because of the PRD's weak influence in the Costa Chica region in 1989, a partisan strategy was probably not an option for Light of the Mountain at that time.

had joined the Alliance by severely restricting their access to federal resources. Light of the Mountain, by contrast, benefited greatly from PRONASOL projects for small producers.[81]

As we have seen, the Coalition of the Costa Grande's partisan strategy brought it into conflict with Figueroa while he was president of the PRI's State Executive Committee. As long as the coalition was the hegemonic force in the coffee sector, Figueroa was unlikely to propose or accept new institutions to coordinate policymaking in that sector. Like Ruiz Massieu, he had few incentives to build new institutions that were likely to be dominated by an independent organization with which he had a long history of hostility.

Light of the Mountain had no such history of confrontation with Figueroa.[82] Thus Light of the Mountain's emergence as Guerrero's most powerful independent producer organization reduced the risk to Figueroa of establishing a State Coffee Council. Because of this diminished threat and the mounting pressure to catch up with the other major coffee-producing states, which already had councils, Figueroa finally agreed to create a new government agency to regulate coffee.

In May 1994 he issued an executive decree establishing the State Coffee Council of Guerrero. Because of the prior tensions between the Coalition of the Costa Grande and the state government, however, conflicts soon developed that delayed the council's operations. These conflicts centered on the issue of how the council's coordinator would be chosen. After months of negotiations, an agreement was finally reached: The producer organizations would propose a list of three candidates from which the governor would choose, supposedly by a random drawing. The independent organizations' third choice was appointed coordinator of the coffee council in October 1994.

---

[81] For example, PRONASOL funds made possible the construction of a large warehouse and dry-processing plant (Ravelo and Avila 1994:61). The fact that Light of the Mountain's membership was almost entirely indigenous futher contributed to its rapid expansion, since the organization was eligible for assistance from the National Indigenous Institute (INI). INI began to play an increasingly important role in the coffee sector as INMECAFE withdrew. The Coalition of the Costa Grande's membership, by contrast, was predominantly mestizo, and thus the organization was far less eligible for INI support.

[82] Furthermore, bitter conflicts for control of the Costa Chica region had occurred between Light of the Mountain and the coalition since 1990, when the coalition sought to expand its influence to that region (Ravelo and Avila 1994:90–1). According to members of Light of the Mountain, "We thought that [the coalition's] intentions were to usurp our union, repeating what the CNC had done to the [Union of Ejidos] Alfredo V. Bonfil when it was an autonomous producer organization" (quoted in Ravelo and Avila 1994:90).

Although the coordinator was a competent, well-respected technician, he lacked the leadership and consensus-inducing skills of his counterpart in Oaxaca – skills that were especially important in Guerrero's polarized climate. The council was handicapped further by state government obstruction of its budgetary allocations. The council received no funding until May 1995 and was allocated only one-third of its programmed budget.[83] Consequently, the council was forced to operate with a skeleton staff that relied on office space and vehicles lent by the federal Ministry of Agriculture.

Figueroa showed little interest in supporting the council and appeared intent on keeping it a technocratic dead space. His strategy seemed to be to strangle the council financially in order to avoid creating new institutional access points that might have helped strengthen the independent organizations and increased their leverage in the policy arena.

Weak support for the council from the producer organizations compounded the debilitating effects of lack of funds. The lukewarm enthusiasm for the council partially reflected the coordinator's poor leadership. His laconic, uninspiring style failed to motivate participation. More important, the council's lack of resources gave the organizations few incentives to focus their energies on participating in it. Their time was better spent lobbying federal agencies with resources to distribute (INI, PRONASOL, SAGAR).[84] Lack of funding led to a vicious circle of inefficacy: Because the council had so few resources, it could not generate the support from producer organizations that might have increased its ability to secure more resources. In sum, lack of support either from above or from below severely handicapped Guerrero's State Coffee Council. As one federal official vividly put it, the coffee council was an "orphan."[85]

Guerrero's post-INMECAFE policy framework thus lacked a solid institutional core. A comparison of how coffee plagues and parasites were managed in Oaxaca and Guerrero highlights the tangible consequences for Guerrero's small producers of this institutional gap. Like Oaxaca,

[83] The council's coordinator did not even receive a salary during his first seven months on the job! Interview, Atoyac, Guerrero, Dec. 1995.
[84] According to one PRONASOL official, the council's coordinator had even asked permission to take personal credit for PRONASOL projects in the coffee sector so that he could potentially stimulate more producer interest in the council. Interview, Chilpancingo, Guerrero, Dec. 1995.
[85] Interview, Chilpancingo, Dec. 1995.

Guerrero experienced a major infestation of the *broca*, a coffee bore, in the early 1990s.[86] According to an estimate from 1995, approximately 15,000 of Guerrero's 50,000 hectares of coffee had been affected by *broca* (Gobierno Constitucional del Estado de Guerrero 1995). In Oaxaca the State Coffee Council launched a comprehensive program in 1993 to combat the *broca* plague. In Guerrero, by contrast, the State Coffee Council was just beginning to design a program for controlling the plague at the end of 1995. Although the program's technical dimensions were sound,[87] the chances for its successful implementation were slim. First, the timing of the initiative was inauspicious. In December 1994 Mexico entered a deep economic crisis that led to sharp cuts in federal and state government spending. In contrast to its counterpart in Oaxaca, Guerrero's coffee council thus faced serious fiscal obstacles to launching its anti-*broca* campaign.

Moreover, the weak participation by the producer organizations in Guerrero's council made it difficult to involve their rank and file and technical staffs in the campaign against the *broca* plague. In Oaxaca collaboration between government and producers had contributed to the efficacy of plague control and greatly reduced the costs borne by the coffee council. In the context of the national economic crisis in which Guerrero's coffee council launched its anti-*broca* program, the inability to collaborate with grassroots organizations proved a major disadvantage. For example, although the council designed a sophisticated survey to measure levels of *broca* infestation and gauge the effectiveness of different pesticides, its staff of three could not even begin to administer it. Without the help of engaged producer organizations, the council's sophisticated plan for managing the *broca* plague was doomed to fail.

In December 1995 the coordinator of Guerrero's coffee council unveiled a comprehensive "five-year development plan" for the coffee sector. The plan included proposals for projects that had already been implemented with great success in Oaxaca, such as concrete patios for drying coffee (*asoleadores*) and microprocessing plants. As of 1996, because of the ongoing economic crisis, it appeared highly unlikely that these projects would in fact be carried out. Even if the necessary funds were secured,

---

[86] See the discussion of the *broca* plague in Oaxaca in the previous chapter.
[87] The program in Guerrero focused both on distributing the same antiparasite mushroom that had been employed successfully in Oaxaca and on breeding a local wasp that fed on *broca*.

Guerrero's exclusionary policy framework offered a weak foundation for implementing and sustaining the projects. Indeed, the leaders of the two most important producer organizations, Light of the Mountain and the Coalition of the Costa Grande, did not even bother to attend the meeting at which the coffee council's plan was unveiled.[88]

In sum, the legacy of polarization in Guerrero's coffee sector stemming from the electoral conjuncture of 1988–91 resulted in a policy framework with little potential to improve the welfare of producers.

Conclusion: Tensions between Neocorporatism and Democracy

The case of Oaxaca showed how the politics of reregulation can result in new institutions that enhance the welfare of small producers. In Oaxaca grassroots producer organizations transformed a neocorporatist reregulation project into a participatory policy framework that improved the ability of small farmers to compete in the global marketplace. The case of Guerrero, however, shows that neocorporatist reregulation projects do not necessarily result in participatory policy frameworks. In an authoritarian political system facing pressure to democratize, a neocorporatist project may be linked to the maintenance of the incumbent authoritarian regime. Producers are citizens too, and if they join struggles for democracy and frame their opposition to the neocorporatist project in partisan terms, then it may be extremely difficult to achieve a participatory outcome.

In Guerrero the dismantling of INMECAFE coincided with a volatile transition toward competitive electoral politics. Consequently, bargaining over the shape of the post-INMECAFE policy framework took place in a political context that narrowed the margins for producer organizations to pursue nonpartisan, productivist strategies. By openly embracing the main opposition party and participating in the struggle to democratize local government, the leaders and rank and file of Guerrero's most important organization of small coffee producers sparked a confrontation with hardline authoritarian elites at the state and local levels. This conflict contributed to politicization of the coffee sector, which resulted in an exclusionary policy framework that delivered few, if any, benefits to producers.

The next two chapters turn to the cases of Chiapas and Puebla, where state governors responded to the withdrawal of INMECAFE not by

---

[88] These leaders were angered by the governor's designation of a CNC leader to speak at the meeting on behalf of all the state's coffee producers.

seeking to resurrect mass-based, corporatist frameworks of controlled interest representation, but by trying to build new regulatory institutions that strengthened the hegemony of oligarchs. As we shall see, these crony capitalist reregulation projects posed challenges for grassroots producer organizations that differed dramatically from those associated with neo-corporatist projects. Thus shifting the focus from neocorporatism to crony capitalism will help strengthen our understanding of the politics of reregulation.

5

Peasants against Oligarchs: Stalemate and Transition to a Participatory Policy Framework in Chiapas

The politics of reregulation in Chiapas was foreshadowed by a curious incident in Texas. At the end of 1987, a District Court in Harris County rendered a $15 million verdict in favor of Quaestor Investments, Inc. Quaestor, an import–export firm based in the United States, had sued several close advisors to the governor of Chiapas. The firm sought compensation for the millions of dollars to buy coffee that it had advanced to a state government regulatory agency, the State Coffee Commission of Chiapas. Although thousands of small coffee farmers had delivered their crops to the State Coffee Commission, Quaestor received only a tiny fraction of the half-million bags it had purchased. Furthermore, most of the farmers had not been paid for their coffee. Quaestor's multimillion dollar investment had mysteriously disappeared, presumably into the hands of the governor's cronies who ran the Coffee Commission.[1]

Quaestor Investments' unfortunate experience is more than just another example of the perils of doing business in so-called emerging markets. This case also highlights a crucial reason why the implementation of neoliberal reforms does not necessarily result in competitive markets: Subnational elites have strong incentives to reregulate local markets to their advantage. The Coffee Commission, established in 1985, four years before the withdrawal of INMECAFE, shows how even in the face of an extensive, national regulatory regime, subnational elites can nevertheless

---

[1] For Governor Absalón Castellanos Domínguez's (1982–8) justification of the Coffee Commision as an effort to help producer organizations escape exploitation by middlemen, see Rojas (1995:35). The vignette regarding the Quaestor incident is based on my interviews with leaders of producer organizations and on documents obtained from the Archives of the State Government of Chiapas. See esp. Velázquez Carmona (1989).

seek independent sources of rents by launching their own regulatory initiatives.

Neoliberal reforms at the national level can intensify the regulatory impulses of subnational actors. Indeed, when the dismantling of INMECAFE began in 1989, the government of Chiapas launched a new, more ambitious regulatory project that went far beyond the Coffee Commission's goal of creating short-term rents for the governor's cronies. The new regulatory initiative aimed to revive the hegemony of the oligarchy that had dominated the coffee sector in Chiapas before INMECAFE. Because it focused on winning political support from the coffee oligarchy, this *crony capitalist* reregulation project contrasts sharply with the neocorporatist projects in Oaxaca and Guerrero, where the state governors saw the dismantling of INMECAFE as an opportunity to strengthen officially sanctioned peasant organizations.

In Chapter 2, I argued that different types of reregulation projects shape the strategies of grassroots producer organizations in distinct ways. Because they focus on generating benefits for oligarchs, crony capitalist projects give grassroots organizations weak incentives to pursue engaged productivist strategies. Hence, depending on factors such as their strength and the availability of allies, grassroots organizations are likely either to try to defeat crony capitalist projects or, alternatively, to ignore them by focusing on autonomous economic development projects. Organizations of small coffee farmers in Chiapas initially chose the latter, *disengaged productivist* option and devoted their energies to building their own statewide marketing cooperative.

As we shall see, both the governor's crony capitalist project and the producers' productivist initiative failed, a situation that resulted in a stalemate. After the Zapatista armed uprising in eastern Chiapas in January 1994, this stalemate was broken by a new alliance between the producer organizations and reformist federal government officials against the state government and coffee oligarchy. This alliance defeated the crony capitalist forces, laying the foundations for a *participatory* policy framework.

The first part of the chapter analyzes the modernizing authoritarian regime of José Patrocinio González Garrido (1988–93). This section links the crony capitalist reregulation project that his government launched in the coffee sector both to González's specific policy preferences and the generic dilemmas of support mobilization faced by state governors across Mexico. González sought to manage these dilemmas not by promoting the PRI's corporatist confederations, as had Ramírez in Oaxaca and Ruiz

Massieu in Guerrero, but by cozying up to the oligarchy in an effort to take advantage of the patron–client networks and paramilitary forces it controlled. The dismantling of INMECAFE gave González's government new opportunities to pursue this coalition-building strategy.

The next section analyzes the crony capitalist project. The focus then shifts to the grassroots producer organizations, as I explore their efforts to build a statewide marketing cooperative. The final section turns to the transition from a stalemate to a participatory policy framework. The analysis highlights how the Zapatista rebellion fostered a new alliance between producer organizations and reformist federal officials. Together they were able to defeat the crony capitalist initiative and achieve a participatory policy framework.

Political Context of Reregulation: The Modernizing Regime in Chiapas

José Patrocinio González Garrido established a modernizing authoritarian regime in Chiapas. Like Ruiz Massieu, who created a similar regime in Guerrero, González had close family and political ties to President Carlos Salinas de Gortari, and he supported the president's agenda of market-oriented reform and economic modernization. González's economic strategy combined privatization of public enterprises[2] with promotion of large-scale external investment in sectors such as tourism, urban consumer goods and services, and nontraditional agricultural exports. Moreover, his proximity to the president gave González compelling reasons to expect a promotion to a top federal government post if he succeeded in maintaining political stability in Chiapas and delivering his quota of votes to the PRI.[3] Thus González faced the same dilemma as Ruiz Massieu – reconciling an economic strategy that benefited a narrow segment of the population with the political tasks of mobilizing support for the PRI and preserving stability. González sought to manage this dilemma by combining repression against autonomous societal organizations with selective alliances with both the traditional oligarchy (large

---

[2] For example, his government privatized the Chiapas Forestry Corporation (CORFO) and the Pujiltic sugar mill (Harvey 1994:9).

[3] This expectation was realized in 1992, four years into González's six-year term, when Salinas offered him the prestigious cabinet-level position of secretary of the interior, an offer he quickly accepted. González held this position until the Zapatista uprising led to his dismissal in early 1994.

landowners and merchants whose wealth was based in cattle, timber, and coffee) and old-guard factions of the PRI's corporatist confederations.

Leadership and Ideology

Like many Mexican governors, González spent most of his prior political career outside his home state. He studied in Mexico City, where he earned his undergraduate degree from the National School of Law in 1956, and subsequently lived abroad, studying law and economics at Cambridge University while working at the Mexican Embassy in London (Camp 1995:298). In contrast to governors like Ramírez in Oaxaca and Cervantes in Guerrero, who were first-generation politicians from humble backgrounds, González belonged to a family that was tightly integrated into the national political elite. His father, Salomón González Blanco, had served as secretary of labor under two presidents, Adolfo López Mateos (1958–64) and Gustavo Díaz Ordaz (1964–70), and had even been considered a possible presidential candidate in 1963. González Blanco had also been interim governor of Chiapas (1978–80).

González's marriage to Patricia Ortiz Salinas extended and strengthened his inherited ties to the national political elite. Ortiz Salinas was the niece of Raúl Salinas Lozano, who had served alongside González's father in President López Mateos's cabinet (as secretary of industry and commerce). She was also the cousin of future president Carlos Salinas. Her father, Antonio Ortiz Mena, had been considered a candidate for the presidency in 1970 and had subsequently served as president of the Inter-American Development Bank (1971–88). During the first two years of Salinas's presidency, he was general director of the National Bank of Mexico (BANAMEX), one of Mexico's leading commercial banks (Camp 1995:528–9).

Given his family's impressive connections, it is not surprising that González began his political career at an early age. When his father was secretary of labor, González, then in his twenties, held several administrative posts in the federal executive branch. In 1967, at the age of thirty-three, he was elected to the federal legislature to represent his home district of Palenque, Chiapas. González's career subsequently shifted away from elected office to technical and administrative positions in Mexico City. In the 1970s González held a series of administrative posts in the municipal government of Mexico City, eventually becoming general director of urban development (1978–82).

137

Like Ruiz Massieu, González had little experience as a PRI cadre. Besides serving as president of his class at the National School of Law, his only formal involvement in the party apparatus was a brief stint during the late 1960s as the PRI's delegate to the states of Oaxaca, Jalisco, and Guanajuato (Camp 1995:298). In contrast to populist governors like Ramírez, González's national-level patrons were not members of the party hierarchy or its affiliated corporatist confederations but rather technocrats in federal ministries.

In 1982, after fifteen years in administrative and technical positions, González returned to elected office, serving as senator from Chiapas. González's election to the senate reflected his ties to the PRI's presidential candidate, Miguel de la Madrid, who had been González's classmate at the National Law School. As noted in Chapter 3, de la Madrid's administration was characterized by a marked increase in the number of technocratic candidates for governorships and other elected positions. In this context, González's administrative credentials and political connections made him a strong candidate for elected office. His subsequent nomination as the PRI's candidate for governor of Chiapas in 1988 reflected the efforts of Carlos Salinas (by then the PRI's presidential candidate) to deepen the "technocratization" of governorships begun by de la Madrid. The fact that his wife was Salinas's cousin surely gave González an additional advantage.

Of the governors of Mexico's major coffee-producing states when INMECAFE withdrew, González had the most extensive connections to national political and economic groups. Because of his close family ties to the president, he, more than most governors, had reason to believe the governorship would be a steppingstone to a swift promotion to a high-level federal government post. Of course, any such promotion would be contingent on his successfully carrying out the basic tasks expected of all PRI governors: delivering his quota of votes for the ruling party and maintaining political stability.

González's links to national business groups complicated these two tasks. Through his network of contacts in Mexico City, González had forged close ties with politically influential financial and business elites who sought to exploit the natural resources of Chiapas by investing in its tourist and tropical fruit industries. González's government catered to these interests by focusing on providing them a favorable investment climate. This economic strategy offered little to the state's predominantly poor, rural inhabitants, who cultivated traditional crops, such as corn and beans. Nor did this development strategy benefit the traditional oligarchy, whose wealth was concentrated in coffee and cattle.

To attract external investment into the tourist industry, González's government promoted a cluster of natural and archaeological tourist destinations that formed the so-called Mayan Route. New luxury hotels were built, including a five-star establishment conspicuously located at a principal entrance to the state capital. The state government also constructed a huge center for the performing arts. In addition to hotels and cultural centers, a flurry of new retail stores and shopping malls appeared in the capital. These shops often carried luxury goods beyond the reach of most of the population. Such ventures were financed by national business groups from outside Chiapas (e.g., the Chedraui group, led by Antonio Chedraui Obeso of Veracruz). State government officials, including González himself, reportedly took kickbacks and bribes from the private firms involved in these projects.[4] These investments in tourism and retail consumer goods benefited only a small segment of the overall population, the urban middle and upper classes. Shopping malls, cultural centers, and five-star hotels did little to address the needs of the impoverished majority of one of Mexico's poorest states.[5]

"Maize, the Crop of Failure": Modernizing the Countryside

González's rural development strategy focused on promoting large-scale, commercial agriculture in the state's tropical fruit and citrus enclave, the Soconusco region. Export crops, such as banana, mango, melon, and citric fruits, received special attention.[6] González's government launched a major project to upgrade the Soconusco's main port, Puerto Madero, through which most of the state's banana exports were shipped.[7] Large agribusiness export firms were the principal beneficiaries of these public works, which helped lower their transportation costs and reduce shipment delays.

González had a personal stake in these agribusiness firms, as he was reportedly a business partner of the multimillionaire, Carlos Cabal

---

[4] González was reportedly a business associate of Chedraui through their shared partnership with the financier, Carlos Cabal Peniche (Albarrán de Alba 1994; Ravelo 1994; and Puig 1994).

[5] For data on poverty and marginalization in Chiapas, see Legorreta Díaz (1995).

[6] Harvey (1994:7); González Esponda and Pólito Barrios (1995:112).

[7] Mota (1994:338–9). Banana production in Chiapas doubled between 1989 and 1992 (Ceceña and Barreda 1995:84).

Peniche, who owned Fresh Del Monte Produce (a former subsidiary of Del Monte Foods that Cabal Peniche purchased in the late 1980s). Cabal Peniche's extensive network of political contacts included President Salinas, his secretary of agriculture, Carlos Hank González, and several state governors.[8] He used this network to help build a vast business empire rooted in exports of tropical fruit (especially bananas) from the states of Chiapas, Tabasco, and Yucatán. In fact, Cabal Peniche had explicitly included the upgrading of Puerto Madero in Chiapas as part of his "business plan," which envisioned a "corridor of ports" across southern Mexico to facilitate his business operations (Ravelo 1994:17).

The responsiveness of González's government to the needs of agribusiness conglomerates contrasted sharply with its neglect of the hundreds of thousands of poor *campesinos* who grew traditional crops like maize and beans. Although González's government took modest steps to improve the welfare of small producers by promoting nontraditional cash crops, such as rubber, tobacco, peanuts, soy beans, sorghum, and safflower, such initiatives targeted relatively well-off producers in the Soconusco region. For example, the sixteen *ejidos* in Chiapas that produced soy beans were all in the Soconusco, where 10 percent of *ejidos* had access to irrigation, as opposed to 4.1 percent of *ejidos* in Chiapas as a whole (Harvey 1994:7–8). Tobacco production was also concentrated in the Soconusco enclave.

Despite the fact that Chiapas produced more maize than any other Mexican state, this crop received virtually no support from the state government.[9] Since 1987, maize productivity in Chiapas had fallen precipitously (as it had across Mexico), largely because producers faced higher input costs, falling prices, and reduced access to credit.[10] González ignored

---

[8] Albarrán de Alba (1994). In an interview with *The Wall Street Journal* in 1994, Cabal Peniche boasted that he had numerous ex-governors as business partners (Puig 1994:13). Before his indictment in late 1994 on charges of violating federal banking regulations, Cabal Peniche had been praised as an "exemplary entrepreneur" by President Salinas and his Secretary of Commerce, Jaime Serra Puche (Puig 1994:6).

[9] In 1990, over 166,000 *ejidatarios* in Chiapas (91% of the state's total) produced maize. Federal agricultural policy had also begun to deemphasize maize production during this period, focusing on nontraditional exports, such as fruits and vegetables.

[10] Harvey (1994:11). By 1987, BANRURAL provided credit for only 37% of the national area under maize cultivation and 43% in the case of beans. By contrast, it financed 52% of the land area dedicated to soy beans and 49% of the area under sorghum cultivation. The Pact for Stability and Economic Growth (PECE), signed in late 1987 to control wages and prices, caused the real value of guaranteed maize prices to fall behind the rate of increase in input costs. According to Hewitt de Alcántara (cited by Harvey), the proportion of maize producers operating at a loss increased from 43% in 1987 to 65% in 1988.

the increasingly difficult plight of most *campesinos*, crassly dismissing maize as "the crop of failure."

In contrast to Ramírez in Oaxaca, who launched a massive campaign of public investment and organizing in the countryside, González aimed first and foremost to satisfy the needs of large agribusiness firms. Like Ruiz Massieu in Guerrero, González thus faced the challenge of reconciling an exclusionary development strategy with the political imperatives of maintaining stability and delivering his quota of votes for the PRI. González sought to achieve these political objectives in part by repressing societal organizations not affiliated with the ruling party. During the initial months of his administration, prominent members of independent *campesino* organizations were assassinated, including two of the state's most important *campesino* leaders.[11] In the municipality of Pijijiapan, local police ambushed a group of peasants, killing eight and wounding five.[12] Although González himself may not have personally ordered the attacks, he did nothing to punish those responsible or to prevent future such incidents.

Thus González's government quickly established a reputation for employing heavyhanded tactics against peasant organizations. According to Hernández Navarro (1994:59), "Practically all democratic *campesino* organizations active in the state had some of their members in prison."[13] A climate of violence prevailed across Chiapas, as indicated by one review of the human rights situation five months after González took office that reported twenty-six assassinations since the start of his term (Legorreta 1994:141).

In addition to fostering and exploiting this climate of fear and violence to deter opposition, González sought to build political support by allying with segments of the landed oligarchy. Waves of land reform that had swept most other states in the wake of the Mexican Revolution had had little impact in Chiapas.[14] Consequently the traditional landed elite continued to play a key role across much of rural Chiapas. The oligarchy

---

[11] For González's own account of the assassination of these two leaders, see the interview with him in Rojas (1995:53–6).

[12] Polito and González Esponda (1996:209–10); Harvey (1994:22). The Centro Fray Bartolomé de las Casas documented numerous abuses of human rights by state police against *campesino* organizations during González's tenure (Rojas 1995:140–1, 203–5).

[13] On government violence against peasant organizations in Chiapas, see Polito and González Esponda (1996).

[14] On the ability of the landed elites in Chiapas to avoid the "federal *agrarista* threat," see García de León (1985:175–218).

initially viewed González with suspicion, regarding him as yet another outsider imposed by the federal government.[15] The governor's obvious preference for external investors and his neglect of traditional agricultural crops (i.e., coffee, beef, and lumber) confirmed their doubts.

Because of his need to build a base of political support, however, González could ill afford to alienate the oligarchy. These elites dominated key patron–client networks across rural Chiapas, and they often had personal paramilitary forces ("white guards") at their disposal. Although their grip on rural society had been weakened somewhat since the 1970s by *campesino* organizations, these elites still controlled on-the-ground "carrots and sticks" in many regions.[16] For González, who had entered office with weak local bases of support, allying with these elites offered a way to solve the problems of maintaining stability and securing his quota of votes for the PRI.

The withdrawal of INMECAFE created an attractive opportunity for González to gain the oligarchy's support by reregulating coffee to its advantage. The elites who traditionally had dominated the processing and marketing of coffee in Chiapas had been partially displaced by INMECAFE, which gave small producers an alternative channel for securing production inputs and marketing their crops. The dismantling of the state-owned enterprise gave the oligarchy a welcome chance to reassert its hegemony. González's crony capitalist project was intended to win the oligarchy's political allegiance by helping it achieve that goal.

Reregulation Project and Producer Response: Crony Capitalism from Above, Disengaged Productivism from Below

The withdrawal of INMECAFE triggered two competing projects in Chiapas. González's government sought to give monopoly control

---

[15] Indeed, members of this elite employed a slang term, "Pichichi" – *pinche chilango chiapaneco* [lousy Chiapan from Mexico City] – to refer to politicians who, like González, had spent their careers outside the state. Interviews with members of the oligarchy, Tuxtla Gutiérrez, Chiapas, Oct. 1995.

[16] On the continued strength of the oligarchy and the prevalence of "private violence" in rural Chiapas, see Guillén Rodríguez (1994:309–20). See also Escalante Gonzalbo (1991); Zuñiga López et al. (1995); and Zuñiga (1995). On paramilitary, "rural defense" groups, with telling names like "Force and Reaction," see Juan Balboa, "Investigan diputados la existencia de grupos paramilitares en Chiapas," *La Jornada*, Oct. 6, 1995, p. 14; and Matilda Pérez U. and Elio Henriquez, "Pide la Aedpch a la Procuraduría frenar la violencia contra indios," *La Jornada*, Oct. 6, 1995, p. 18.

over coffee processing and marketing to a small group of elite agro-industrialists and exporters. By contrast, grassroots producer organizations formed a statewide cooperative through which small producers themselves could manage processing and marketing. Although they did not explicitly challenge the crony capitalist initiative, the participants in this productivist project sought to prevent the exploitation of small producers by private elites.

In the end, both projects failed, resulting in a stalemate. Neither the crony capitalist vision of atomized small producers selling their unprocessed coffee to private-sector agro-industry, nor the grassroots dream of producer-controlled processing and exporting were fully realized. Instead, the dismantling of INMECAFE resulted in an uneven, patchwork market structure in which private-sector elites dominated some regions and cooperatives of small producers controlled others.

Cozying up to the Oligarchy: The Special Subcommittee for Coffee Production and Marketing

In March 1989, as the dismantling of INMECAFE was about to begin, González's government created a Special Subcommittee for Coffee Production and Marketing. Formed under the auspices of the State Planning Commission (COPLADE), the subcommittee would spearhead the crony capitalist project.

The subcommittee's composition reflected its mission. González appointed Estéban Figueroa Aramoni as the subcommittee's coordinator. Figueroa, a close friend of the governor, owned a major coffee-exporting firm. The subcommittee's deputy coordinator, Gabriel Orantes Balbuena, belonged to a prominent elite family (the Orantes) that owned extensive coffee plantations and processing facilities in the Jaltenango region.[17] The subcommittee had five representatives of big producers and agro-

---

[17] See "Café: Oro Verde, Sabor Amargo," *La Republica en Chiapas*, Oct. 10, 1994 for an interview with a member of the Orantes family. The coffee oligarchy in Chiapas combined extensive landholdings with ownership of processing and other agro-industrial facilities. It was thus what I described in Chapter 2 as an "agrarian-industrial" elite. On the official (probably underreported) holdings of the Orantes Balbuena family in the municipality of La Concordia, see INMECAFE (1992). According to official figures, Aniceto Orantes Balbuena owned 200 hectares of coffee-producing land; Amado Balbuena owned 150 hectares; and Pedro Aguilar Balbuena owned 150 hectares. The holdings of 400 hectares by Jesús Orantes Aramoni recorded in INMECAFE's census indicate that the Orantes and Aramoni families intermarried.

industrial firms, including the leaders of the local coffee industry's most important private-sector associations: the Regional Agricultural Union of Coffee Producers Tacaná, based in the Soconusco region; the Union of Producers, Industrialists, and Exporters of Coffee of the Yajalón Region, located in northern Chiapas; and Coffee Agroindustries of Chiapas, which drew its membership from across the state.[18] By contrast, the subcommittee included just three representatives for the more than 70,000 small producers in Chiapas, and all three were old-guard CNC leaders. Producer organizations *not* affiliated with the ruling party had no formal representation.

The minutes of the subcommittee's meetings during 1989 clearly reveal its primary objective: reestablishing the oligarchy's hegemony over coffee processing and exporting after twenty years of competition from INMECAFE. The principal tool for achieving this goal would be the regulation of coffee exports through quotas and licenses.

At the subcommittee's initial sessions, its members focused on wresting control of export quotas from INMECAFE.[19] In a letter to the governor in April 1989, for example, the subcommittee expressed its dissatisfaction with how INMECAFE was managing export quotas. They complained that INMECAFE consistently undermeasured Chiapas's production of export-quality coffee and had denied local firms their fair share of national export quotas. To rectify this problem, the subcommittee proposed a "state register of exporters" that it would administer and on which INMECAFE's subsequent distribution of export quotas would be based.[20]

After the rupture of the International Coffee Agreement (ICA) in July 1989, which caused the immediate collapse of the national export quota system, the subcommittee sought autonomous power to issue export licenses at the state level. Thus the subcommittee proposed that firms exporting coffee from Chiapas should be required to obtain licenses from the state government.[21] In addition to creating an important source of rents, this new regulatory power would allow the subcommittee to block the efforts by small-producer cooperatives to export their coffee directly instead of selling it at exploitively low prices to elite-controlled exporting firms. Ironically, the subcommittee justified its move to establish a new

[18] Subcomité Especial de Producción y Comercialización del Café (1989a).
[19] Subcomité Especial de Producción y Comercialización del Café (1989b).
[20] Subcomité Especial de Producción y Comercialización del Café (1989c).
[21] Subcomité Especial de Producción y Comercialización del Café (1989d).

system of export licenses by claiming that this regulatory power would actually protect small producers by helping the subcommittee "exclude speculators [and] coyotes" from local markets.[22]

The subcommittee also tried to promote what it called "direct links" between small producers and private-sector exporters.[23] It proposed that "the group of exporters-industrialists" should protect the welfare of small producers by providing them marketing assistance. As one document put it, "We consider that the best way to help the small producer would be, among other things, establishing contacts with the various exporters, with the obligation on the part of the exporters to provide administrative, financial, and marketing assistance . . . in order to help [the small producers] realize their own exporting in the future."[24] The document made no mention, however, of aiding the ongoing efforts by many small producers to control production and marketing by forming their own autonomous cooperatives.

In a perverse twist on the dominant *campesino* strategy of achieving self-management of the production process, the subcommittee cast private-sector exporters and agro-industrialists as the small producers' principal allies in their struggle to take control of processing and marketing. Through charity or noblesse oblige, the agro-industrial elite would eventually relinquish its control of these activities to small producers. Despite such rhetorical nods to the welfare of small producers, the subcommittee's real objectives were described more accurately by one member of a grassroots cooperative: "Producers should produce, exporters should export."[25]

The subcommittee's attempt to promote direct marketing relations between small producers and private-sector exporters generated little enthusiasm among the former. The earlier scam by the State Coffee Commission of Chiapas during the administration of Governor Absalón Castellanos Domínguez (1982–8) had made small producers wary of state

---

[22] Subcomité Especial de Producción y Comercialización del Café (1989d). "Coyote" is a derogatory term for an exploitive middleman. This justification was ironic, given that many small producers felt the subcommittee was composed of the principal speculators and coyotes. According to the leader of one grassroots producer organization, the export firms represented by the subcommittee tried to differentiate themselves from middlemen by claiming, "We are not coyotes, we are exporters." Interview, Tuxtla Gutiérrez, Chiapas, Oct. 1995.

[23] Subcomité Especial de Producción y Comercialización del Café (n.d.).

[24] Subcomité Especial de Producción y Comercialización del Café (n.d.).

[25] Interview, Tuxtla Gutiérrez, Chiapas, Oct. 1995.

145

government export schemes.[26] As one farmer put it, no one wanted to risk delivering coffee on consignment or for a small advance to a "den of thieves."[27]

Moreover, the subcommittee lacked funding. Mexico's extreme fiscal centralization severely limited the size of most state government budgets, and, in 1989, the principal government agencies with money to spend in the coffee sector of Chiapas were the federal National Indigenous Institute (INI) and PRONASOL. These agencies were in the process of launching a joint national program to help small coffee producers cope with both a global price crash and the disruptive effects of INMECAFE's withdrawal.[28] As we shall soon see, INI and PRONASOL officials in Chiapas were not inclined to support initiatives intended to benefit wealthy private sector elites. Rather than aid the subcommittee, these federal agencies backed an alternative marketing project launched by small-producer organizations themselves. This alternative project further weakened the incentives for small producers to participate in the scheme with private exporters that the subcommittee had proposed.

By the end of the harvest of 1989–90, the subcommittee had ceased its unsuccessful efforts to bring together private exporters and small producers. Through the rest of 1990, the subcommittee functioned as little more than an advocate through which private sector firms lodged complaints about petty corruption by government officials.[29] The subcommittee was disbanded at the end of 1990. González's crony capitalist project had failed.

An Alternative Project from Below: The Social Enterprise Council

In 1987 grassroots organizations of small coffee producers from across Chiapas formed a joint-marketing cooperative called the Coffee Network.[30]

---

[26] See the vignette about this scam at the beginning of this chapter.

[27] Interview, Comitán, Chiapas, Oct. 1995.

[28] For an overview of the INI-Solidaridad program, see INI-Solidaridad, Dirección del Programa de Apoyo a Productores de Café (1994). For a critical appraisal, see Hernández Navarro and Célis Callejas (1994).

[29] Subcomité Especial de Producción y Comercialización del Café (1990).

[30] The Coffee Network included the following organizations: Union of Ejidos La Selva, based near the town of Las Margaritas; the Union of Ejidos San Fernando, located near the state capital of Tuxtla Gutiérrez; Independent Central of Agricultural Workers and Peasants (CIOAC)-Simojovel, located in the northern part of Chiapas; and the ARIC-Union of Unions. Interviews with leaders of these organizations, Chiapas, Oct. 1995.

These organizations were not affiliated with the officially sponsored CNC, and most were led by former members of the Maoist-inspired Proletarian Line, which had established a powerful presence in Chiapas in the mid-1970s.[31] The Coffee Network's goal was to help small producers take control of coffee processing and marketing. In addition to exchanging information about marketing and production strategies, the organizations affiliated with the Coffee Network sold their coffee jointly, thereby securing higher prices through increased volume. The Coffee Network targeted niche, "solidarity" markets in Western Europe (especially in Holland and Germany), where "socially responsible" coffee grown by grassroots organizations of small farmers commanded a premium price.

In mid-1989, when INMECAFE began to withdraw and González's government launched its crony capitalist project, the Coffee Network accepted an invitation from organizations affiliated with the CNC's State Union of Coffee Producers (UEPC-CNC) to join forces and form a massive statewide marketing cooperative. The CNC organizations that sought to ally with the Coffee Network were linked to productivist factions of the PRI's peasant confederation that did not support the state government's crony capitalist initiative. The new marketing cooperative, the Social Enterprise Council of Coffee Producers of Chiapas (CESCAFE), included some thirty organizations from across Chiapas and united well over 5,000 producers in an ambitious joint venture.[32]

To understand how such a curious joint project between independent and officially sponsored producer organizations was possible in Chiapas, it is necessary to consider key developments in Mexico's *campesino* movement that occurred at the national level in the late 1980s. In 1989 the top leaders of the most important independent national *campesino* organization, the National Union of Autonomous Regional Peasant Organizations (UNORCA), accepted high-level government offices in the Salinas administration. These UNORCA leaders turned government officials justified their new positions by claiming a convergence between the neoliberal economic polices of the Salinas administration and the *campesino* struggle for self-management of production and marketing.

---

[31] On the Proletarian Line see Moguel (1987) and (1994).
[32] CESCAFE was composed of four Regional Committees. The eleven organizations that comprised the three Regional Committees of the Soconusco, Sierra, and Coast alone included 5,245 producers (García Aguilar and Pontigo Sánchez 1993:129).

In August 1989 one of UNORCA's founders and leaders, Hugo Andrés Araujo, took office as the CNC's secretary for organization.[33] Araujo sought to rejuvenate the PRI confederation by recovering the ground it had lost during the previous decade to independent producer organizations like UNORCA. To achieve this goal, Araujo and his protégés tried to reform the CNC by shifting its focus from securing votes for the PRI to promoting economic projects and self-managed peasant enterprises. Through what Mackinlay (1996:207) appropriately calls the "Unorcaization" of the CNC, Araujo and his reformist team aimed to strengthen the official confederation by using the very tactics they had previously employed against it.[34]

Araujo's reformist project faced strong opposition from inside the CNC itself. Old-guard factions, especially those linked to the territorially based Agrarian Leagues, felt threatened by the new focus on productivist projects and on cooperating with independent organizations. These internal cleavages were especially intense at the subnational level, where old-guard CNC groups often had support from state governors and other local elites. Consequently, reformist CNC cadres committed to productivist projects often found they had more in common with nonpartisan, independent *campesino* organizations than with many of their fellow CNC members.

CESCAFE spearheaded Araujo's reformist initiative in Chiapas. The CNC reformists hoped CESCAFE would weaken old-guard CNC factions, whose leaders supported the governor's crony capitalist project despite the fact that it offered few benefits to their rank and file. By offering an attractive alternative to the governor's project, CESCAFE was intended to undermine the old-guard CNC groups. At the same time the CNC reformists also hoped that CESCAFE would counteract the threat to the CNC's hegemony posed by independent organizations, such as those affiliated with the Coffee Network. By embracing their productivist strategy and incorporating them into a CNC-led project, CESCAFE would steal these organizations' thunder.

---

[33] Araujo would subsequently be elected secretary general of the CNC in 1992 (Mackinlay 1996:201). In addition to Araujo, other prominent UNORCA leaders who accepted positions with the Salinas administration included Gustavo Gordillo de Anda, who was appointed undersecretary of agriculture, and Jesús Rubiell, who joined INI-PRONASOL.

[34] Gustavo Gordillo's *concertación* strategy, which focused on channeling to CNC affiliates the resources of state-owned enterprises that were being dismantled by the neoliberal reforms, was an important complement to Araujo's strategy.

The CNC's privileged access to government resources attracted the independent organizations to CESCAFE, as did the possibility of achieving greater market power by collectively selling enormous volumes of coffee. For many independent organizations, benefits such as these outweighed the risks of allying with CNC groups.[35] Furthermore, many CNC cadres involved in the CESCAFE project had worked previously with the independent organizations. These ties further facilitated the alliance between the independent organizations and the CNC that formed around CESCAFE's productivist project.

Araujo's protégé, Rafael Arellanes Caballero, was named director of CESCAFE. Before joining the CNC with Arajuo, Arellanes had worked as an advisor to major independent organizations in Chiapas, such as the ARIC Union of Unions. Under Arellanes's leadership, CESCAFE quickly cashed in on its government support by securing an unusually large loan through INI-PRONASOL to help finance coffee purchasing in the 1989–90 harvest.[36]

CESCAFE's links to powerful CNC and federal government patrons soon proved double-edged. Tensions developed between the dual objective of marketing coffee, on the one hand, and rejuvenating the CNC, on the other. Arellanes began to treat CESCAFE as a personal springboard to a national CNC position, a move that contributed to overexpansion and mismanagement of funds. Within only few months of its founding, CESCAFE had opened five offices and hired excessive staff, which caused administrative expenses to soar. Numerous participants in CESCAFE attributed this rapid expansion to Arellanes's career ambitions. They pointed out that because large-scale projects were likely to attract the most attention from Arellanes's superiors, he had strong incentives to quickly increase the organization's size.[37] This focus on rapid expansion also created pressure for CESCAFE to admit new organizations regardless of whether they were capable of producing high-quality coffee.

---

[35] Several prominent independent organizations, such as the Organization of Indigenous People of the Sierra Madre of Motozintla (ISMAM) and the Majomut Union of Ejidos and Coffee-Producing Communities, chose not to join CESCAFE.

[36] Instituto Nacional Indigenista, Delegación Estatal Chiapas (n.d.a). Since at least the early 1980s, INI had played an active role supporting autonomous campesino organizations in Chiapas (Hernández Navarro 1994:54–5).

[37] Interviews with leaders of non-CNC producer organizations, Chiapas, Oct. and Nov. 1995.

Despite the generous start-up loan from INI-PRONASOL, CESCAFE soon experienced financial difficulties. By the beginning of the 1990–1 harvest, the organization had repaid a paltry 17 percent of INI-PRONASOL's loan from the previous year.[38] These financial troubles severely hampered CESCAFE's ability to purchase coffee from affiliated producers. For example, in the Soconusco, Coast, and Sierra regions, where CESCAFE had bought approximately 20 percent of the estimated production of its members during the 1989–90 harvest, it was able to purchase just 6 percent of estimated production during the 1990–1 harvest (García Aguilar and Pontigo Sánchez 1993:130).

In addition to these internal problems, CESCAFE's links to Araujo's national project to reform the CNC drew it into conflict with old-guard CNC groups who backed the governor's crony capitalist project. The governor supported these groups and even threatened to imprison Arellanes, charging him in late 1991 with misuse of public funds. Araujo soon pulled his protégé out of Chiapas and appointed him to the leadership of the CNC's National Union of Coffee Producers. INI-PRONASOL officials who had supported CESCAFE also faced growing pressure from González's government. In early 1992 the state government jailed several of these federal officials, accusing them of stealing public funds.[39] The effects of Arellanes's departure, the state government's attack against reformist federal officials, and mounting financial difficulties soon led to CESCAFE's collapse.

Despite its demise, CESCAFE had an enduring impact on the evolution of the post-INMECAFE policy framework in Chiapas. Their participation in CESCAFE solidified the linkages among the independent producer organizations.[40] With help from the national-level independent coordinating network, CNOC, the organizations in Chiapas would sub-

---

[38] Depressed global coffee prices also contributed to CESCAFE's financial problems. By July 1991, however, at least one major producer-managed cooperative, ISMAM, had repaid all of the previous year's credits from INI-PRONASOL (García Aguilar and Pontigo Sánchez 1993:130). Moreover, an INI-PRONASOL document names CESCAFE as one of "the only debtors" during the 1989–90 cycle (Instituto Nacional Indigenista, Delegación Estatal, n.d.a). Hence, even in the face of depressed prices, it was not impossible for producer organizations to service their debts.

[39] These arrests occurred just several months after hotly contested federal elections in August 1991. According to one of the arrested officials, the governor suspected them of having campaigned for the PRD. Interview, Tuxtla Gutiérrez, Chiapas, Oct. 1995.

[40] Their participation in CESCAFE also demonstrated to the independent organizations the great risks of allying with productivist CNC groups.

sequently join forces and carry out a successful initiative to build a participatory policy framework. As we shall see, some of the same federal
officials who had backed CESCAFE would provide crucial support for this
new initiative. Although González defeated the federal reformists in 1992,
many would reemerge in 1994, when the Zapatista uprising opened fresh
opportunities for launching productivist projects.

From Stalemate to Exclusion: The State Coffee Council of Chiapas

At the end of 1992, González received his anticipated invitation back to
Mexico City when President Salinas offered him the prestigious cabinet
position of secretary of the interior. González immediately accepted and
named Elmar Harald Setzer Marseille (1993–4) to complete the remaining two years of his term.[41] Setzer, who one observer described as a "Boer-
style rancher of European extraction," belonged to a wealthy family of
coffee producers and exporters based in the northern part of the state.[42]
Not surprisingly, given his strong family ties to the coffee industry, Setzer
soon launched a new policy initiative for the sector.

In February 1993 he issued an executive decree establishing the State
Coffee Council of Chiapas (COESCAFE) (Gobierno del Estado de
Chiapas 1993). According to the decree, the council would coordinate
planning and policy for the coffee sector. Thus COESCAFE's formal
responsibilities closely resembled those of Oaxaca's State Coffee Council
as analyzed in Chapter 3. Despite these similarities, the two councils
differed in key respects. First, COESCAFE's director was granted a far
greater degree of discretion. The governor's decree stipulated that the
director could "invite" (or not invite) representatives of producer organizations to join the council's board of directors.[43] Because the decree did
not *guarantee* seats on the board to any producer organizations, the
council's director had the power to include or exclude organizations at his
discretion.[44]

---

[41] As one observer put it, "González left the keys to his ranch to Setzer."
[42] Reding (1994:14). The Setzers' wealth was located principally in the municipality of
Yajalón.
[43] The decree states that "representatives of the social sector of coffee producers" will have
votes in the council and that these representatives "will be invited by the president of the
board of directors" (Gobierno del Estado de Chiapas 1993:12).
[44] In Oaxaca, by contrast, the legislation establishing the coffee council guaranteed seats to
specific producer organizations.

Second, COESCAFE formally included municipal presidents from coffee-producing regions. Although they were granted "voice without vote," the municipal presidents of the eight most important coffee-producing municipalities in Chiapas (Tapachula, Motozintla, Yajalón, San Cristobal de las Casas, Las Margaritas, Jaltenango, Simojovel, and Tapilula) had the authority to name "representatives of the coffee regions" to the council, and these regional representatives *did* hold votes.[45] In Chiapas municipal presidents were often local political bosses linked closely to the PRI's clientelist networks. Their designation as members of COESCAFE thus signaled that promoting rural development would not be at the top of the new agency's agenda.

Finally, in contrast to their counterparts in Oaxaca, the producer organizations in Chiapas had not been consulted about the coffee council's design. Governor Ramírez had organized a grandiose public forum (analyzed in Chapter 3) to unveil his proposed legislation. Governor Setzer convened no such event – he simply created the council by executive fiat.

Because of its exclusionary design and birth by imposition, the new coffee council failed to generate enthusiasm among the small-producer organizations. The council's lack of funds reinforced this disinterest.[46] Although the council's first director did elaborate a plan of action, lack of resources prevented its implementation. During its first year, COESCAFE was little more than an empty shell imposed on the coffee sector by a weak interim governor.

The Coffee Council as a Political Weapon

In its second year, the coffee council began to play an increasingly active role. At the end of January 1994, as a result of the armed Zapatista uprising that erupted in Chiapas earlier that month, Setzer was forced to resign as governor. His replacement, Javier López Moreno (1994), appointed a new director to the coffee council, José Damas Damas. Damas was a promi-

---

[45] According to a document from a major producer organization critical of the council's institutional design, this framework of "regional representatives [resulted in] the extreme case that the representative of the coffee producers from the Los Altos region was named by the municipal president of San Cristobal, where there is not even a single coffee plant" (CNOC-Chiapas 1995).

[46] As discussed below, most small producer organizations focused their energies instead on federal assistance programs administered by INI-PRONASOL.

nent member of the local PRI machine who had served on the party's State Committee and had been municipal president of the town of Catazajá, located near Palenque.[47] He sought to convert the coffee council into a political weapon that would serve his party and advance his career.

Damas focused on strengthening old-guard CNC factions by channeling federal and state government resources to them. The dramatic increase in federal funding for rural development in Chiapas following the Zapatista uprising put considerable resources at Damas's disposal.[48] Damas received additional support from Governor López Moreno, whose strategy for managing the crisis of governability in Chiapas was to grease the wheels of the PRI's political machine and its affiliated corporatist confederations.[49]

Under direction of Damas, the coffee council diverted federal resources intended for small producers toward financing electoral campaigns by local CNC leaders. Public funds managed by the council reportedly bankrolled successful bids for seats in the federal and state legislatures by CNC leaders from the regions of Palenque and the Soconusco.[50] An internal INI document summarized the role of the council in the following terms: "According to the producers, [the council] has not reactivated coffee production, it has only focused on helping political campaigns of [PRI] deputies." The document criticized Damas for devoting his energies to running his own political campaign for the state legislature, stating that he had "completely forgotten his obligations [as director of the council] and was using his position to promote his personal interests."[51]

Although Damas focused on using public resources to fuel clientelist networks controlled by old-guard CNC leaders, he did not ignore the powerful coffee oligarchy. Damas ensured that large producers affiliated with the PRI's CNPP[52] were the principal recipients of federal funds

[47] Instituto Nacional Indigenista, Delegación Estatal Chiapas (n.d.b).
[48] On the increase in federal funding for Chiapas, see, for example, Yolanda López Ordaz, "Chiapas, un 'estado prioritario' para la federación: Rojas," *La Jornada*, May 19, 1995, p. 7.
[49] However, López Moreno did seek to negotiate with some opposition groups and had poor relations with a number of hard-line PRI municipal presidents (Correa and López 1994).
[50] This information is based on my interviews with leaders of both independent and CNC organizations as well as with INI and PRONASOL officials, Chiapas, Oct. and Nov. 1995.
[51] Instituto Nacional Indigenista, Delegación Estatal Chiapas (n.d.b).
[52] Although formally called the National Confederation of Smallholders, the CNPP included large property owners. Indeed, the leader of the CNPP's national coffee union reportedly owned large coffee estates in the Soconusco region that exceeded the legal limits on landholdings. The CNPP later changed its name to the National Confederation of Rural Smallholders (CNPR).

earmarked for a program to combat parasites and plagues (e.g., *broca* and coffee rust). COESCAFE administered the funds and transferred most of the program's $700,000 budget to wealthy plantation owners in the Soconusco region.[53] Impoverished small producers, who lacked the resources to manage such parasites and thus stood to benefit most from the government program, received virtually no support.[54]

In sum, under Damas's direction, the coffee council served the interests of the two power blocs in the coffee sector linked most closely to the PRI: old-guard CNC groups and private-sector coffee barons affiliated with the CNPP. In the context of the Zapatista uprising, Damas had vigorous support from state government hardliners, who sought to solve the governability crisis by strengthening traditional mechanisms of social control. From this hardline perspective, neither grassroots organizations with a productivist focus nor reformist CNC factions were to be tolerated.[55]

The excluded producer organizations were not powerless, however. They enjoyed support from reformist officials in federal agencies, such as INI, PRONASOL, and SARH. Although these federal officials had previously been defeated by González (who, as noted above, had jailed several), the Zapatista uprising strengthened their hand.[56] In the context of armed rebellion, their focus on supporting nonviolent productivist organizations gained new currency at the highest levels of the federal government. Confrontations between federal government reformists and state government hardliners would soon reshape the post-INMECAFE policy framework.

Scaling Down: Productivism Retreats to the Grassroots

After the collapse of the Social Enterprise Council (CESCAFE) in 1992, productivist organizations (both independent and CNC-affiliated) shifted

---

[53] Instituto Nacional Indigenista, Delegación Estatal Chiapas (n.d.b).
[54] According to INI's internal evaluation of this program, it had "ignored the social sector" (Instituto Nacional Indigenista, Delegación Estatal Chiapas, n.d.b).
[55] According to an internal INI document, "social sector producers are notably absent from the events organized by the [coffee] council . . ." (Instituto Nacional Indigenista, Delegación Estatal Chiapas, n.d.b).
[56] Several key federal officials forced to leave Chiapas during González's tenure returned to their old positions after the Zapatista uprising.

their focus to a series of federal programs for small coffee producers launched by INI-PRONASOL.[57] The organizations sought to increase their role in the implementation and administration of these programs. Because of Damas's politicization of the State Coffee Council, INI-PRONASOL was virtually the only source of financial support available to productivist organizations.

Governor González's attacks in early 1992 against the leadership of INI's delegation to Chiapas had forced the federal agency to decentralize the administration of many programs from its easily monitored offices in the state capital (Tuxtla Gutiérrez) to the less visible Indigenous Coordinating Centers (CCIs) spread across the state. Consequently, federal officials working in field offices outside the state capital played an increasingly important role administering INI-PRONASOL's programs. Productivist organizations thus faced new incentives to scale down and focus on local issues of program implementation, monitoring, and evaluation.

The launching in October 1992 of the federal Emergency Program for Small Coffee Producers further strengthened the incentives for productivist organizations to emphasize local issues of program implementation. The Emergency Program, which resulted from negotiations at the national level between producer organizations and INI-PRONASOL, established more than fifty Regional Operating Groups (GORs) across Mexico's coffee-producing states. The GORs, which were charged with administering and monitoring the distribution of emergency federal loans, integrated representatives of regional organizations of small producers and INI-PRONASOL field staff.[58] In Chiapas the Emergency Program was administered by twelve GORs in which a total of fifty-five producer organizations participated.

During 1993 and 1994, this widespread network of GORs provided local havens for the organizations excluded from the State Coffee Council of Chiapas. The GORs met frequently to review and revise lists of producers who were eligible for federal funds and to monitor the distribution and repayment of government loans. Independent organizations secured

---

[57] An overview of these programs can be found in INI-Solidaridad (1994).
[58] Grupo Operativo Nacional del Programa Emergente de Apoyo a Productores de Café del Sector Social (1992). These Regional Operating Groups were linked to a National Operating Group (GON), which brought together the leaders of national producer organizations with federal officials from INI, PRONASOL, and BANRURAL.

loans and technical support through the GORs.[59] Furthermore, the GORs fostered and helped sustain ongoing interaction among producer organizations and between them and the field staff of federal agencies. The GORs thus served to strengthen ties among these various actors, a process that led to the construction of a dense network of local alliances.

These alliances helped productivist organizations survive in the hostile policy environment created by Damas. They also helped protect INI and PRONASOL officials from attacks by local authoritarian elites. The alliances forged inside the GORs would soon serve as a springboard for an initiative to oust Damas and reform the State Coffee Council.

Dinosaurs versus Reformers

Damas felt threatened by the GORs, and he attempted to destroy the alliances they were nurturing at the local level between INI field staff and productivist organizations. His main weapon for achieving this goal was a campaign of misinformation about the rules and operating procedures of federal assistance programs. Damas hoped that by spreading false information he could arouse suspicion among producers that local INI officials were withholding or stealing funds.

In mid-1994, Damas launched a misinformation campaign about the federal Program of Direct Assistance for Coffee Producers. The program offered eligible producers a loan of 700 pesos per hectare that was distributed in two installments – an initial payment of 400 pesos in the spring and a subsequent payment of 300 pesos in the fall.[60] Despite the fact that the leaders of national producer organizations, the directors of INI and PRONASOL, and two cabinet ministers (the secretary of social development, and the secretary of agriculture) had signed a pact stipulating the program's rules, Damas falsely announced that producers were entitled to receive the full 700 pesos per hectare in a *single* payment. This misinformation generated much suspicion and anger toward local INI officials in Chiapas when they correctly informed producers that the program provided an initial credit of just 400 pesos. Damas's allies in the CNC helped spread

---

[59] The GORs' activities during this period are documented in Instituto Nacional Indigenista, Delegación Estatal Chiapas (n.d.a). According to the document, which was probably prepared in late 1993, "The GORs are considered the most viable avenue for advancing toward defining a new strategy for the coming year for the coffee producers of the social sector."

[60] Programa de Apoyo a Productores de Café (1994).

the false information, and, in several instances, disgruntled producers actually seized INI field offices and took their staffs hostage.[61]

Productivist organizations played an important role defusing Damas's attack against their federal government allies. Local and national leaders of these organizations clarified the program's rules and procedures, and they met with rank and file across Chiapas to explain why the producer organizations had agreed to abide by these rules. The confrontations between the State Coffee Council and its old-guard CNC partners, on the one hand, and productivist organizations and their federal reformist allies, on the other, intensified in the spring of 1995, when a new federal program for small coffee producers was launched.[62]

This national financial assistance program, which was unveiled by President Ernesto Zedillo Ponce de Leon (1994–2000) in April 1995, made subsidized commercial bank loans available to small producers to help them take advantage of an upsurge in global coffee prices that had begun in late 1994. After five years of severely depressed prices, most producers (both small and large) were so undercapitalized that they had difficulty covering even the basic costs of the year's harvest. Extremely high interest rates (around 100 percent) and the general reluctance of commercial banks to lend to indebted farmers made it virtually impossible for them to secure the preharvest financing needed to take advantage of the price increase. The new government program aimed to help producers surmount these impediments by providing access to commercial bank loans.

Sustained pressure against the government from producer organizations affiliated with CNOC and productivist CNC currents had played an important role motivating the new program. In fact the rules and procedures of the program reflected the input of these organizations, which had mobilized repeatedly in early 1995 to demand federal assistance. Eligibility for the subsidized credits was restricted to producers who had repaid their outstanding debts to INI-PRONASOL. And before they could receive fresh credits, producers had to make a cash payment to a loan guaranty fund.[63]

---

[61] Occupations of INI facilities were clustered in municipalities in the northern part of the state (e.g., Tila, Sabanilla, Chilón, and Tumbalá), where old-guard CNC unions were especially strong. See Méndez Arcos (1994); López (1994); and Cruz Galdámez (1994).

[62] Elena Gallegos and Emilio Lomas, "Anuncia Zedillo un plan de apoyo a caficultores: Se capitalizará a 260 mil pequeños productores," *La Jornada*, April 26, 1995, p. 49.

[63] Instituto Nacional Indigenista, Delegación Estatal Chiapas (1995b).

157

These rules disadvantaged old-guard CNC unions, because their members often had poor loan repayment records. The members of such unions tended to see government credits as handouts to which they were entitled with no expectation of repayment. Thus traditional CNC unions strongly opposed the requirement that producers make an initial contribution to a loan guaranty fund before receiving fresh credits.

In Chiapas Damas actively fomented such opposition to the rules of the new program by falsely announcing that *all* producers were eligible for new loans, whether or not they had liquidated their prior debts with INI-PRONASOL. Furthermore, Damas asserted that access to new credits would *not* be contingent on making a prior payment to a loan guaranty fund.[64] Through the State Coffee Council, Damas and his cronies also worked to inflate the number of individuals eligible for subsidized loans through the program. In the six coffee-producing municipalities of the Selva region (Altamirano, Ocosingo, Chilón, Sitalá, Salto de Agua, and Palenque), where old-guard CNC groups had especially strong bases of support, the coffee council reported a remarkable threefold expansion of the total acreage employed for coffee-production (from 29,000 to 90,000 hectares) in just one year.[65] By manipulating these figures, Damas sought to hijack the federal program and use it to help fuel patronage networks controlled by local CNC bosses. Ironically, these efforts soon led to Damas's demise.

Institutional Outcome: A Participatory Policy Framework

In December 1994 Eduardo Robledo Rincón took office as governor of Chiapas. Robledo, who had served as president of the PRI's Executive Committee for Chiapas during González's administration, had close links to both the oligarchy and old-guard factions of the PRI's peasant and labor

---

[64] This misinformation campaign focused on the Ocosingo region, which includes the municipalities of Altamirano, Ocosingo, Chilón, and Sitalá. Interviews with INI officials, Tuxtla Gutiérrez, Chiapas, Oct. 1995. See Instituto Nacional Indigenista, Delegación Estatal Chiapas (1995b).

[65] Because the amount of credit available to producers through the federal financial assistance program depended in part on the size of their coffee holdings, this threefold increase meant more money for producers in the Selva region (Instituto Nacional Indigenista, Delegación Estatal Chiapas 1995b). According to the INI document, even 29,000 hectares was considered to be "much higher than the amount really cultivated."

confederations.[66] Robledo's election did not bode well for those who opposed Damas's management of the coffee council.

Robledo's government proved short-lived, however. The legitimacy of his election had been strongly challenged by supporters of the defeated PRD candidate, Amado Avendaño. On the very day of Robledo's inauguration, Avendaño's supporters held their own inaugural ceremony, naming their candidate the "people's governor" of "zones in rebellion against the usurper Robledo" (Correa et al. 1994:23). Thus the new PRI governor took office amid a mounting political crisis.[67] In February 1995 the growing threat of instability in Chiapas led President Zedillo to force Robledo's resignation and install a federally sponsored interim government led by Julio César Ruiz Ferro.

In contrast to Robledo, Ruiz Ferro did not owe allegiance to local elites. He had been appointed by Zedillo and was accountable directly to him. Ruiz Ferro entered office with a presidential mandate to restore stability in Chiapas, even if achieving this goal meant sacrificing the interests of local elites. Through his previous work in the federal National Basic Foods Company (CONASUPO), Ruiz Ferro had links to reformist policy currents that tolerated and, at times, even supported nonpartisan, grassroots *campesino* organizations.[68] The new governor showed a strong preference for reform and negotiation, seeking to open channels for dialogue with producer and civic organizations. In the coffee sector, Ruiz Ferro reached out to the very grassroots organizations that Damas had excluded from the State Coffee Council. He would offer crucial support for the project to reform the council that these organizations soon launched together with INI and PRONASOL officials.

Because of the ongoing armed Zapatista rebellion that erupted in January 1994, promoting nonviolent, productivist organizations had become a top priority for reformist federal officials. According to an internal INI planning document prepared soon after Ruiz Ferro took office, the key to resolving the rebellion was "promoting and reactivating one of the most important productive activities [in Chiapas]: coffee farming."[69]

---

[66] Robledo had also been secretary general of government in the administration of Absalón Castellanos Domínguez (1982–8) (Correa, López, and Vera 1994:21).

[67] Correa and López (1994); Correa et al. (1994).

[68] Correa (1995a, b). On reformist CONASUPO policy currents, see Fox (1993).

[69] Instituto Nacional Indigenista, Delegación Estatal Chiapas (1995a).

The document emphasized that achieving this task would not require "establishing new [institutional] structures," rather it would involve "strengthening" existing ones. From the perspective of reformist federal officials, the State Coffee Council was perhaps the most obvious candidate for such strengthening: Instead of greasing the palms of corrupt CNC elites who had dubious bases of mass support, the State Coffee Council could be put to better use addressing the demands of productivist organizations that had thus far rejected the Zapatista path of armed resistance.[70]

According to INI's plan, the GORs would serve as launching pads for an initiative to reform the coffee council. The twelve GORs, which the internal INI document praised as "transparent, plural, and reliable institutions of intermediation between government agencies and coffee producers," would each elect representatives to a reformed coffee council.[71] Since 1992, when González's attacks forced INI to decentralize its activities, the federal agency had been nurturing the network of GORs through its local Indigenous Coordinating Centers (CCIs). Consequently, the GORs were well positioned to serve as wedges for prying open the State Coffee Council.

As INI's national and state leadership plotted from above, the producer organizations pressured from below. Independent organizations affiliated with CNOC spearheaded the initiative to reform the coffee council. These organizations (many of which had previously worked together in the ill-fated Social Enterprise Council) had joined forces in 1994 by forming CNOC-Chiapas. Through their participation in CNOC, they learned of the benefits enjoyed by their counterparts in Oaxaca through its coffee council. In fact, CNOC-Chiapas invited key members of Oaxaca's coffee council to visit Chiapas and share their advice about how to build a similar institution.[72]

CNOC-Chiapas endorsed INI's strategy of using the GORs to reform the coffee council. CNOC-Chiapas aimed to make the GORs a formal

---

[70] Some of these productivist organizations were nevertheless quite supportive of and sympathetic to the Zapatista forces.

[71] Instituto Nacional Indigenista, Delegación Estatal Chiapas (1995a). It should be noted that INI's interest in reforming the coffee council was motivated in part by the goal of ending Damas's attacks against it.

[72] Both the coordinator of the State Coffee Council of Oaxaca and the leadership of CNOC's main affiliate in Oaxaca (CEPCO) were invited to visit Chiapas in order to discuss their experiences. Interviews with leaders of CNOC-Chiapas, Chiapas, Oct. and Nov. 1995.

component of the council, and it demanded that a representative from each GOR should be elected to the council's board of directors. Moreover, CNOC-Chiapas proposed that the power to appoint the council's director should be transferred from the governor to this expanded board (CNOC-Chiapas 1995).

With the help of INI's delegate to Chiapas, representatives from CNOC-Chiapas obtained an audience with Governor Ruiz Ferro in May 1995. They demanded Damas's removal as director of the coffee council, charging that his efforts to subvert the new federal financial assistance program had violated a national policy initiative sponsored by the president himself. The governor agreed that Damas had greatly overstepped his authority and decided to dismiss him immediately.

The governor's appointment of Andrés Bejarano Ortega as the council's new director demonstrated his commitment to transform the council in a participatory direction. In contrast to Damas, who had held numerous political posts before becoming director of the coffee council, Bejarano had not previously served in public office. Rather, his career had focused on running his family's large coffee business. Bejarano did not appear to harbor political ambitions, and, because he was in his late sixties, his appointment as the coffee council's director was unlikely to kindle such ambitions. Moreover, Bejarano enjoyed an honest reputation, and, although he belonged to a wealthy family of coffee plantation owners, he had a solid record of genuine concern for the welfare of small producers.[73] Bejarano's lack of political ambition and his status as a large producer, which would help assuage the oligarchy's fears that small-producer organizations had seized control of the coffee council, made him an attractive candidate to head a reformed council.

Bejarano and his staff soon invited all the independent organizations to participate in the coffee council. Furthermore, the new director adopted CNOC-Chiapas's proposal to integrate the GORs into the council. Thus the GORs were renamed Regional Operating Councils (CORs) and expanded to include officials from the federal Ministry of Agriculture, Livestock, and Rural Development (SAGDR), the state government's Ministry of Agriculture, and a liaison from the State Coffee Council.[74]

---

[73] Interviews with members of producer organizations, Chiapas, Oct. and Nov. 1995.

[74] None of these agencies had participated in the GORs, which had served to link producer organizations only to INI and SEDESOL. Also, a new regional council was established in the Soconusco region. No GOR had been formed in the Soconusco because the small number of indigenous producers in that region had precluded INI from operating there.

With the addition of these agencies, the regional councils now included all major government actors involved in the coffee sector. In addition to administering the loans for small producers distributed through the national financial assistance program, the new regional councils managed key components of the federal Ministry of Agriculture's phytosanitary program.

As of late 1995, hopes ran high that this renovated state coffee council and its new network of regional affiliates would deliver the kinds of benefits to small producers in Chiapas that small producers in Oaxaca had enjoyed since 1990. The active role played by grassroots organizations in the regional councils in Chiapas certainly offered a far stronger basis for optimism than in the case of Guerrero, where, as we saw in the previous chapter, the coffee council had lackluster support from producers. However, the national economic crisis that engulfed Mexico in 1995 tightly restricted government spending and thus raised doubts about the capacity of the coffee council of Chiapas to deliver the type of agro-industrial infrastructure and production supports seen in Oaxaca.

Although their grip on the policy framework in Chiapas had been broken, the coffee oligarchy and local CNC bosses still posed a threat. In late 1995, as part of President Zedillo's New Federalism initiative, the federal government started to devolve increasing authority over economic development programs to state and local government. (See Chapter 6.) In Chiapas the Zapatista rebellion delayed this devolution. Nevertheless, a peaceful resolution of the armed conflict could clear the way for federal retrenchment, which might unleash a new round of struggle between subnational authoritarian elites and grassroots producer organizations. If such struggles were to occur, the producer organizations would probably find themselves in a weaker position than in 1995, because the New Federalism would make it harder for them to locate federal government allies. Thus the future of the fledgling participatory policy framework in Chiapas was uncertain.

Conclusion: Crony Capitalism and Participatory Policy Frameworks

The case of Chiapas illustrates how neoliberal reforms can create opportunities for traditional elites to reassert their hegemony. Neoliberal policies get the central state off the backs of subnational elites, allowing them to return to business as usual, which means enjoying monopoly control over local markets. If these oligarchs command significant societal control through patron–client networks, as in Chiapas, politicians should have powerful incentives to seek their support by launching crony capitalist reregulation projects. Rather than leading to competitive markets, neoliberal reforms in places with resilient local elites are likely to result in new institutions for market governance that generate monopoly rents for oligarchs.

The case of Chiapas also shows how powerful grassroots organizations can block crony capitalist efforts to reregulate markets to the advantage of oligarchs. By implementing their own development project from below (that is, the Social Enterprise Council), organizations of small coffee producers in Chiapas opened alternative marketing channels that contributed to the demise of the governor's crony capitalist scheme.

Strong grassroots organizations can do more than just defeat crony capitalism; they can also help forge participatory policy frameworks. In Chiapas an alliance between organizations of small producers and reformist federal government officials offset the power of local elites, allowing the construction of a participatory policy framework even in a polarized context with strong oligarchs. Thus the case of Chiapas illustrates an alternative path to a participatory policy framework to the path seen in Oaxaca, where the politics of reregulation resulted in a participatory outcome because a powerful grassroots movement was able to modify the governor's neocorporatist project. In Chiapas, by contrast, grassroots organizations faced a crony capitalist project that supplied weak incentives and poor institutional ingredients for a Oaxaca-style reworking from below. Despite this unfavorable context, the producer movement in Chiapas was able to achieve a participatory outcome by forming an alliance with reformist federal government officials that defeated the crony capitalist coalition. When neoliberal reforms are launched in places with powerful oligarchies, such alliances are probably a necessary condition for participatory policy frameworks.

The case of Puebla, which is analyzed in the next chapter, highlights the difficulties of building successful reformist alliances in the face of weak grassroots movements. As we shall see, under such conditions the politics of reregulation is likely to result in exclusionary institutions that strengthen the hegemony of oligarchs.

6

Oligarchs as the Dominant Force: An Exclusionary Policy Framework in Puebla

In the state of Puebla, as in Chiapas, the governor responded to the withdrawal of INMECAFE by launching a crony capitalist reregulation project intended to win political support from a powerful coffee oligarchy. In Chiapas, a strong movement of small producers blocked the governor's project and was eventually able to forge a participatory policy framework by allying with reformist federal government officials. By contrast, the producer movement in Puebla was extremely weak, and thus the crony capitalist project faced no significant opposition. Consequently, the politics of reregulation resulted in an exclusionary policy framework that generated monopoly rents for oligarchs.

The chapter begins by analyzing the crony capitalist project launched by Governor Mariano Piña Olaya (1987–93). The next section focuses on Puebla's small producer movement and shows how the weakness of their grassroots organizations prevented a coherent response by small producers to the crony capitalist project. The analysis then turns to the impact on the politics of reregulation of President Ernesto Zedillo's New Federalism program, a major national policy initiative launched in 1995 to decentralize government. The governor of Puebla, Manuel Bartlett Díaz (1993–9), was a leading supporter of the New Federalism, and he boldly exploited the opportunities this program offered to expand his authority. Bartlett's efforts to take advantage of the federal government's decentralizing reforms were especially strong in the coffee sector, where his government sought to wrest control from federal agencies of a financial assistance program targeting small producers. In addition to analyzing the financial program's contested implementation in Puebla, the concluding sections explore the sobering implications of this case for Mexico's grassroots organizations in the face of a growing national trend toward political decentralization.

164

Political Context of Reregulation: The Regime in Puebla

The government of Mariano Piña Olaya (1987–93) was extremely weak and unpopular. According to Reynoso (1995:6), "before becoming governor, [Piña] had practically nothing to do with the state of Puebla."[1] Thus the challenge of building a support base that confronted many state governors in Mexico was especially daunting in Piña's case.[2] His tenure was characterized by haphazard, largely unsuccessful attempts to find a base of support by allying with local elite groups. Moreover, in contrast to the governors of Mexico's other major coffee-producing states in the late 1980s, who pursued either populist or modernizing agendas, Piña failed to define a coherent strategy and often vacillated between corruption and inaction.

Soon after entering office, Piña launched a campaign of repression against a powerful street-vendor movement that had organized in the city of Puebla.[3] In addition to signaling his willingness to use heavyhanded tactics against groups mobilized outside the PRI's corporatist confederations, Piña's attack was an effort to build support among the merchant sector, which vigorously opposed the street vendors. Although the merchants applauded Piña's actions and initially backed his government, they later withdrew their support. By the middle of the governor's term, the Chamber of Commerce of the city of Puebla spoke of a "divorce" between the governor and the business sector. In 1991 approximately one thousand local businesses declared a strike against the state government, complaining that it had failed to reduce municipal taxes and satisfactorily resolve the street-vendor problem. The local business sector also objected to the governor's chief advisor, Alberto Jiménez Morales, who was seen as holding far too much influence over governmental affairs.[4]

---

[1] Piña had studied at the UNAM's National School of Law during the mid-1950s, where he was a classmate of Miguel de la Madrid. Piña and de la Madrid were later colleagues on the law school's faculty. These links to de la Madrid help explain how Piña became governor of Puebla. Prior to serving as governor, Piña held a variety of federal administrative and political positions. He served as general delegate of the PRI's National Executive Council and as director general of the ruling party's National Chamber of Sugar and Alcohol Industries (1972–3). He was later appointed director general of administration for the Federal Electric Commission (1973–6) and administrative director of Aeromexico (1977–80). Piña was subsequently elected federal deputy from Puebla (1982–5). See Camp (1995:559–60 and 189).

[2] See Chapter 2 for an analysis of the career incentives of Mexico's state governors.

[3] On the street-vendor movement, see Castillo Palma (1986, 1994).

[4] Jiménez Morales was the brother of Piña's predecessor, Guillermo Jiménez Morales (1981–7) and a key link to landed elites in the Sierra Norte region. Jiménez Morales's

165

Piña devoted much of his energies to illicit self-enrichment.[5] He reportedly purchased vast tracts of land in the Sierra Norte region of the state and took several lavish trips to Germany at the invitation of the president of Volkswagen-Mexico, which was based just outside the city of Puebla.[6] By the end of his term, Piña had alienated most of Puebla's population. According to one assessment, the governor was so unpopular that he "literally could not show his face in public" (Reynoso 1995:12). During the national independence day celebration in 1992, he was publicly booed. To avoid further public embarrassment (and in violation of the state constitution), Piña did not even attend his last State of the State address.

The First Round of Crony Capitalism: The Coffee Council of the State of Puebla

Piña's government responded to the withdrawal of INMECAFE by launching a reregulation project intended to generate large rents for Puebla's powerful coffee oligarchy. This crony capitalist initiative was an effort to cultivate the support of this key rural elite group. Like most policy initiatives during Piña's tenure, however, the crony capitalist project was short lived and unconsolidated.

In November 1988, as the dismantling of INMECAFE was becoming increasingly likely, Piña issued an executive decree creating the Coffee Council of the State of Puebla.[7] The council had an exclusionary design that put it firmly under the discretionary control of the governor and

presence in the governor's cabinet reflected Piña's efforts to ally with a powerful rural elite group from the town of Huachinango in the Sierra Norte. The wealth of this *Grupo Huachinango* was rooted primarily in cattle and lumber. Piña supplemented these efforts to establish a base of support in the countryside by aiding the semiofficial, paramilitary peasant organization, *Antorcha Campesina* (Peasant Torch).
[5] Piña was subsequently investigated on charges of corruption and illicit enrichment. See "Mariano Piña Olaya fue exculpado de acusaciones de la IP," *La Jornada*, Sept. 12, 1995, p. 13.
[6] The president of Volkswagen-Mexico, Martín Josephi, also acquired large coffee holdings during Piña's administration, including a 2,000-hectare farm named Green Gold (*Oro Verde*) that reportedly produced more coffee than any other farm in Latin America. See Sergio Cortés Sánchez, "La solución a la caficultura compete a productores: Albin," *La Jornada de Oriente*, May 10, 1995, p. 14.
[7] Puebla's coffee council was, in fact, the very first such council in Mexico. Although the governor of Oaxaca had also introduced legislation to create a coffee council in late 1988, the legislation was delayed by the efforts of grassroots producer organizations to modify it (see Chapter 3).

allowed little room for producer participation. According to the decree, the council would be led by a Committee of Directors which the governor or his chosen representative would chair (Gobierno Constitucional del Estado de Puebla 1988:3). The Committee of Directors was composed entirely of federal and state government officials.[8] The governor's decree did stipulate that any producer organization was eligible to "apply" to join the council; however, all applications were subject to the committee's approval.

Although the coffee council's formal mission was to "promote the integrated development of the coffee producing areas [of Puebla]" (Gobierno Constitucional del Estado de Puebla 1988), it actually served to generate rents for corrupt government officials and large-scale agro-industrialists. In fact, the council's only accomplishment was to secure a multimillion dollar loan for Puebla's coffee-exporting industry from the federal National Development Bank (NAFINSA). When it solicited the loan, the council claimed the funds would benefit Puebla's small producers by subsidizing the sale of their crops to large export firms and by promoting "joint ventures" between *campesino* organizations and exporters. The resources the council received from NAFINSA never reached the small producers, however. Small-producer organizations later charged that the coffee council had never actually intended to involve them in joint ventures with exporters and had strategically misrepresented its objectives to NAFINSA in order to convince the federal bank to approve its loan application. As one member of a major organization of small producers put it, the coffee council was a "ghost agency" that had pretended to speak for *campesinos* in order to secure federal funds for elite exporters.[9]

The promised exporter–campesino joint ventures never materialized. Moreover, because of misuse of funds and the crash of global coffee prices in the summer of 1989, Puebla's exporters failed to repay the NAFINSA loan. By 1990 Piña's coffee council ceased operations, having achieved little more than the delivery of an enormous, single-shot rent to the coffee export oligarchy and a handful of corrupt state government officials.

The government of Puebla did not intervene in the coffee sector again until 1993, after Manuel Bartlett Díaz (1993–9) had succeeded Piña.

---

[8] The legislation explicitly named as directors the delegates of the federal Ministry of Agriculture and Water Resources (SARH), the Ministry of Agrarian Reform, and INMECAFE, as well as the secretary of agriculture of the state of Puebla.

[9] Interviews, Xicotepec, Puebla, Sept. 1995; and Cuetzalan, Puebla, Aug. 1995.

Bartlett created a new state government agency and launched a second round of crony capitalism that benefited the same export elite as had Piña's project. As we shall see, however, Bartlett had grander visions for the coffee sector. Although he initially focused on serving the interests of the coffee oligarchy, Bartlett soon shifted his attention to a broader, *neofederalist* project to wrest control of public policy from federal government agencies and transfer it to the state government. Before turning to Bartlett's project, we first need to explore how Puebla's producer organizations responded both to the withdrawal of INMECAFE and Piña's crony capitalist initiative.

A Weak Producer Movement: Disorganization at the Grassroots

The dismantling of INMECAFE triggered important processes of expansion and consolidation among small-producer organizations across Mexico. As analyzed in previous chapters, INMECAFE's withdrawal created new opportunities for these organizations to broaden their bases of support by recruiting producers who previously had belonged to INMECAFE's extensive network of Economic Units for Production and Marketing (UEPCs).[10] The dismantling of INMECAFE also gave these organizations a chance to move into new areas of the production process. The case of Oaxaca, where grassroots producer organizations dramatically expanded their ranks and formed a statewide coordinating network (CEPCO), provides the most vivid example of organizational consolidation in the wake of INMECAFE's exit.

In Puebla, by contrast, the dismantling of INMECAFE had a different effect. Although several mature independent producer organizations operated in Puebla when INMECAFE withdrew, no broad-based producer movement emerged. Puebla's organizations failed to join forces, a situation that left them dispersed and weak. One measure of this weakness is the low percentage (46 percent) of producers who belonged to an organization in Puebla after INMECAFE's dismantling (see Table 2.5). In Oaxaca, by contrast, approximately 79 percent of the producers were affiliated with an organization. And in Guerrero and Chiapas nearly 100 percent of producers belonged to an organization. Another indication of the weakness of Puebla's producer movement is the absence of a statewide

[10] As explained in Chapter 2, the UEPCs were collective credit associations that linked small coffee producers both to INMECAFE and the CNC.

alliance of producer organizations like those that emerged in Oaxaca and Chiapas.

Because of their weakness, Puebla's producer organizations were unable either to challenge the governor's reregulation project (as had their counterparts in Guerrero and Oaxaca) or to launch a counterproject to coordinate production and marketing from below (as had their counterparts in Chiapas). Instead, Puebla's producer organizations ignored the governor's project and pursued uncoordinated economic development projects. This disengaged and disorganized productivist response to the governor's reregulation project cleared the way for unmitigated crony capitalism and an exclusionary institutional outcome. What explains the weakness of Puebla's producer movement? Why were small-producer organizations unable to expand their ranks and join forces after the withdrawal of INMECAFE?

Structural Barriers to Collective Action: A Powerful Oligarchy and Weak Penetration by INMECAFE

Until the late 1980s the organizational profiles of the coffee sectors in Puebla and Oaxaca were strikingly similar. In both states a handful of powerful independent producer organizations had formed in the late 1970s. Nevertheless the vast majority of producers were either disorganized or affiliated with INMECAFE's UEPC's and, in the case of Oaxaca, with the CNC's State Union of Coffee Producers.[11] After INMECAFE's exit, however, the organizational profiles of the coffee sectors in the two states diverged dramatically. In Oaxaca independent producer organizations expanded rapidly by recruiting former members of the UEPCs. Moreover, these independent organizations soon formed a statewide confederation, CEPCO (see Chapter 3). In Puebla, by contrast, independent producer organizations, such as the "We Shall Overcome" Regional Agricultural

---

[11] In Puebla, the CNC had a limited presence in the coffee sector because it had concentrated mainly on organizing wheat and corn farmers in the state's grain-producing Altiplano region. The limited effort that the CNC gave to organizing coffee producers can be explained in large part by the fact that the federal Ministry of Agrarian Reform had formally classified the majority of Puebla's small coffee farmers as "private property" owners, rather than *ejidatarios* or communal property owners. This classification put Puebla's small coffee producers under the jurisdiction of the PRI's National Confederation of Smallholders (CNPP) rather than the CNC. The CNPP lacked the CNC's resources and, as of 1994, had organized only about 1,400 of Puebla's 30,000 coffee producers (FIDECAFE 1994).

Cooperative (CARTT) and the Independent Regional Union of Autonomous Coffee Producers (URICAA),[12] reaped no such benefits from the withdrawal of INMECAFE. They failed either to expand their bases of support or form a statewide coalition.

The strength of Puebla's coffee oligarchy partially explains why the independent organizations were unable to capitalize on the dismantling of INMECAFE.[13] In the second most important coffee region in Puebla, which centered on the municipality of Cuetzalan del Progreso, five elite families controlled approximately 90 percent of the coffee processing industry both before and after INMECAFE's withdrawal. The oligarchy's strength partly reflected INMECAFE's weakness. Not only had this government enterprise failed to displace local elites, but it had actually depended on them to help carry out its processing and marketing activities. In Puebla INMECAFE lacked its own dry-processing plants and was thus forced to rent such facilities from the oligarchy. It passed the rental costs on to small producers as part of its "marketing fee."[14] Because INMECAFE failed to weaken the oligarchy's grip on local production and marketing networks, its departure created few opportunities for producer organizations to recruit new members by taking over economic activities previously controlled by the government enterprise.

The weakness of INMECAFE can also be seen in the comparatively small amount of agro-industrial infrastructure it owned in Puebla. As Table 6.1 shows, INMECAFE owned *no* dry-processing plants, which forced it to make the kinds of rental arrangements with local elites described above. Moreover, INMECAFE had only eight wet-processing plants to serve Puebla's 30,000 small producers, an average of one plant per 3,750 producers. In Guerrero, by contrast, INMECAFE had six plants for 10,000 producers, an average of one plant per 1,667 producers.

In other states, the goal of purchasing INMECAFE's agro-industrial machinery – especially its large, dry-processing mills – gave producers strong incentives to mobilize when the government enterprise withdrew.

[12] CARTT was located in the Cuetzalan region, whereas URICAA was located near Xicotepec.
[13] On Puebla's coffee oligarchy, see Agüilar Ayon and Mora Aguilera (1991); Paré (1975); Nolasco (1985:66–7); and Martínez Borrego (1991, esp. ch. 4).
[14] Agüilar Ayon and Mora Aguilera (1991:60–2). As suggested by the small number (11) of producers with more than 100 hectares (see Table 2.3), land ownership was not the key source of wealth for Puebla's coffee oligarchy. Their income came principally from the marketing and processing of coffee grown by small producers.

Table 6.1. *Distribution of INMECAFE's Agro-Industrial Machinery by State, 1989*

	Dry-Processing Plants	Drying Centers	Wet-Processing Plants
Oaxaca	2	1	0
Guerrero	1	1	6
Chiapas	2	1	0
Puebla	0	0	8

Notes: In Oaxaca and Chiapas, many small producers had their own small-scale wet-processing facilities (*beneficios familiares*), which explains the absence of INMECAFE wet-processing plants.
Sources: INMECAFE (1989b); INMECAFE (1990b).

Furthermore, in the case of several organizations (e.g., CEPCO), agro-industrial infrastructure purchased from INMECAFE served as a potent resource for recruiting new members because it enabled the organizations to take over the critical production-related services (for example, dry processing) that the government enterprise previously had managed.[15] INMECAFE's sparse agro-industrial capacity in Puebla deprived producer organizations of the chance to acquire such resources for mobilizing and recruiting new members.

In Puebla the strength of the oligarchy and the weakness of INMECAFE thus posed important obstacles to the kinds of organizing processes seen in Oaxaca and Chiapas after the dismantling of INMECAFE. Yet powerful oligarchies also existed in those two states. Indeed, in Chiapas the coffee oligarchy was stronger in size and political clout than in Puebla. The ability of producer organizations in Chiapas and Oaxaca to surmount barriers to collective action similar to those faced by their counterparts in Puebla suggests that such structural factors alone cannot explain the variation in the strengths and fortunes of producer movements across the cases. Moreover, numerous small coffee producers *were* able to organize in Puebla despite the powerful oligarchy and the limited penetration by INMECAFE. For example, in the late 1980s

[15] Infrastructure purchased from INMECAFE was not always a blessing for producer organizations, however. The machinery was often outdated and in poor condition, and the loans required to purchase the equipment saddled many producer organizations with heavy debts. Moreover, the scale of INMECAFE's machinery often exceeded the production capacities of the organizations that acquired it, a situation that resulted in severe inefficiencies.

CARTT had more than 8,000 members and was one of the most sophisticated and consolidated independent producer organizations in Mexico.[16] To explain the overall weakness of Puebla's coffee producer movement, we thus need to shift the focus from structural factors to the strategies of producer organizations.

Strategic Barriers to Collective Action: Dilemmas of a Full-Service Campesino Organization

When INMECAFE withdrew, CARTT was the obvious candidate to lead an effort by Puebla's small producers to build a statewide coalition like CEPCO in Oaxaca. Why did CARTT fail to play this role? The organization's strategy for promoting *campesino* welfare helps answer this question. CARTT aspired to achieve "integrated" rural development by functioning as a full-service *campesino* organization that addressed the basic needs of its membership (e.g., health, nutrition, etc.).[17] This goal fostered an inward orientation that strongly deemphasized external alliances with other organizations.

In contrast to more specialized organizations, like CEPCO, which focused primarily on issues of coffee production, CARTT sought to address the full range of *campesino* needs. CARTT was founded around issues of consumption and had developed its own food distribution network to challenge the monopoly of local elites over sugar and other comestibles.[18] Even after CARTT had broadened its focus to include production activities (primarily the processing and marketing of coffee and allspice), the organization retained its initial commitment to addressing basic needs. As one member explained, "Coffee is important for the welfare of *campesinos* during just three or four months of the year [during the harvest], but *campesinos* have to eat every day." This perspective was reflected in programs that CARTT launched to promote the cultivation of mushrooms and macadamia nuts in order to help meet local consumption and nutritional needs.[19]

---

[16] The figure of 8,000 is from Masferrer Kan (1986:15). Not all of CARTT's members grew coffee.

[17] This point is emphasized in Agüilar Ayon and Mora Aguilera (1991:100).

[18] On CARTT's origins, see Agüilar Ayon and Mora Aguilera (1991:95–107); and Martínez Borrego (1991:ch. 6).

[19] Although they expressed hopes that macadamia nuts could eventually be exported, CARTT's agronomists emphasized their immediate nutritional value for the local population (interviews, Cuetzalan, Puebla, Aug. 1995).

CARTT's emphasis on integrated rural development led it to prioritize deepening over expanding its base of support. This inward focus was reflected in CARTT's ambivalent, arm's length relationships with national-level producer organizations, such as UNORCA and CNOC.[20] CARTT's leadership criticized these national organizations for failing to grasp the needs of its rank and file. According to one of CARTT's founders, UNORCA's leadership did not understand the importance of basic consumption issues for the very poor indigenous producers who were the core of CARTT's support base. He attributed this lack of understanding to the fact that most of UNORCA's top leaders had worked in relatively wealthy agricultural regions in northern Mexico. Moreover, he described the disgust and confusion he and other CARTT members felt when a top UNORCA leader "defected" to the CNC. As he put it, " [Hugo Andrés] Araujo always told us the CNC was our enemy, and the next thing we know, he turns around and joins it!"[21] Incidents such as these fostered a mistrust of external organizations that reinforced CARTT's parochialism.

CARTT's ongoing efforts to consolidate political control in the four municipalities where its base of support was concentrated further illustrate the organization's inward focus. In 1981 CARTT entered the electoral arena by fielding candidates for local government office. By participating directly in municipal government, the *campesino* organization aimed to weaken the hegemony of the oligarchs who had traditionally controlled local government (Agüilar Ayon and Mora Aguilera 1991:1–4, 116–24). In the 1981 elections, CARTT-affiliated candidates won four seats at the submunicipal level (for the *Juntas Auxiliares*), and in 1983 CARTT's candidates captured four municipal presidencies (Agüilar Ayon and Mora Aguilera 1991:119). In 1986 CARTT formally allied with the PRI in an effort to take advantage of national reforms of the party that promised greater local participation in the candidate selection process. Because the PRI had been the only political party to field candidates in the region, the

---

[20] UNORCA was Mexico's most important independent national *campesino* organization in the 1980s and early 1990s; CNOC was the national-level umbrella organization for independent organizations of coffee producers.

[21] Interview, Cuetzalan, Puebla, Aug. 1995. As explained in Chapter 5, Araujo was an important UNORCA leader during the 1980s who subsequently became the CNC's secretary general during the Salinas administration. CARTT also had an important negative experience with CNOC. In 1988 CNOC's first representative to the state of Puebla advised the organization to take a massive loan to purchase a dry-processing plant. In the wake of the global crash of coffee prices in mid-1989, this debt became a major albatross around CARTT's neck.

majority of CARTT's rank and file saw themselves as "*priistas* by custom."[22] CARTT's decision to participate in municipal politics both reflected and strengthened the organization's local focus.

Challenges from a rival peasant organization – the semiofficial, paramilitary Antorcha Campesina (Peasant Torch) – further focused CARTT's energies on the internal tasks of defending and consolidating its base of support. Antorcha Campesina was founded in the mid-1970s by radical students and faculty at the National Agricultural University who were affiliated with the National Federation of Bolshevik Organizations (FNOB). Although Antorcha Campesina would eventually become a national organization, its initial base was in the town of Tecomatlán in southwest Puebla.[23] In 1981 Antorcha Campesina started to expand into CARTT's region (the Sierra Norte) with support from both the state government and high-level federal officials of the National Basic Foods Company (CONASUPO).

Antorcha Campesina's arrival in the Sierra Norte posed an immediate threat to CARTT, especially because the former's strategy was to hijack preexisting, community-level organizations (Agüilar Ayon and Mora Aguilera 1991:87). Throughout the 1980s, and especially between 1986 and 1990, much of CARTT's energies were absorbed by local conflicts with Antorcha Campesina. Confrontations occurred in approximately twelve of the sixty-six communities where CARTT had bases of support.[24]

[22] CARTT's leaders felt the PRI was more likely than an opposition party (e.g., the center-right National Action Party, PAN) to respect the organization's autonomy (Agüilar Ayon and Mora Aguilera 1991:122–3). It is important to point out that the conflicts between CARTT and local oligarchs also played out inside the PRI. For example, prior to local elections in Nov. 1986, an intense confrontation erupted over the party's internal nominating procedures. According to Agüilar Ayon and Mora Aguilera (1991:129), local oligarchs complained, "Los indios huarachudos se apoderen de nuestro palacio municipal" (Sandal-clad indians have taken over our town hall), and vigorously opposed the nomination of CARTT's candidates. After the elections, members of the oligarchy attempted unsuccessfully to use their links to high-ranking members of the PRI's state-level machine to have the victory by CARTT's candidates annulled.

[23] Tecomatlán was the home of Antorcha's quasi-charismatic leader, Aquilles Córdova Moran. On Antorcha Campesina, see Rappo (1991) and Jiménez Huerta (1992).

[24] In the 1986 elections, Antorcha Campesina fielded candidates in five municipalities (Agüilar Ayon and Mora Aguilera 1991:90–1). The conflict between Antorcha Campesina and CARTT, which had previously taken the form of assassinations and grassroots confrontations, thus spilled over into the electoral arena. CARTT therefore had new incentives to participate in local electoral politics in order to counter the threat from Antorcha Campesina.

When INMECAFE began to withdraw in 1989, Puebla's most important independent producer organization thus faced intense pressures to focus on defending its grassroots base. Under these conditions, it would have been difficult for CARTT to have launched a statewide initiative to shape the emerging post-INMECAFE policy framework. The organization's integrated rural development strategy, which further inclined it to look inward, helps explain why it did not even try.

The structural factors analyzed above (a powerful oligarchy and INMECAFE's weak penetration into Puebla) combined with the parochialism of Puebla's most important small-producer organization, CARTT, explain why the kinds of organizing processes observed in other states after INMECAFE's withdrawal did not occur in Puebla. Puebla's small-producer organizations thus emerged from the conjuncture defined by the dismantling of INMECAFE exactly as they had entered it: weak and divided.

A New Political Context: The Transition to a Modernizing Regime

In 1993, four years after the first round of crony capitalism in Puebla, Manuel Bartlett Díaz was elected governor. Bartlett was a prominent figure in national politics who had held cabinet positions in both the de la Madrid and Salinas presidential administrations. Under de la Madrid, Bartlett served as secretary of the interior (1982–8) and had been considered a possible PRI candidate for the presidency in 1988. Although he did not win his party's nomination, Bartlett played a key role in the elections in his capacity as president of the Federal Electoral Commission. Opposition parties subsequently accused him of masterminding a last-minute breakdown of the computerized voting tabulation system that they claimed had saved the PRI from defeat by enabling a fraudulent victory.[25] Many analysts saw Bartlett's appointment as secretary of education (1988–92) and his subsequent selection as the PRI's candidate for governor in Puebla as expressions of gratitude from President Salinas to Bartlett for his adept electoral engineering.[26]

---

[25] For Bartlett's version of his actions during the 1988 elections, see Bartlett Díaz (1995).

[26] Prominent members of Salinas's cabinet (e.g., Secretary of the Treasury Pedro Aspe) apparently did not support Bartlett's candidacy for the governorship. According to Reynoso (1995:24), however, "It appears that only the vote of one person [i.e., President Salinas] actually mattered, and this was for Bartlett."

For a politician with Bartlett's impressive credentials, becoming governor of Puebla meant a *loss* of power and prestige. In the status hierarchy of Mexico's centralized political system, federal cabinet ministers far outranked state governors. Bartlett, who was only in his midfifties when he became governor and thus in the prime of his political career, had already held two cabinet positions, including the prized office of secretary of the interior. For him, the presidency was the only avenue remaining for upward mobility.[27]

Yet Bartlett's tenure as governor occurred at a time when new opportunities were emerging for Mexico's state governments to expand their power and authority. During the 1990s, mounting pressures for political democratization caused divisions inside the national PRI machine that increased the autonomy of subnational party elites. Furthermore, President Zedillo's laissez-faire approach to state and local governments signaled a weakening of Mexico's centralized, presidentialist tradition. Finally, as part of Zedillo's New Federalism reforms, federal agencies were starting to devolve resources and administrative responsibilities to state and local governments.

Bartlett, who was accustomed to holding the reins of power in federal ministries, quickly seized these new opportunities for expanding the authority and prestige of his government. He became a leading supporter of the New Federalism, allying with other governors (including some affiliated with the opposition National Action Party (PAN)) who sought to accelerate the decentralization process. To his critics, Bartlett's government soon came to symbolize the "dark side" of Mexican federalism, confirming their fears that decentralizing reforms would unleash a brutal "refeudalization" of Mexico.[28]

Bartlett's efforts to assert state government control over public policy were especially vigorous in the coffee sector. As we shall see, federal government officials tried to resist these efforts by allying with grassroots producer organizations. However, the New Federalism gave Bartlett's government resources that helped it undercut these alliances by inducing key producer organizations not to join. The case of Puebla thus provides an excellent optic for exploring the process of political decentralization in a federal system and for understanding how such reforms shape the politics of reregulation.

---

[27] Indeed, Bartlett subsequently made an unsuccessful bid to be the PRI's candidate for the presidency in the elections of 2000.
[28] See, for example, López Obrador (1995:186–7).

From Crony Capitalism to Neofederalism

Bartlett's government evolved in two distinct stages. In an initial phase, the governor focused on building a support base by allying with local elite groups. Bartlett's links to Puebla were tenuous. He had never worked there, and the fact that his father, Manuel Bartlett Bautista, had been governor of the state of Tabasco led many to doubt Bartlett's status as a son of Puebla. In an effort to overcome these problems and strengthen his support, Bartlett allied with a powerful business group led by Rafael Cañedo Benítez, whom he proposed as the PRI's candidate for municipal president of the city of Puebla (Reynoso 1995:25). In the countryside, Bartlett sought the support of traditional elites by launching a crony capitalist project in the coffee sector.[29]

After Bartlett had consolidated internal support his government entered a second phase characterized by efforts to wrest power from federal government agencies. In the coffee sector, Bartlett's government attempted to seize control of a national financial program launched by the federal government in 1995. The resulting confrontation between federal and state government agencies resulted in a stalemate that denied Puebla's 30,000 small coffee producers access to the resources enjoyed by their counterparts in other states.

Debt Relief for Oligarchs: The Second Round of Crony Capitalism

In March 1993 Bartlett issued an executive decree creating a new state government agency, the Pueblan Coffee Council, to replace the defunct council established by his predecessor, Piña (Gobierno Constitucional del Estado de Puebla 1993). Bartlett hoped to use the new council to gain the coffee oligarchy's support, and he appointed one of Puebla's wealthiest coffee industrialists and exporters, Omar Soto Velazco, to direct it. Soto's

---

[29] In addition, Bartlett's government implemented a massive program of urban renewal and development in the city of Puebla, the "Angelopolis" project. Bartlett's government also focused on modernizing the educational system, especially the Autonomous University of Puebla (BUAP), which had been a stronghold of leftist political opposition since the early 1960s. The state government commissioned an international consulting firm to evaluate the BUAP. The firm's report, which was published only in English, focused on depoliticizing the university and proposed innovations such as "Trilateral Front-Line Research Exchanges by TV Forums" (International Council for Educational Development 1994). On the BUAP's long history of political conflict, see Yáñez Delgado (1988) and Pansters (1990:chs. 5 and 6).

family dominated the processing industry in the important coffee zone centered on the municipality of Cuetzalan del Progreso in the Sierra Norte region. In addition to supervising his family's business, Soto also owned a coffee-importing firm in the United States. He had a history of tense relations with CARTT, which was also based in Cuetzalan.[30]

As the coffee council's director, Soto focused on the financial restructuring of the sector, which meant renegotiating the enormous debt that large producers and agro-industrialists had acquired with commercial and government banks during the bust in coffee prices in the early 1990s.[31] The extensive personal ties Soto had forged with bankers through his own business helped him negotiate favorable terms for the indebted large producers, and in some cases he achieved 70 percent reductions of their debts. Within two years, the council claimed to have either liquidated or restructured about 90 percent of the overall debt in the coffee sector.[32] Soto's success mediating between banks and Puebla's coffee elite is evidenced by the enthusiastic praise he received from Mexico's most important private-sector producer association, the Mexican Confederation of Coffee Producers (CMPC). National CMPC leaders portrayed the Pueblan Coffee Council as the model that other states should emulate.[33]

By contrast, small-producer organizations had a strikingly different evaluation of Soto's performance. National leaders of CNOC harshly criticized Puebla's coffee council, describing it as an exclusionary institution that served wealthy elites for whom debt renegotiation was the top priority.[34] CNOC leaders saw financial restructuring as a secondary issue for most small producers, who faced more pressing problems, such as a lack of basic production infrastructure. Although most peasant producers had

---

[30] According to Agüilar Ayon and Mora Aguilera (1991:126), in the mid-1980s Soto had led the oligarchy's opposition to CARTT's effort to win control of the municipal government of Cuetzalan.

[31] Consejo Poblano del Café (1993a). The sustained depression of global coffee prices since mid-1989 had thrown most of Puebla's producers (both large and small) into severe debt. According to one estimate, at the beginning of 1993, the total coffee sector debt was approximately 430 million pesos, of which roughly 135 million was held by commercial banks and 295 million by federal government development banks (Consejo Poblano del Café 1993b).

[32] Interviews, Puebla, Puebla, March, 1995.

[33] Interviews, Mexico City, Oct. 1994 and March 1995.

[34] Interviews, Mexico City, March and April 1995.

also fallen into debt, their debt was held mainly by federal government agencies such as INI and BANRURAL, not by the private banks on which the coffee council had focused its negotiating efforts. Thus the council's achievements in the area of financial restructuring did little to address the needs of most small producers.

In addition to securing debt relief for the coffee elite, Soto used his position as director of the coffee council to promote his own private business. Through the council, Soto launched a technical assistance program for poor producers in his home region of Cuetzalan. When he left the council in 1995, Soto absorbed the program's infrastructure and employees into his own private firm, Integrated Agricultural Consulting Services, and started to charge producers for services that had previously been provided at no cost by the coffee council. After Soto left the council, his personal employees continued to oversee government-funded nurseries. When asked whether the nurseries belonged to Soto or the coffee council, workers seemed not to understand this distinction.[35]

For two years, Soto ran the coffee council at his discretion. By 1995, however, as the governor shifted his focus from building alliances with local elites to wresting power from federal agencies, Soto had outlived his usefulness. As part of his neofederalist strategy, Bartlett undertook a major administrative reorganization in order to prepare state government agencies to take over functions previously performed by federal agencies. Soto's arbitrary style and his status as a private citizen outside the regular bureaucratic chain of command (he had never formally registered as a government employee) posed potential obstacles to the implementation of the governor's reforms. In May 1995, in the face of growing charges of corruption against Soto from small-producer organizations, the governor replaced him with a midlevel technocrat from the state government's Ministry of Agriculture.[36] Soto's departure marked the transition from crony capitalism to neofederalism.

---

[35] Interviews, Cuetzalan, Puebla, Aug. 1995. The fact that Soto was never formally a public employee and had no government salary contributed to the blurring of his public and private roles, as did the council's lack of a government budget and its reliance entirely on voluntary contributions from producers.

[36] Representatives of producer organizations opposed the appointment and demanded that a coffee farmer be chosen instead. Their complaints were ignored. See "Sesionó el Consejo Poblano del Café sin aprobar el plan especial de financiamiento," *Sintesis*, May 25, 1995, p. 9.

Neofederalism and the Perils of Political Decentralization

In March 1995 President Zedillo launched a major policy initiative to decentralize government functions from the federal to the state and municipal levels. Zedillo portrayed his New Federalism program as the solution to a broad array of social, political, and economic problems that supposedly stemmed from Mexico's "centralist" tradition, which he vilified as "oppressive, backwards, socially insensitive, and inefficient."[37]

Behind the rhetoric touting decentralization as a magic bullet that would cure the country's ills lay a series of substantive administrative reforms.[38] Several federal agencies started transferring control of infrastructure and personnel from their state-level delegations to state and municipal governments. This devolution was intended to give state and local governments chief responsibility for the coordination and implementation of programs. The streamlined federal delegations to the states, whose resources had previously dwarfed those of state governments, would limit themselves to the tasks of oversight and evaluation. The two federal agencies that had played the most important roles in the coffee sector after the dismantling of INMECAFE – that is, the Ministry of Social Development (SEDESOL) and the Ministry of Agriculture, Livestock, and Rural Development (SAGAR)[39] – were among the first slated for decentralization.[40]

Bartlett responded quickly to these reforms. In addition to trying to wrest control of policymaking from the delegations of federal agencies in Puebla, he also sought national attention by casting himself as a leading supporter of the New Federalism and portraying his state as a kind of neofederalist laboratory. In April 1995, one month after the president had unveiled his policy initiative, Bartlett held a National Forum on Federalism in the city of Puebla to which he invited several other governors, including two affiliated with the PAN (the governor of

[37] "Se compromete Ernesto Zedillo a dar la batalla contra el centralismo," *La Jornada*, March 30, 1995, p. 3.
[38] Fiscal decentralization also figured prominently in policy debates about the New Federalism. Mexico's federal government controlled approximately 80% of the national tax revenue, state governments controlled 16%, and municipalities a mere 4%. See Díaz Cayeros (1995).
[39] Formally SARH.
[40] On SEDESOL's decentralization, see Jorge Cruz Escalante, "La regionalización del Pronasol, base del nuevo federalismo," *La Jornada*, Sept. 28, 1995, p. 12. The Ministry of Health was also slated for rapid "federalization."

Chihuahua, Francisco Barrio Terrazas, and the governor of Guanajuato, Carlos Medina Plascencia). In his keynote address at the forum, Bartlett echoed Zedillo, remarking that "centralization has ceased to be an instrument for mobilizing the forces of the nation." He also criticized federal government policies for causing "blurred responsibilities, duplicated efforts, and perpetuation of local backwardness" and praised the New Federalism as a project "to strengthen the nation by benefiting its constituent parts – states and municipalities."[41] Bartlett translated his rhetoric into action by working to consolidate his government's control over policy and resources. Under the banner of decentralization, he aimed for "recentralization" at the state level.

"Federalizing" Agricultural Policy: The Rural Development Council

In September 1995 the federal secretary of agriculture (a former state governor himself) announced that 85 percent of the agency's functions and resources would be devolved to state governments in the coming months.[42] The government of Puebla was poised to seize the new resources and responsibilities.[43] In fact the devolution of agricultural policy had already begun in Puebla, as Governor Bartlett had previously appointed the SAGAR's delegate to his state, Manuel Villa Issa, to serve simultaneously in his cabinet as Puebla's secretary of agriculture.

Villa Issa was well qualified to supervise the consolidation of agricultural policymaking at the state level. Like Bartlett, Villa Issa had previously held high-level federal office, serving as undersecretary of agriculture for forest resources (1986–8) (Camp 1995:916). Thus he had an inside understanding of the centralist logic of federal agencies and knew how to reproduce that logic at the state level. Because the prestige and power of his earlier position as a federal undersecretary far exceeded those of his position in Puebla as secretary of agriculture for the state government, the New Federalism offered Villa Issa a chance to regain lost professional status

---

[41] "No se avanzará en la democracia si no se considera a los estados: Bartlett." *La Jornada*, April 26, 1995, p. 20.

[42] Matilde Pérez U., "Labastida: no será traumática le desincorporación de la SAGDR" *La Jornada*, Sept. 10, 1995, p. 46. See also Néstor Martínez, "Descentralización definitiva de la Secretaría de Agricultura, en 96" *La Jornada*, May 5, 1995, p. 17; SAGAR 1995, esp. ch. 8; and Comisión Intersecretarial del Gabinete Agropecuario (1995).

[43] Indeed, the state of Puebla would soon be touted as a model for how the decentralization of the Ministry of Agriculture should proceed.

by expanding the authority of state government. His aspiration to be Puebla's governor strengthened his incentives to pursue this goal.[44]

In addition to overseeing a rapid transfer of the federal Ministry of Agriculture's resources to Puebla's state government, Villa Issa moved to seize control from the various other federal agencies that intervened in the rural sector, most of which had not yet been targeted for decentralization. The Rural Development Council of the State of Puebla served as his weapon for achieving this objective. The Rural Development Council was established in 1993 as an interagency coordinating committee for the more than thirty federal and state government agencies involved in Puebla's rural sector. During its first two years, the council's role was limited because it relied on nonbinding agreements among these various government agencies.[45]

In 1995, however, Villa Issa drafted legislation to transform the Rural Development Council into the cornerstone of Bartlett's neofederalist project to recentralize control over public policy at the state level. The legislation gave the council, which Villa Issa chaired, new authority over federal agencies operating in rural Puebla. Although state government officials argued that the legislation would help promote coherent, integrated rural policy, the initiative was fiercely opposed by federal officials, especially the delegates of INI and SEDESOL.[46] The resulting intergovernmental conflict would be especially visible in the coffee sector, where state and federal officials struggled for control of the national financial assistance program launched by President Zedillo in April 1995.[47]

Subnational Rogues and Grassroots Defectors: The Battle over the Federal Financial Assistance Program

The director of the State Coffee Council of Chiapas subverted the rules of several federal government programs. As analyzed in Chapter 5, these systematic violations of federal law ultimately contributed to his downfall

---

[44] Villa Issa had been considered a potential PRI candidate during the 1993 gubernatorial elections, but he had been passed over for Bartlett. Interviews, Puebla, Puebla, Aug. 1995.

[45] According to an official document written by Villa Issa, the council had achieved limited results "since in the central offices of each federal agency, national programs are defined ... which do not always coincide with the necessities and proposals at the state level." See Secretaría de Agricultura, Ganadería y Desarrollo Rural, Delegación Estatal en Puebla (1995).

[46] Interviews, Puebla, Puebla, Sept. 1995.

[47] Elena Gallegos y Emilio Lomas, "Anuncia Zedillo un plan de apoyo a caficultores," *La Jornada*, April 26, 1995, p. 49.

when a reformist governor (Ruiz Ferro) took office. In Puebla, by contrast, state-level deviations from federal norms and operating procedures did not reflect the actions of wayward middle-level officials. Rather, the governor himself sanctioned such deviations as part of his neofederalist project to strengthen Puebla's state government. Resistance by state government officials to federal policies was especially notable in the case of the national financial assistance program for small coffee producers.[48]

Problems of Program Implementation. The financial assistance program encountered serious difficulties in Puebla. In the weeks following Zedillo's unveiling of the program, Bartlett's government made clear that it would not play by the national rules. Bartlett faced a growing threat from the center-right PAN, which was mobilizing for state elections scheduled for November 1995.[49] In response to this partisan threat, Bartlett sought to use the financial assistance program to solidify the PRI's rural base of support. Although the program's rules stipulated that *all* producer organizations were eligible to help supervise the distribution of government-subsidized loans,[50] the governor tried to grant monopoly control over the disbursement process to the credit union of the CNC's State Union of Coffee Producers.[51] The leader of the credit union, Omar Lechuga, had recently been nominated by the PRI as a candidate for the state legislature. Thus giving the CNC control of the distribution of credits was a way for Bartlett to boost his party's chances in the upcoming elections.[52]

---

[48] See the analysis of this program in the previous chapter. The program made government-subsidized loans available to small coffee producers.

[49] On political tensions preceding the elections, see "Decide el PAN no dialogar con Manuel Bartlett," *La Jornada*, Oct. 7, 1995, p. 6; Rosa Icela Rodríguez, "Toman perredistas comités de districtos electorales en Puebla," *La Jornada*, Oct. 21, 1995, p. 5; "Se prepara en Puebla fraude electoral: López Obrador," *La Jornada*, Nov. 5, 1995, p. 6; "Acusa Manuel Bartlett al PAN de concertacesión y falta de ética," *La Jornada*, Nov. 8, 1995, p. 12.

[50] According to the rules, the organizations would supervise the distribution of credits through newly formed Regional Operating Councils, which were responsible for validating producers' requests for credits, certifying their eligibility to receive credits, providing lists of approved producers to BANRURAL, and guaranteeing repayment of the credits. See Programa de Fomento a la Cafeticultura (1995).

[51] Interviews, Mexico City and Xicotepec, Puebla, Aug. 1995. This move would have made the ruling party's peasant confederation the exclusive intermediary between the federal bank responsible for making the subsidized loans (i.e., BANRURAL) and all producers in Puebla enrolled in the financial program.

[52] Bartlett's strategy resembled Damas's efforts in Chiapas to use the State Coffee Council to finance political campaigns of CNC leaders. See Chapter 5.

Curiously, Lechuga did not belong to an old-guard CNC group. The union he directed was part of a broad productivist project to form a massive credit union uniting more than thirty thousand producers across several states.[53] In fact the national CNC faction sponsoring this credit union initiative had allied with CNOC and other independent organizations to defend the uniform application of the financial program's rules.[54] By supporting Bartlett's efforts to subvert these rules in Puebla, Lechuga tacitly broke with the national leadership of his organization. The governor's offer to support his bid for a seat in the state legislature had apparently induced Lechuga to switch loyalties.

Independent producer organizations, INI officials, and CNC groups not linked to the credit union project challenged Bartlett's plan to make Lechuga's union the exclusive intermediary between small coffee producers and BANRURAL.[55] Together they succeeded in blocking the governor's initiative. Bartlett responded to this situation by shifting his tactics from seeking to control the financial program to delaying and sabotaging it.

Despite the fact that Bartlett, like the governors of Mexico's other coffee-producing states, had signed an agreement in the presence of President Zedillo affirming his support for the financial program, the government of Puebla refused to create the state loan guaranty fund mandated by the program.[56] The Pueblan Coffee Council, firmly under the control of Puebla's secretary of agriculture since Soto's dismissal, took additional steps to block the financial program's implementation. Although the governments of other states had employed INMECAFE's 1992 census to determine which producers were eligible to participate in the financial program, the government of Puebla insisted on using a different census carried out by its own coffee council. This insistence slowed the implementation of the program, because many producers who had been counted in INMECAFE's census had not been counted in the council's census. To

---

[53] This Credit Union of the Gulf (Unión de Credito del Golfo) project is described in Unión Nacional de Productores de Café, CNC (n.d.).

[54] This CNC faction was headed by Rafael Arellanes Caballero, who, as analyzed in Chapter 5, had previously led the ill-fated CESCAFE project in Chiapas.

[55] See Alma N. López Pérez, "Fricciones entre SAGDR e INI obstruyen programa cafetalero," *El Financiero*, Aug. 21, 1995; Alma N. López Pérez, "Sin definirse, la operación del programa cafetalero para el sector social," *El Financiero*, Sept. 20, 1995.

[56] State governments were required to contribute at least 200 pesos per hectare to a loan guaranty fund. See Programa de Fomento a la Cafeticultura (1995).

be eligible for loans from the financial program, those not included in the council's census were required to complete a complicated certification process.

The Pueblan Coffee Council also required producers who wished to participate in the financial program to submit credentials with photographs and offical stamps from their municipal governments. Because many peasants lacked birth certificates, this was an onerous requirement that posed a formidable barrier to their enrolling in the program. Moreover, the requirement that producers obtain official stamps from the municipal government created ample opportunities for corruption and cooptation, especially in places where producer organizations and municipal governments were in conflict. In other states, by contrast, a simple sworn document from two witnesses had sufficed.

In poor rural settings, implementing a new government program with unfamiliar, complex rules is a difficult task, especially when the beneficiaries are expected to play an active role in the program's operation. In states such as Oaxaca, where the State Coffee Council strongly supported the financial program, the work of informing producers about the new program and helping them enroll strained the capacities of producer organizations and government agencies alike. The bureaucratic obstacles erected by Puebla's coffee council should thus be seen not as mere administrative nuisances, but rather as important barriers to the implementation of the program. The effects of these obstacles are evident in the program's extremely low enrollment rate in Puebla (see Table 6.2 on the number of producers approved by Regional Operating Councils).

Bartlett's friendship with BANRURAL's regional director for the state of Puebla, Guillermo Funes Rodríguez, gave the governor another way to impede the implementation of the financial assistance program. In Puebla, BANRURAL arbitrarily excluded producers from the program and refused to disclose the names of ineligible producers. In other states BANRURAL had published lists of those who were ineligible for credits, a disclosure that helped the producer organizations dispute cases and serve as advocates for excluded farmers. In Puebla, by contrast, BANRURAL's decision to keep these lists confidential hindered the organizations' abilities to play such a role.[57]

---

[57] On producer organizations' complaints about BANRURAL's activities in Puebla, see Hipólito Contreras, "Banrural no cumple con el programa de financiamiento," *Cambio de la Sierra*, Aug. 1995.

Table 6.2. *Implementation of the Federal Financial Assistance Program*

	Eligible for Credits		Approved by Regional Operating Councils		Credits Granted (as of mid-October 1995)
	Producers	Hectares	Producers	Hectares	
Oaxaca	49,225	102,464	37,432	67,694	$66,753,750
Guerrero	7,465	18,455	4,082	9,623	$9,079,000
Chiapas	67,010	131,874	57,768	119,734	$111,230,000
Puebla	29,551	41,638	3,800	8,310	$0

Notes: Figures for "credits granted" are in new pesos. Eligible producers were those with no more than 5 hectares of coffee according to INMECAFE's 1992 census. The Financial Assistance Program offered a loan of 1,000 pesos per hectare approved by the Regional Operating Councils.
Source: Consejo Mexicano del Café 1995.

Bartlett did not disguise his opposition to the financial program. He and high-ranking members of his government openly criticized it as an inefficient measure that failed to address the structural causes of poverty in the coffee sector. State government officials argued that funds earmarked for the financial assistance program should be distributed instead through the state government's proposed Integrated Program for Indigenous Zones, which was scheduled to begin the next year.[58] This program was designed to help marginal coffee farmers diversify their production by shifting out of coffee into other, more viable crops. State government officials argued that their Integrated Program was superior to the federal financial program because it would redeploy resources to more efficient uses rather than give producers new incentives to invest in coffee farming, an activity where they lacked competitive advantages.

State government officials also justified their opposition to the federal financial program by appealing to fiscal stability. Since the beginning of Bartlett's administration, Puebla's government had significantly reduced its overall debt. Officials claimed that participating in the financial assistance program would undermine the state government's fragile fiscal health,

[58] Interviews, Puebla, Puebla, Aug. and Sept. 1995. The government of Puebla's program is outlined in Secretaría de Agricultura, Ganadería y Desarrollo Rural, Delegación Estatal en Puebla, Programa de Atención a Poblaciones Indígenas (1995).

because it required the government of Puebla to make a large contribution to a loan guaranty fund and because many producers were sure to default on their loans.[59]

Finally, as statewide elections in November 1995 approached, Bartlett's government announced that it opposed distributing fresh resources to coffee producers, because these funds would invite vote-buying and other clientelistic abuses that would tarnish the elections. Bartlett's apparent concern about the politicization of public resources was ironic in light of his efforts several months earlier to channel public funds exclusively to the CNC's credit union.

Despite these vocal concerns about transparent elections and balanced budgets, Bartlett's move to block the financial assistance program seemed driven more by political motives. His government's proposal that the distribution of the program's funds be delayed until the following year so that they could be allocated instead via the state government's Integrated Program for Indigenous Zones would have guaranteed it full control over the resources. Moreover, because of the Zedillo administration's ongoing efforts to decentralize government authority, the longer the financial program could be postponed, the greater the probability that the state government would be able to control its implementation. Thus even if it ultimately proved impossible to transfer the federal program's funds to their proposed Integrated Program, state government officials nevertheless had good reasons for dragging their feet. Finally, because Bartlett had proven unable to control how the financial program would be implemented in Puebla,[60] he had strong incentives to prevent the release of funds, because they were likely to benefit his federal government enemies, the delegates of INI and SEDESOL.

Defections at the Grassroots. Bartlett's attempt to undermine the financial program did not go unchallenged. National producer organizations pressured Puebla's state government to obey the program's rules. Official and independent organizations publically denounced Bartlett's

---

[59] Interviews, Puebla, Puebla, Aug. and Sept. 1995.
[60] As noted, independent producer organizations, INI officials, and a number of CNC organizations had successfully challenged Bartlett's move to make the credit union of the CNC's State Union of Coffee Producers the exclusive intermediary for the financial program in Puebla.

government at a national meeting to evaluate the financial program's performance.[61] They issued a resolution censuring the government of Puebla "for not contributing its share of the funds to the program ... consequently affecting thousands of peasant and indigenous farmers." The resolution demanded "that the governor comply with the commitment to support the national program that he signed in the presence of the President of the Republic" and that "legal retribution should be sought against the governor for affecting the patrimony and sovereignty of the *campesino* organizations of Puebla that have not been able to incorporate themselves into the program."[62] Federal officials from INI and SEDESOL supported this initiative to force the government of Puebla to comply with the financial program's rules.

This alliance between national-level producer organizations and federal officials against Bartlett's government failed to win support from Puebla's producer organizations. As discussed above, the leader of the CNC's credit union in Puebla, Omar Lechuga, defected from the position of his national sponsors and supported Bartlett instead. Such subnational defections were not limited to the CNC, however: Puebla's most important independent organization, CARTT, chose a similar strategy.

CARTT's leadership criticized the financial program in terms remarkably similar to those used by Bartlett's government – they rejected it as an inefficient consumption subsidy that would neither improve productivity nor help small coffee farmers diversify their crops.[63] Thus CARTT's leadership urged their rank and file not to join the program. According to leaders of CNOC (the national producer organization with which CARTT was affiliated), CARTT's leadership tried to sabotage the financial program. They charged that CARTT's delegate to the Pueblan Coffee Council had falsely claimed to speak for all CNOC affiliates in Puebla when he announced that his organization had decided not to endorse the financial program.[64] This claim misrepresented and undercut the position of CNOC's other affiliates in Puebla, such as the Independent Totonaco

---

[61] The meeting was held in Mexico City in Nov. 1995. Because the financial program was intended primarily to support the purchase of inputs and fertilizers as well as initial maintenance of coffee plants, the credits should have been distributed prior to the harvest (i.e., in August and September). Hence, by the date of this national meeting, it was clear that the window for implementing the program in Puebla had already closed.
[62] Reunión Nacional de Consejos Operativos Regionales de Café (1995).
[63] Interviews, Cuetzalan, Puebla, Aug. 1995.
[64] Interviews, Mexico City, Aug. and Sept. 1995.

Organization (OIT) and the Tunkuwini Social Solidarity Society (SSS), that did in fact support the program.

Why would CARTT pursue such a strategy and risk straining its relationship with its national umbrella organization? As analyzed above, CARTT's focus on integrated rural development had made the organization skeptical about the value of external allies. The New Federalism greatly strengthened this skepticism. As federal agencies increasingly transferred their resources and personnel to state and local governments, grassroots organizations had new incentives to participate in subnational policy arenas. As one CARTT leader put it, serving the rank and file increasingly required "good relations with the governor."[65] From the perspective of grassroots producer organizations like CARTT, political decentralization weakened the rationale for affiliating with a national organization. In the old, highly centralized system, support from a national organization like CNOC, which had direct access to top federal officials in Mexico City, could yield crucial advantages. As control over public policy and resources shifted from Mexico City to the state capitals, however, such national allies were becoming increasingly dispensable. Consequently, when the governor opposed the federal financial program, Puebla's producer organizations had powerful incentives to break with their national organizations – incentives to which both CARTT and the CNC's credit union responded.

CARTT's longstanding strategy of trying to control municipal governments and its decision to affiliate with the PRI in the mid-1980s made the organization especially vulnerable to the state government's efforts to induce it to defect from CNOC. In mid-1995, as the federal financial program was being launched, the leaders of the PRI machine in Puebla took steps to strengthen their relationship with CARTT by inviting it to participate in a new State Political Council for the ruling party. A key leader of CARTT was appointed vice-president of indigenous affairs for this council and put in charge of organizing a state-wide forum on challenges facing indigenous people.[66]

CARTT's strategy of participating in the local political arena in order to secure resources for its development projects had started to pay off. By

---

[65] Interview, Cuetzalan, Puebla, Aug. 1995.

[66] Rosa Rojas, "En Cuetzalan, logran indígenas meterle una 'cuña al racismo,'" *La Jornada*, Aug. 18, 1995, p. 40. Approximately 1,500 representatives of indigenous groups from Puebla and neighboring states were invited to the forum. In exchange for organizing this event, CARTT demanded more community control over local police forces.

promising to devolve more resources to state and municipal governments, the New Federalism strengthened CARTT's commitment to this strategy.[67] To CARTT's leadership, the immediate, short-term benefits offered by the financial assistance program were not worth jeopardizing the important advances the organization had achieved by cultivating the favor of the governor and Puebla's ruling party elites.[68] The centrifugal forces unleashed by the New Federalism made it increasingly likely that these subnational elites, not national producer organizations or federal agencies, would control the distribution of public resources in the future. From CARTT's perspective, the rewards of defection from its national affiliate thus outweighed the benefits of loyalty.

The fact that Puebla's two most important producer organizations did not support the financial assistance program greatly strengthened Bartlett's claim that the efforts of federal officials and national-level organizations to force the program's implementation were illegitimate assaults against his state's sovereignty. Without the crucial support of their affiliates in Puebla, the national producer organizations and their federal government allies were unable to make Bartlett comply with the rules of the financial program. Consequently, as summarized above in Table 6.2, Puebla was the only major coffee-producing state where the financial program was not implemented. In Chiapas, recalcitrant state government elites also tried to undermine the program. However, as analyzed in Chapter 5, they were defeated by an alliance between producer organizations and federal officials. In Oaxaca the participatory policy framework that had been consolidated several years prior to the financial program resulted in its smooth implementation. Even in Guerrero, which had an exclusionary policy framework, powerful producer organizations (aided by national allies) were nevertheless able to enforce the financial program's rules. In Puebla, by contrast, opposition from the state government and grassroots defections combined to prevent the implementation of the program. Thus Puebla's 30,000 poor producers were denied access to some $7 million in loans that they could have obtained had they been able to participate in the federal financial program.

---

[67] In 1995, for example, CARTT sought to elect one of its members to the state legislature for the first time.

[68] Moreover, the leaders of national organizations were often seen as misunderstanding local needs and subordinating local interests to their own national agendas and quests for power – perceptions that were justified in many instances.

Conclusion: Political Decentralization and the Resurgence of Oligarchs

Rather than leading to competitive markets, neoliberal economic reforms in places with powerful oligarchies and weak grassroots organizations are likely to result in new regulatory institutions that generate monopoly rents for oligarchs. The case of Puebla shows why. When private elites are strong, neoliberal reforms give politicians incentives to seek their support by launching crony capitalist reregulation projects. In Puebla, two different governors initiated crony capitalist projects in response to the dismantling of INMECAFE. Moreover, if grassroots organizations are weak, crony capitalist projects are likely to face little opposition. This scenario was also seen in Puebla, where disorganization at the grassroots resulted in unmitigated crony capitalism and an exclusionary policy framework.

The case of Chiapas showed how alliances between strong grassroots organizations and reformist federal officials can offset the power of local elites and authoritarian state government officials. In Chiapas such an alliance was able to achieve a participatory policy framework. By contrast, reformist federal officials in Puebla lacked the support of a powerful producer movement. Without this pressure from below, they were unable to break the grip of subnational elites on the post-INMECAFE policy framework.[69]

The case of Puebla also highlights the potential perils of "centrifugal" reforms that decentralize government. In political systems with subnational authoritarian regimes or enclaves, such reforms can actually strengthen local authoritarian elites, rather than increase the responsiveness of government to ordinary citizens.[70] The federal financial assistance program provides a vivid example of this scenario. The decentralizing reforms launched by President Zedillo gave Puebla's small-producer organizations powerful inducements to defect from their national-level organizations and cultivate the favor of an authoritarian state government. Before the decentralizing reforms were implemented, rural policymaking

---

[69] In Fox's (1993) terms, the weakness of the producer movement meant that no "sandwich strategy" was possible in Puebla.

[70] The potential dangers of decentralization are also emphasized in Fox and Aranda (1996) and Fox (1999). For optimistic assessments of decentralizing reforms, see Interamerican Development Bank (1994) and Shah (1994). A useful overview of the current trend toward political decentralization in Latin America is Willis, Garman, and Haggard (1999).

in Mexico was a process in which federal agencies and national producer organizations commanded great influence. Under the old, centralized policy regime, local and state organizations thus had strong incentives to affiliate with and seek support from national actors. The New Federalism transformed the policy regime by dramatically increasing the control of state governments over agricultural policy. In this new context, Puebla's small-producer organizations decided that they could best defend their interests by bargaining directly with the state government. Consequently, they were increasingly willing to cut their ties with national organizations.

Thus political decentralization threatened to reverse the important advances that Mexico's small-producer organizations had achieved during the 1970s and 1980s by building national alliances. These alliances had not only strengthened the capacity of small producers to defend their interests in the policy arena, they had also improved the ability of producers to compete in the marketplace by lowering their transaction costs and helping them create economies of scale. Moreover, national alliances had helped small producers escape from exploitation by local oligarchs. From the perspective of Mexico's small farmers, the New Federalism thus seemed unlikely to deliver on its promise of expanding their opportunities to participate in policymaking. Rather, political decentralization appeared to be leading to a dismal situation in which disorganized, isolated producers struggled alone against the exploitive designs of resurgent oligarchs.

Although this outcome was most likely in places such as Puebla, where grassroots organizations were weak, it was becoming increasingly possible even in cases where such organizations were strong. As analyzed in earlier chapters, the impressive achievements of powerful grassroots organizations in Oaxaca and Chiapas depended in large part on their ability to forge effective alliances both with national producer organizations and with federal government officials. By undercutting the potential for such multilevel alliances, political decentralization posed daunting new challenges for Mexico's small farmers.

PART III

Conclusion

7

After Neoliberalism: What Next?

Neoliberal policy reforms result in different kinds of new institutions for market governance, not in the triumph of free-market forces. That is the main finding of this study. This finding challenges the expectations of both the supporters and the opponents of neoliberal policies, who share the assumption that, for better or worse, these policies result in a convergence on unregulated markets. The evidence analyzed in this study shows instead that neoliberal reforms unleash a new round of politics – the politics of reregulation. As we have seen, the politics of reregulation leads to varying institutions for market governance with contrasting consequences for economic efficiency and social justice.

Neoliberal shocks create institutional vacuums, a situation that gives political entrepreneurs opportunities to reregulate sectors of the economy. Politicians seize these opportunities because reregulation generates divisible benefits and targetable rewards that help them gain and keep power. Societal groups also have a stake in how markets are reregulated, and politicians' reregulation projects can give them compelling incentives to mobilize. Hence, reregulation is a *political* process in which politicians and societal groups bargain over the rules of new institutions for market governance that replace those destroyed by neoliberal reforms. The relative strengths and strategies of politicians and societal groups who participate in this bargaining determine the distinct institutional outcomes of reregulation.

To cast this argument in a systematic form, in Chapter 1 I proposed a framework for analyzing the politics of reregulation. The framework consists of two steps with a dual focus on politicians' choices of reregulation projects and on subsequent strategic interactions between politicians and societal groups regarding the terms of reregulation. First, incumbents' reregulation strategies are explained from a politician-centered perspective that connects societal forces, regime institutions, and policy repertoires to the shaping of policy choice. Second, institutional outcomes are explained from an interactive perspective that focuses on bargaining between politicians and societal groups as they compete to influence the terms of reregulation. These two steps explain why neoliberal reforms in Mexico led to exclusionary institutions that served the interests of oligarchs in some states and to participatory institutions that benefited small producers in others.

By shifting the focus to institutional reconstruction after neoliberalism, this study goes beyond most recent work on the political economy of development. Previous analyses focus mainly on the dismantling of statist ancien régimes. From that perspective, the goal is to explain how old institutions for market governance are destroyed, not how new institutions are built. Consequently, prior studies leave us without a framework for addressing what is perhaps the most important question for understanding the political economy of the contemporary era: *What kinds of new institutions have replaced those destroyed by the global wave of neoliberalism?* I have attempted to fill this gap by providing conceptual and analytic tools for answering that question.

The first section of this chapter revisits the distinct patterns of reregulation analyzed in the case chapters. This exercise affords an opportunity to explore the broader implications of these patterns for understanding post-neoliberal politics in the contemporary developing world. The next section concludes by proposing a research agenda for a comparative political economy of post-neoliberalism.

Post-Neoliberal Pathways: Lessons from Mexico

The discovery of four different reregulation scenarios in a single economic sector in just one country provides a strong basis for expecting that a rich array of varying reregulation processes have unfolded across sectors and nations. From the Mexican case, we can distinguish two plausible patterns of reregulation after neoliberalism: innovation along corporatist lines and, alternatively, hegemony by oligarchs. Although these two patterns do not exhaust the full range of possibilities, they help dispel the widely held belief that neoliberal reforms set countries on a convergent path toward laissez-faire markets. The evidence from Mexico suggests that, instead of converging on free markets, countries that implement neoliberal reforms travel multiple pathways leading to distinct institutional frameworks for market governance.[1]

Making Corporatism Work: Institutional Innovation along Corporatist Lines

Students of comparative political economy are increasingly skeptical about the efficacy of corporatist institutions for managing challenges of economic adjustment.[2] This skepticism is based largely on the experiences of European countries, such as Sweden and Austria, where pressures from globalization of markets (for example, increasing demand for labor flexibility) eroded social democratic corporatist institutions that, until the 1980s, had delivered political stability and economic growth.

Despite such skepticism, the case of Oaxaca shows that innovation along corporatist lines is still feasible.[3] As analyzed in Chapter 3, a neocorporatist reregulation project, originally intended to strengthen authoritarian modes of policymaking, unexpectedly supplied incentives and institutional raw materials with which a grassroots producer movement was able to forge a participatory policy framework. The State Coffee Council of Oaxaca served as a centralized arena for mobilizing consensus among competing interests in the coffee sector and for launching collaborative projects between government and producers. These collaborations creatively combined producer organizations' social capital with government's state capital in ways that improved the efficiency and quality of coffee production. Thus the case of Oaxaca shows how grassroots organizations can transform exclusionary corporatist institutions into participatory policy frameworks that help them compete in the global marketplace.

Viewed this way, corporatist heritages – even those of the top-down, state corporatist variety[4] – may offer important institutional comparative advantages for reconciling the often conflicting imperatives of political

---

[1] This study thus links with the burgeoning literature on varying forms of capitalism. The literature has focused on advanced industrial countries, generally neglecting developing countries. See, for example, Berger and Dore (1996); Hollingsworth and Boyer (1997); Kitschelt, Lange, Marks, and Stephens (1999); and Huber and Stephens (in press).
[2] See, for example, Pontusson (1992); Streeck and Schmitter (1991); and Haggard and Kaufman (1995:340–5).
[3] For a different perspective on the viability of corporatist institutions in the context of globalization, see Garrett (1998).
[4] On "state corporatism," see Schmitter (1974).

stability and economic growth. The task in developing countries with such heritages, for example, Brazil, Venezuela, Egypt, Ghana, Ivory Coast, and Thailand may therefore be to make corporatism work by making it inclusive and participatory, rather than to get rid of it.[5] To assess this intriguing possibility, we need to explore the generalizability of the path to a participatory policy framework seen in the case of Oaxaca.

State-Builders and Reregulators. Politicians with state-building agendas are probably a necessary ingredient for participatory policy frameworks. Such politicians seek to advance their careers by constructing new public institutions and expanding the role of government (for example, through reregulation). These new institutions in turn provide incentives and focal points that can trigger and help sustain mobilization by societal actors. The combination of institution building from above and organized pressure from below is a basic building block of participatory policy frameworks.

In Oaxaca a populist political regime supplied institutional raw materials that grassroots organizations reworked into a participatory policy framework. The governor of Oaxaca when INMECAFE withdrew, Heladio Ramírez López, was a relic of a bygone era of statist policies, and he surrounded himself with advisers who shared his ideological formation. Their policy repertoires, especially their perception of the appropriate economic role for government, diverged dramatically from those of the neoliberals at the national level who championed orthodox, market-oriented reform. Moreover, the officials who launched the neocorporatist project in Oaxaca were not insulated technocrats driven by technical policy goals and ideological blueprints. Rather, they were political actors motivated mainly by the objective of strengthening the incumbent regime's base of support.

The supply of political entrepreneurs with state-building proclivities should be abundant in the contemporary developing world. The ideological mold of state-led development that defined the governor of Oaxaca's policy repertoire was by no means unique to Mexico. This ideology held sway across the developing world from the 1950s until the 1980s.[6] In many

---

[5] On corporatism in Brazil and Venezuela, see Collier and Collier (1991); in Egypt, see Vitalis (1995) and Waterbury (1993:ch. 9); in Ghana and Ivory Coast, see Widner (1994); and in Thailand, see Laothamatas (1992).

[6] One of the pivotal events in the ascendance of this statist ideology was the Bandung Summit in Indonesia in 1955. See Yergin and Stanislaw (1998:ch. 3).

countries, we should thus expect to find numerous holdovers from the pre-neoliberal era, who, like the governor of Oaxaca, reject the neoliberal creed and regard state intervention as a legitimate tool for pursuing their goals.

The number of state-building entrepreneurs should not be limited to old-guard survivors from a bygone developmental era, however. This study has shown repeatedly how imperatives of political survival give politicians powerful incentives to intervene in markets. Consequently, regardless of their ideological persuasions, political incumbents may have strong incentives to behave like populists by using government regulatory authority as a tool for building support. Because of the coalitional dilemmas created by neoliberal reforms (for example, their tendency to inflict high costs on well-organized interest groups), potential state-builders and reregulators should be easy to find.[7]

Work on the politics of neoliberal reform has often lamented the lack of insulated technocratic agencies in developing countries, arguing that weak state capacity undermines economic adjustment by exposing the policy process to the distortions of political ambition.[8] The case of Oaxaca casts political ambition in a different light: Politicians in pursuit of power may unintentionally supply institutional raw materials ripe for transformation into participatory policy frameworks. In Oaxaca the governor's neocorporatist reregulation project provided incentives for a reworking from below by grassroots producer organizations that resulted in participatory institutions for market governance. Rather than insulating policymakers, then, the challenge facing developing countries may instead involve reconfiguring political institutions so that ambition induces incumbents to supply the institutional ingredients for participatory policy frameworks. Viewed from this perspective, the "soft state" may have a silver lining.

Coordinated Pressure from Below. Politicians who launch neocorporatist projects are not sufficient conditions for participatory policy frameworks. In the absence of coordinated pressure from societal organizations, such projects are likely to result in state-controlled corporatist institutions that serve to generate political support, rather than promote economic performance. Mobilized societal actors with the capacity to make policy

---

[7] These coalitional dilemmas are analyzed in Collier (1992); Waterbury (1993); Haggard and Kaufman (1995); Levitsky and Way (1998); and Burgess (1999).
[8] See, for example, Callaghy (1990) and Nelson (1990a).

proposals and hold government officials accountable are an important additional element for participatory policy frameworks.[9]

To achieve the kinds of welfare-enhancing institutions seen in Oaxaca, however, societal organizations need to do more than just lodge demands, pressure for inclusion, and monitor government performance – they should also shoulder new economic responsibilities. The State Coffee Council of Oaxaca was able to curtail costly externalities because producer organizations participated actively in its program to recycle environmentally hazardous production byproducts (e.g., the pulp of coffee cherries). By helping control free-rider problems in the management of pests and parasites, the producer organizations played a crucial auxiliary role that buttressed the council's efforts to police the commons. By taking responsibility for marketing crops, the organizations freed government agencies to focus on the area where they could make the most valuable contribution: targeted interventions to plug leaks in the production process that undermined quality and efficiency. Finally, the information the producer organizations provided to help identify these leaks and their active participation in the design and implementation of government programs proved essential for the success of Oaxaca's participatory policy framework.

In sum, the producer organizations in Oaxaca did far more than just pressure and shout. They also embraced new economic roles (e.g., self-management of production and marketing) that enabled novel divisions of labor between them and government that exploited the comparative advantages of each. *Engaged* productivist organizations willing to defend their interests by challenging government policy, yet committed to self-management of core economic activities, seem crucial for making corporatism work.

By disciplining the producer organizations and imposing constraints against rent seeking, the bureaucrats who ran the State Coffee Council helped the organizations carry out their new economic roles. As illustrated by the *microbodega* program, where the council's staff prevented unnecessary project duplication by forcing rival producer organizations to cooperate and share bodegas, the council disciplined the organizations in ways that enhanced efficiency. Just as the capacity of the producer organizations to monitor the council's staff gave it incentives to perform effectively, the

[9] The advantages for economic performance of combining social capital with government capacity is a central theme in Evans (1995, 1996a,b). See also Schneider and Maxfield (1997) as well as the insightful analysis by Tendler (1997) of subnational development programs in Brazil.

staff's power to discipline the organizations gave them incentives to act responsibly. Mutual checks and balances and reciprocal accountability between producers and government bureaucrats worked to prevent shirking and predatory rent seeking on both sides of the public–private divide. Reciprocal accountability between public officials and private organizations is probably a key building block for participatory policy frameworks that improve welfare and efficiency.[10]

Downsized Corporatism?   Scholars who take a dim view of the prospects for future innovation along corporatist lines argue that neoliberal reforms undermine the collective actors necessary to sustain centralized bargains and policy coordination. In Mexico's coffee sector, however, these reforms often had the opposite effect, as the challenge of managing economic activities previously controlled by government actually catalyzed and helped sustain collective action by producers in a number of instances. Moreover, self-management of their economic activities enabled producers to overcome the subordinate roles they had previously played under the old, state-dominated corporatist system. This new autonomy equipped the producer organizations to act as equal partners in collaborative relationships with government agencies.

Although neoliberal reforms can have disorganizing effects that erode the potential for collective action, this study shows that such effects are by no means universal. Policies aimed at reducing state intervention can cause societal actors to mobilize in order to manage economic activities disavowed by the state. Politicians' reregulation projects can have a similar impact by providing incentives that help societal actors overcome disorganizing pressures from global markets and neoliberal policy shocks. In Oaxaca, for example, the governor's neocorporatist project motivated previously dispersed producer organizations to join forces and form an encompassing, statewide organization, CEPCO.

The national level is probably the wrong place to look for innovation along corporatist lines. National-level, macrocorporatist institutions do seem increasingly difficult to sustain because they depend on the stability and internal coherence of large-scale, peak-level interest groups –

---

[10] The concept of reciprocal accountability is from Roeder (1993), who uses it to analyze bureaucratic politics in the Soviet Union. However, Roeder emphasizes negative effects of reciprocal accountability, showing how it can be a source of institutional rigidity and policy stagnation.

conditions that may be hard to achieve in the fragmented social landscape of the neoliberal era. However, the present analysis shows that these conditions can be met on a smaller scale. Indeed, it is precisely at the regional and local levels that the solidarities for sustaining coherent and stable interest associations are most likely to exist.[11]

As seen in the case of Oaxaca, where strong village and ethnic solidarities provided a firm basis for a cohesive, encompassing federation of small producers, parochial underpinnings can provide the kinds of social ties needed to sustain a downscaled, *mesocorporatism* in the face of disorganizing pressures from the global economy.[12] Contrary to the claims of skeptics, centralized peak associations can still be formed. However, the "peaks" may lie well below the national level. It bears emphasis that such mesocorporatist institutions (in contrast to their macro antecedents) will probably not center on macroeconomic policy issues, such as exchange rates and national wage and price agreements, but rather on narrower, sector- or region-specific issues, such as how to coordinate public investment in a particular policy area.

In addition to a shift to subnational levels of analysis, exploring the possibilities for institutional innovation along corporatist lines requires a focus on new mass actors. Because of the declining size of the industrial labor force in many countries (and the fact that industrial labor has never played a decisive political role in many developing countries), the classic model of corporatism as tripartite bargaining between labor, business, and the state may be outmoded. Post-neoliberal corporatism, besides being meso in scale, is likely to involve new groups, such as productivist peasant unions, informal urban sector associations, and new social movements mobilized around issues like local environmental degradation.[13] The challenges confronting political and societal leaders who seek to organize these groups as

---

[11] Locke (1995) makes a similar argument for the case of Italy. See esp. his critique of "national models" schools of comparative political economy (Locke 1995:ch. 6).

[12] On the role of "parochial underpinnings" and "preexisting, smaller-scale groupings" in sustaining mass mobilization, see Perry (1993:251–2). On mesocorporatism in the European context, see Cawson (1985) and Contarino (1995). Haggard and Kaufman (1995:345) mention a similar possibility. See Martin (1997) for an argument that the term "corporatism" should not be used to describe the new patterns of interest representation emerging in Latin America.

[13] Post-neoliberal corporatism may also be bipartite, rather than tripartite. That is, such arrangements may be based on bilateral state–group linkages. On the varying forms of corporatism in the Latin American context, see Collier (1995) and O'Donnell (1977). On new forms of state–business linkages in Latin America, see Durand and Silva (1998).

well as the ideal and material incentives that could anchor post-neoliberal corporatist bargains are exciting, unexplored research frontiers.[14]

A further issue for future research concerns how nonsectoral organizations – such as political parties – can strengthen or undercut sectoral organizations that participate in corporatist-type bargains. This question is especially relevant for countries experiencing simultaneous pressures for political and economic liberalization. The case of Guerrero highlights the difficult trade-off such simultaneity can create between the goal of building effective economic institutions and the goal of achieving political democracy. In a nondemocratic system under pressure to liberalize politically, a neocorporatist reregulation project in a particular sector of the economy may be linked to the maintenance of the incumbent authoritarian political regime. Producers are citizens, too, and if they become embroiled in struggles to democratize the political regime, framing their opposition to the neocorporatist project in partisan terms, as occurred in Guerrero, then it may be extremely difficult to establish a participatory policy framework. Spillover into the sector of contentious issues related to democratization may lead to politicization, causing the government to rigidify and refuse to bargain with a producer movement it sees as part of the political opposition. Furthermore, producers motivated by partisan and civic goals may be reluctant to negotiate with the government for inclusion in the policy arena, because they may decide that gaining admission is not worth compromising their struggle for political democracy. Thus polarization and an exclusionary policy framework are the likely outcomes.

The contrasts between the cases of Oaxaca and Guerrero, where neocorporatist projects led to distinct policy frameworks, suggest powerful tensions between political democratization, on the one hand, and the construction of participatory institutions for market governance, on the other. In the context of an authoritarian or semidemocratic regime undergoing neoliberal reforms, one of the costs of choosing to be a democrat first, and a producer second, may be forfeiting the opportunity to build economic institutions that could help improve welfare and competitiveness.[15]

---

[14] See Hagopian (1998a,b) for a suggestive analysis of how neoliberal policy shocks have reconfigured institutions for interest representation in the Latin American context. See also Chalmers et al. (1997).

[15] Because corporatist frameworks explicitly limit contestation about policy issues in order to coordinate societal demands, it is open to debate whether participatory policy frameworks should be considered fully democratic. Such frameworks may be highly inclusionary yet not permit competition among groups with distinct policy viewpoints.

Countries with corporatist traditions of interest intermediation exist across the developing world. In such places, neoliberal reforms should give politicians strong incentives to launch neocorporatist reregulation projects to mobilize mass support. Mobilizing mass support is not always the strategy that politicians prefer, however. In cases where societal elites are powerful, political incumbents may face compelling pressures to ally with them by choosing crony capitalist projects. Indeed, crony capitalism, not neocorporatism, may well be the modal pattern of reregulation in the contemporary developing world. The following section develops this proposition and explores its sobering implications for the kinds of post-neoliberal policy frameworks likely to emerge in most developing countries.

Protecting Elite Interests: New Forms of Oligarchic Control

During the 1960s and 1970s, policymakers across the developing world favored state intervention in the economy as an instrument for promoting modernization and national development.[16] These interventions were often cloaked in a populist rhetoric of promoting social justice by displacing traditional elites – chiefs, bosses, oligarchs, landlords, rich peasants, and clan leaders – in order to forge direct links between the state and subaltern groups. Despite high expectations, state-led development projects had uneven success, as states confronted what Joel Migdal calls "weblike" societies characterized by fragmented social control and multiple, autonomous power centers.[17] In these kinds of societies, local elites frequently derailed state-led development efforts by coopting the field-office and line-agency officials responsible for implementing policies.[18] Consequently, instead of destroying traditional elites, state intervention often had the opposite effect by providing them access to fresh resources.[19] Even

---

[16] Yergin and Stanislaw (1998:ch. 3); Evans (1997). According to one observer, "A new 'can-do' spirit gripped many who aspired to state leadership. The state organizations became the focal point for hopes of achieving broad goals of human dignity, prosperity, and equity . . ." (Migdal 1988:4).

[17] As Migdal (1988:37) puts it, "Numerous Third World societies have been as resilient as an intricate spider's web; one could snip a corner of the web away and the rest of the web would swing majestically between the branches, just as one could snip center strands and have the web continue to exist."

[18] On such line–agency problems in the Mexican case, see Grindle (1977). See also Migdal (1988:ch. 7).

[19] See, for example, Hagopian's (1996) analysis of the Brazilian case.

204

when state intervention did not serve to strengthen local elites, it did not necessarily displace them. In many developing countries, therefore, tenacious traditional elites endured.

Neoliberal reforms create opportunities for traditional elites to reassert their hegemony. As seen in the cases of Chiapas and Puebla, neoliberal policies get the government off the backs of local elites, allowing them to return to business as usual, which means enjoying monopoly control over local markets. If these elites command significant social control through patron–client networks, politicians may have strong incentives to seek their support by launching crony capitalist reregulation projects. Rather than leading to efficient allocation of resources by competitive markets, neoliberal reforms in places with powerful traditional elites may instead result in reregulated markets that generate monopoly rents for oligarchs.[20] Because most developing countries have weblike, fractionalized societies, elite resurgence supported by crony capitalist reregulation projects should be widespread.[21]

Crony capitalist patterns of reregulation need not result in the resurgence of traditional elites, however. In Latin America, for example, reregulation of sectors such as telecommunications and finance has often served to create monopoly rents for a *new* class of private entrepreneurs.[22] Moreover, as illustrated by the post-Communist countries, where prior episodes of social revolution and totalitarian rule often decimated traditional elites, reregulation can play a central role in the making of new oligarchic classes. In the post-Soviet context, for example, reregulation has served as a tool for reconfiguring the old political elite into a new economic one. The phenomenon of "nomenklatura buyouts" illustrates this process of elite role change via reregulation. In anticipation of losing political power, regime incumbents across the Soviet bloc sought to convert their political capital into economic capital by controlling the privatization of state enterprises in ways that allowed them to parachute into lucrative management and ownership positions. In a process of "privatization without marketization," these incumbents mobilized to erect

---

[20] This finding challenges the facile equations of decentralization with participatory governance that are common in the development literature. See, for example, Interamerican Development Bank (1994).

[21] Migdal (1988:38) found that well over half of all Third World countries had highly fractionalized societies.

[22] Schamis (1999). On the Mexican case, see Concheiro Bórquez (1996).

regulatory barriers to entry that protected the monopoly rents of the newly privatized firms.[23]

Reregulation can also play an important role in the emergence of new oligarchies comprised of actors who did not hold political positions in the old regime. In an intriguing analysis of the "politics of partial reform" in post-Communist countries, Joel Hellman shows how economic distortions introduced by neoliberal reforms can create large rents for new private entrepreneurs, such as commercial bankers and investment fund managers. These actors, who did not hold political power in the old communist system, may be able to exploit opportunities for rent seeking created by price differentials between liberalized and nonliberalized sectors of the economy.[24] Hellman argues that the beneficiaries of these differentials have a stake in blocking further reforms by maintaining a "partial reform equilibrium" that protects their gains.

From the standpoint of the present analysis, the politics of partial reform, while important, should be viewed as a short-term prelude to the politics of reregulation. The politics of reregulation framework predicts that political entrepreneurs will seek to win support from the beneficiaries of partial reform by launching reregulation projects to protect and perhaps expand their rent-seeking opportunities. Thus the politics of reregulation perspective focuses attention not only on how political actors try to veto further reforms, but also on *how political actors take proactive measures to lock in and extend the benefits they reap from partial reform*.

Oligarchic outcomes are not inevitable, however. First, the kinds of political institutional factors emphasized in this study (for example, how the rules of office structure accountability) can give incumbents autonomy from societal actors.[25] In places with powerful private elites, therefore, politicians do not necessarily launch crony capitalist projects. This possibility is seen in the case of Oaxaca, where the governor chose a neocorporatist project despite the presence of a powerful coffee oligarchy.

---

[23] Stark and Bruszt (1998). See esp. their discussion of new laws (e.g., the Law on Business Associations) that promoted concentration of wealth in the Hungarian economy (pp. 70–1). Furthermore, in the post-Soviet context, local government officials have often sought to prevent the formation of competitive markets in their regions in order to protect their share of local monopoly rents. See also Treisman (1998).

[24] Hellman (1998:219). Hellman also discusses how pivotally positioned members of the former Communist elite (e.g., state enterprise managers, collective farm chairmen, party officials, and ministerial bureaucrats) have had ample rent-seeking opportunities.

[25] See Kohli (1987) on the importance of regime institutions for explaining varied policy outcomes in contexts characterized by similar societal forces.

Second, even if politicians *do* choose crony capitalist projects, powerful grassroots organizations may nevertheless be able to forge participatory policy frameworks, especially if they receive assistance from external allies. The case of Chiapas, where support from reformist federal government officials helped a strong grassroots movement defeat a local crony capitalist initiative, shows how external allies can enable grassroots organizations to offset the power of private elites.[26] If reformist government officials are absent or weak, transnational nongovernmental organizations (NGOs) and solidarity networks may serve as partial substitutes by providing resources that help sustain grassroots mobilization. However, such external organizations often cannot give durable, long-term support.[27]

The alternative scenario is seen in the case of Puebla, which illustrates the difficulties of building and sustaining reformist alliances in the face of weak grassroots movements. Thus, in Puebla, where reform-oriented federal officials lacked organized pressure from below, they failed in their efforts to break the grip of local elites on the post-INMECAFE policy framework. This case serves as a sobering reminder that, rather than leading to efficient, unregulated markets, neoliberal reforms in contexts with weak grassroots organizations are likely to result in new regulatory institutions that generate monopoly rents for oligarchs.

Toward a Comparative Political Economy of Post-Neoliberalism

This book has developed new tools for understanding why and how institutions for market governance are reconstructed after neoliberal reforms. The analysis of the Mexican coffee sector confirmed the value of these tools by showing that they help explain why neoliberal reforms led to exclusionary institutions in some Mexican states and to participatory institutions in others. The Mexican evidence in turn offered intriguing insights about how the politics of reregulation can work across a wide range of

---

[26] It took an armed rebellion by the Zapatistas, however, to induce federal government officials to challenge local authoritarian elites. As seen in the case of Puebla, "neofederalist" trends toward political decentralization can undercut the potential for these kinds of multilevel alliances.

[27] On transnational peasant solidarity networks, see Edelman (1995). Religious institutions, such as the Catholic Church, may be better equipped to play an enduring, transformative role. On transnational NGO networks, see Keck and Sikkink (1997) and Fox and Brown (1998).

cases. Having used these insights to explore alternative patterns of reregulation, let us turn to the questions the book raises for future research. These questions form a promising agenda for a comparative political economy of post-neoliberalism.

What Are the Effects of Federalism?

One intriguing area for future research concerns how federalism affects the politics of reregulation. The Mexican case shows that a neoliberal policy shock in a federal system can trigger varying reregulation processes at the subnational level. Does reregulation in other federal systems also result in divergent institutional outcomes across subnational policy arenas? To address this question we should differentiate federal systems in terms of the distribution of power and authority between local and central governments. In cases of "robust" federalism, where local governments are weakly constrained by the center, the dynamics of reregulation may vary widely at the subnational level.[28] Brazil exemplifies robust federalism. By contrast, in more centralized federal systems, such as Argentina, India, and China, reregulation processes may vary to a lesser degree across subnational units.

Although the distinction between robust and centralized federal systems is important, the Mexican case suggests that the balance of power between center and periphery cannot by itself predict how reregulation works in federal systems. In Mexico the federal government's tight control over public revenues and the president's discretionary power to appoint and dismiss state governors significantly weakened subnational governments.[29] Despite the extreme centralization of power in Mexico, this study discovered political regimes and reregulation processes with distinct dynamics at the subnational level. This finding challenges the conventional view that Mexico has a single, uniform system of politics.[30] It also has important implications for research on other centralized federal systems.

National-level elites in centralized federal systems do not necessarily use their power to impose policy uniformity across subnational units. Rather, they may pursue "heterogenizing" strategies that deliberately

[28] The term robust federalism is from Mainwaring and Samuels (1998).
[29] Cornelius (1996) and Rodríguez (1997:ch. 2).
[30] For an analysis and critique of this conventional view, see Rubin (1997).

208

create subnational deviations from their policy preferences.[31] In contemporary Mexico, for example, reform-oriented elites at the national level often protected and even promoted antireformist enclaves at the subnational level in order to secure the political stability and support they needed to achieve their policy goals.[32] As seen in the case of Oaxaca, where President de la Madrid chose a populist governor (Ramírez López) whose policies did not conform to his own neoliberal agenda, such center-orchestrated policy heterogeneity can be an important source of subnational variation in reregulation dynamics. Explaining reregulation in centralized federal systems thus requires an understanding of the strategies of national elites, especially the conditions under which they use their power to limit or, alternatively, to promote policy diversity across subnational units.[33]

A related area for future research involves the politics of reregulation in *unitary* systems. Because unitary systems usually lack the potential for autonomous policy jurisdictions at the subnational level, reregulation is likely to be a territorially more uniform process than in federal systems. Nevertheless, a unitary system, too, could experience varied reregulation dynamics, with variation occurring across economic sectors, rather than administrative units, and involving interagency, rather than intergovernmental bargaining. Furthermore, the territorially uneven distribution of economic sectors within most countries may cause the politics of reregulation to vary widely along territorial lines, even in a unitary system.[34]

A focus on unitary systems should strengthen our understanding of how political institutions influence reregulation. One intriguing question

[31] Alternatively, they may lack the monitoring capacity to know when subnational governments deviate from the national line. Of course, lack of such capacity might be considered an indicator of a weakly centralized, or robust, federal system.

[32] See, for example, Fox (1994c, 1996); and Snyder (1999b). The cases of Chiapas and Guerrero illustrate this "selective feudalization." The case of Argentina also shows how national-level elites in federal systems may selectively shield subnational units from national reforms in order to secure political support. See Gibson and Calvo (in press).

[33] A focus on the strategies of national elites in centralized federal systems should also help explain when subnational units can operate as if they were autonomous policy jurisdictions, a condition that increases the probability of varied reregulation processes at the subnational level.

[34] In the case of Chile, for example, mining and agricultural exports are concentrated in different parts of the country.

concerns whether unitary systems shape the strategic options of grassroots organizations in ways that make oligarchic outcomes more likely than in federal systems. This study found that in federal systems grassroots movements may be able to defeat local crony capitalist projects by allying with reformist federal government officials. The case of Chiapas illustrated this scenario. In a unitary system, by contrast, grassroots organizations may have fewer opportunities for building multilevel alliances against crony capitalist projects because the policy positions of officials at the local level are likely to mirror those of their national-level superiors.[35] In unitary systems, therefore, crony capitalist initiatives may have a higher probability of success than in federal systems. How unitary systems shape the strategic options of grassroots organizations is an exciting issue for future research.

Does the Structure of Political Competition Matter?

This study includes two cases with semicompetitive two-party systems – Oaxaca and Guerrero.[36] The transition to competitive politics in these cases had profound, yet divergent, effects on the politics of reregulation. In Oaxaca, the ability of the coffee producer movement to sustain a nonpartisan strategy despite the growing strength of the center-left opposition party, the PRD, helped explain why a participatory policy framework resulted. In Guerrero, by contrast, the producer organizations allied with the PRD, thereby choosing a partisan strategy that threatened the ruling party and contributed to an exclusionary outcome.[37] These different outcomes raise intriguing questions about how nonsectoral organizations, such as political parties, shape the politics of reregulation by interacting with sectoral organizations, such as producer associations.

One important issue concerns the capacity of mass-based sectoral organizations to use the threat of supporting an opposition party as a way to elicit government support for participatory policy frameworks.[38] Work

[35] As noted earlier, transnational organizations and networks, while important, may not be able to offer the kind of durable support needed to defeat crony capitalist initiatives.
[36] The study also includes two cases of noncompetitive party systems: Chiapas and Puebla.
[37] During the time frame of this study (1980–96), the center-right National Action Party (PAN) had a minor presence in Oaxaca and Guerrero.
[38] See Bates (1997:chs. 2, 3) for an exemplary analysis of how the structure of political competition can shape the formation of economic institutions. Bates focuses on the Colombian and Brazilian coffee sectors.

needs to be done on the factors that make such threats credible. By providing information about how much control the leadership has over the rank and file, data on the internal structure of sectoral organizations should improve our understanding of their capacity to make credible threats. The degree of leadership control over followers is important because it helps determine an organization's ability to enforce binding agreements. In competitive political systems, the sectoral organizations that command the most influence in the politics of reregulation may be those that can efficiently coordinate their members' votes and thus make credible commitments with political parties to deliver or to deny their support.

A focus on party systems should also improve our understanding of reregulation in the context of competitive politics. Even if the internal structure of sectoral organizations equip them to make binding agreements with political parties, the threat of allying with opposition parties can be rendered credible only if viable partisan allies exist. In both Oaxaca and Guerrero, for example, the threats that organizations of small coffee producers made to the ruling party were credible because the most important opposition party, the PRD, had a center-left agenda compatible with the demands of small farmers. Work should be done on how different kinds of party systems shape the incentives and strategic options of sectoral organizations involved in reregulation processes. This task affords an excellent opportunity to link the study of reregulation to previous work on how party systems affected the implementation of neoliberal reforms.[39]

This book has focused on poor, rural settings where clientelist or corporatist frameworks of interest representation coordinate votes into blocs. In many places around the globe, however, clientelist and corporatist mechanisms have either eroded or never existed. In such contexts, which include most advanced industrial countries as well as many urban areas in developing countries, voting is an increasingly atomized, individualistic act.[40] How does reregulation work in polities with atomized, mobile voters? In such polities, the power of societal organizations to influence reregulation should derive not from the ability to command votes, but rather from other sources, such as the ability to make campaign contributions. Where voting is atomized, the most effective societal actors may be advocacy organizations that use mass mailings to solicit contributions and are led by telegenic opinion mongers with celebrity status in the mass

---

[39] See, for example, Haggard and Kaufman (1995).
[40] See Roberts (1995); Weyland (1996, 1999); and Hagopian (1998a,b).

media. Future research should explore the dynamics of reregulation in electoral systems with atomized voting.

Does Reregulation Work Differently in Advanced Industrial Countries?

As noted in Chapter 1, studies of advanced industrial countries have devoted considerable attention to reregulation. These studies have typically deemphasized the distributive effects of regulatory policy and instead portrayed reregulation as a relatively apolitical process led by technocrats who strive to promote economic performance, codify rules, or expand their bureaucratic prerogatives. This book takes a very different approach, because it argues that the impulse to reregulate stems from politicians, not from technocrats. From this perspective, understanding the dynamics of reregulation requires a framework that puts politicians and their efforts to retain power at the center of analysis. The evidence from Mexico confirmed the value of this politician-centered approach.

An important task for future research involves specifying the range of cases where a focus on politicians or, alternatively, on technocrats offers better leverage for explaining reregulation. In developed and developing countries alike, the distributive effects of regulatory policy generate powerful incentives for political action. If autonomous bureaucratic agencies insulated from "capture" by political actors are nonexistent or scarce, as is the case in most developing countries, understanding how reregulation works requires a framework that highlights politicians' efforts to gain and keep power. By contrast, in contexts where bureaucratic agencies exert independent control over policymaking, a framework that focuses on technocratic actors may be more appropriate.

How much insulation bureaucratic agencies have from political pressures varies widely both across and within countries. Consequently, although autonomous bureaucratic agencies are scarce in the developing world, they are not totally absent. State organizations in some developing countries have "pockets of efficiency" formed by government agencies with meritocratic norms of recruitment and technocratic operating procedures.[41] In policy areas dominated by this kind of bureaucracy, a technocrat-centered perspective on reregulation could prove fruitful.

Just as pockets of efficiency exist in contexts where autonomous bureaucratic agencies are scarce, pockets of *inefficiency* can thrive in contexts

[41] See Evans (1995:60–6) on "pockets of efficiency" in the Brazilian case.

where such agencies are abundant. Thus, even in advanced industrial countries with relatively insulated government bureaucracies, a politician-centered perspective could prove indispensable for explaining how rereg-ulation works. Recent studies of the relationship between legislators and technocrats in advanced industrial countries strengthen this possibility because they show that previous work may have greatly overestimated how much control technocrats have over policymaking.[42] These studies provide a solid basis for inferring that the politician-centered perspective devel-oped in this book can offer important insights about reregulation in advanced industrial nations.

What Role Do Sectors Play?

This book has employed a *one sector, many places* strategy of research that combines a focus on a single industry (coffee) with the comparative analy-sis of distinct subnational political units (four Mexican states). The strength of this approach is that, by holding the economic sector constant, it highlights how variation in political factors results in contrasting pat-terns of reregulation. Moreover, because each of the four Mexican states represents a different kind of politics in terms of the strategies of politi-cians and the relative power of grassroots organizations and economic elites, these cases can help us understand the dynamics of reregulation far beyond Mexico.

Like all methodologies, however, focusing on a single economic sector has limitations. Most significantly, such a focus sheds little light on the role that variation in sectoral characteristics plays in the politics of rereg-ulation. This limitation raises an important question for future research: Does reregulation work differently in other kinds of sectors? As an initial step toward addressing this question, it helps to reflect on how much the characteristics of coffee affect the generalizability of my argument about the politics of reregulation.

In Mexico, coffee is an industry with a large number of small produc-ers. As we have seen, this fact had important implications for the politics

---

[42] See McCubbins and Schwartz (1984) on the United States. Recent work on what many regard as the paradigmatic case of the autonomous bureaucratic state, contemporary Japan, suggests that previous studies underestimated how much control Japanese politicians exert over technocrats. See Ramseyer and Rosenbluth (1993) and McCubbins and Nobel (1995). For the alternative view, which treats the Japanese case as an exemplar of the autonomous bureaucratic state, see Johnson (1982).

of reregulation. Because of the large number of producers, politicians saw coffee as a politically strategic, *high-vote* sector. Consequently, they had strong incentives to use reregulation as a strategy for securing votes.[43] Moreover, the large number of producers posed formidable collective action problems for coffee farmers.[44] These problems help explain why politicians and not societal actors made the first move in the politics of reregulation.

An intriguing issue concerns how reregulation works in sectors with a small number of producers or firms. In such sectors, producers should face less formidable barriers to collective action than in sectors with many producers.[45] Thus societal actors may have a greater capacity to make the first move in reregulation processes. In sectors with few actors, the politics of reregulation should have a greater probability of starting from below, as a consequence of lobbying by societal groups, than from above, as a consequence of initiatives by politicians.[46] Studies that analyze reregulation processes in different kinds of sectors will improve our understanding of how reregulation starts.

The number of producers should also have an important effect on politicians' motives for reregulating. From the perspective of political entrepreneurs, industries with few employees are likely to be seen as *low-vote* sectors. In such contexts, politicians will probably not try to use reregulation as a tool for mobilizing mass support, and thus neocorporatist projects should be unlikely. Rather, in low-vote sectors, politicians' reregulation projects should often be motivated by goals such as the pursuit of campaign contributions or bribes. Reregulation may therefore mainly involve back-room lobbying and secretive collusion between politicians and powerful business interests.[47] Noisy public demonstrations and mass

---

[43] As explained in Chapter 2, even in cases *without* competitive party systems, such as Chiapas and Puebla, state governors nevertheless faced the imperative of getting out the vote in order to deliver their expected quota of votes to the ruling party.

[44] Although important local and regional-level organizations of small producers did emerge, these groups often had difficulty coordinating their activities at the state and national level.

[45] For the classic statement of the logic behind this assertion, see Olson (1965). For an application of this logic to rural politics, see Bates (1981:87–90).

[46] Even if reregulation initiatives are launched from below, political regime institutions will nevertheless shape the responsiveness of politicians to such efforts.

[47] Industries with few employees may nevertheless qualify as high-vote sectors if a large number of *consumers* are linked to them. In such instances, political entrepreneurs should have incentives to use reregulation as a strategy for competing for the votes of consumers. Mobilizing consumers may prove more difficult than mobilizing producers, however, because people usually have a far greater stake in something they produce than in some-

mobilizations, as seen in the high-vote Mexican coffee sector, should be infrequent.[48]

Another distinctive feature of the coffee sector involves its low degree of asset specificity: The main production requirements – land and labor – can be redeployed with relative ease to other economic activities.[49] Asset flexibility lowers barriers to exit, which, in turn, tends to weaken producers' incentives to lobby.[50] This characteristic of coffee may further help to explain why reregulation was a process launched from above by politicians. By contrast, in sectors with large sunk costs and low asset flexibility, barriers to exit are high, and, hence, producers should have stronger incentives to lobby. Consequently, in sectors such as industrial mining, petroleum, and heavy manufacturing, societal actors may be more likely to make the first move in the politics of reregulation.

A final characteristic of coffee – the fact that it is an export – raises questions about how reregulation works in nonexport sectors. For example, rather than involving small producers competing for access to international markets, reregulation in import-competing sectors is likely to involve small, medium, and sometimes large producers struggling to maintain their domestic market share in the face of cheap imports. Thus the politics of reregulation in such sectors is likely to pivot around issues of protectionism and pit producers against consumers. Moreover, in import-competing sectors, the range of reregulation strategies available to politicians may be more tightly constrained by external factors such as the international rules of free trade. Membership in free-trade agreements like the World Trade Organization (WTO), the Common Market of the South (MERCOSUR), or the North American Free Trade Agreement

thing they consume. Despite this potential barrier to mobilization, consumer movements do exist. In advanced industrial countries, for example, such movements have organized around issues like environmental protection and product safety standards. In poor countries, consumer movements have organized around issues like the price of basic goods (for example, food staples) and the cost of public transportation and public utilities. In sectors with such movements, consumer demands should play a pivotal role in the politics of reregulation.

[48] The absence of noisy "public-square politics" in low-vote sectors may help explain why studies of reregulation in advanced industrial countries, which have tended to focus on such sectors, offer apolitical explanations of reregulation.

[49] However, the assets involved in coffee *processing* are far less flexible.

[50] Frieden (1991:21–2); Shafer (1994:ch. 2). According to Frieden (1991:21), "the returns to lobbying for specific government policies increase with asset specificity. . . . The greater the cost of moving their human or physical assets to other activities, the greater the incentive to lobby."

(NAFTA) may make it difficult to regulate the price of imports. Despite such constraints, reregulation may nevertheless occur because international treaty organizations and national governments vary in their capacities and incentives to monitor and enforce the rules of free trade. Consequently, national commitments to international treaties do not necessarily tie the hands of domestic political actors, and rogue subnational governments – especially in federal systems – may be able to implement regulatory policies that transgress national treaty obligations.[51] This potential slack in international free-trade regimes provides a further basis for inferring that the global wave of neoliberalism has not set countries on a convergent path toward unregulated markets: Even in import-competing sectors, where the external constraints on domestic policy options should be especially strong, we may nevertheless find varying patterns of reregulation.[52]

In sum, cross-sectoral variation in the number of producers, the flexibility of assets, and dependence on trade should have an important impact on how reregulation works. Depending on the sector, politicians may be more or less likely to make the first move in reregulation processes, international factors may impose stronger or weaker constraints on the strategies available to domestic actors, and the politics of reregulation may pivot around distinct issues ranging from access to export markets to protection from cheap imports. Despite differences such as these, the findings of this book provide a strong basis for expecting the following core regularities: (1) neoliberal reforms will result in a new politics of reregulation, not an end to regulation; (2) different kinds of new institutions for market governance will emerge; and (3) these institutions will result from strategic interactions among ambitious politicians and organized societal interests as they compete to control the policy areas vacated by neoliberalism.

---

[51] Such subnational protectionism should be especially likely in weakly centralized federal systems. In such cases, we may see complex, multilevel strategic "games" involving subnational jurisdictions, national governments, and international organizations competing to define the rules of trade.

[52] Of course, international treaties are not the only potential constraints on domestic policy options in the contemporary period: Financial markets, international financial institutions (IFIs), and transnational corporations (TNCs) may also limit the range of reregulation strategies available to domestic actors. It would also be interesting to explore how these kinds of external factors shape the politics of reregulation across sectors and countries. See Keohane and Milner (1996) for a recent analysis of how such international constraints affect domestic politics.

Coda

This book began with the observation that the global wave of neoliberal policy reform is over. It then showed why existing studies leave us without a framework for understanding the new politics that emerge after neoliberalism. The rest of the analysis sought to fill this gap by developing such a framework. The case of the Mexican coffee sector confirmed the value of the framework for explaining the different types of new institutions that replace those destroyed by neoliberal policy shocks. The concluding chapter has explored how the framework can be extended to other polities and sectors and raised questions for future research. In sum, this book has aimed to open and define a new research agenda for comparative political economy: the study of politics *after* neoliberalism.

References

Adams, F. Gerard, and Jere R. Berhman. 1976. *Econometric Models of World Agricultural Commodity Markets*. Cambridge, Mass.: Ballinger Publishing Company.

Agüilar Ayon, Alvaro, and Sergio Mora Aguilera. 1991. "Participación de la Cooperative Agropecuaria Tosepan Titataniske en la estructura del poder regional y su influencia en el desarrollo rural." Mexico City: Universidad Autónoma Metropolitana, Xochimilco, División de Ciencias Sociales y Humanidades.

Aguirre Benítez, Adán. 1995. *Guerrero: Economía campesina y capitalismo*. Chilpancingo, Guerrero: Universidad Autónoma de Guerrero, Dirección de Investigación Científica.

Albarrán de Alba, Gerardo. 1994. "Preguntas en la permanente: Ajuste de cuentas, venganza política, 'quinazo' financiero?" *Proceso* 932 (Sept. 12, 1994): 11.

Alianza de Organizaciones Campesinas Autónomas del Estado de Guerrero. 1990. Letter from Coordinating Commission to Lic. José Francisco Ruiz Massieu, Constitutional Governor of the State of Guerrero (March 1).

Anderson, Jeffrey J. 1992. *The Territorial Imperative: Pluralism, Corporatism, and Economic Crisis*. Cambridge: Cambridge University Press.

Aranda Bezaury, Josefina. 1992. "Camino andado, retos y propuestas: La Coordinadora Estatal de Productores de Café de Oaxaca." *Cuadernos del Sur* 1 (Sept.–Dec.): 89–112.

Bailón, Moisés Jaime. 1995. "*Municipios*, Opposition Mayorships, and Public Expenditure in Oaxaca." In Victoria E. Rodríguez and Peter M. Ward, eds., *Opposition Government in Mexico*. Albuquerque: University of New Mexico Press.

Balderas, Antonio. 1989. "Análisis de la coyuntura política en Guerrero, Trimestre: Octubre, Noviembre y Diciembre 1989." Unpublished document.

Barabas, Alicia, and Miguel Bartolomé, eds. 1986. *Etnicidad y pluralismo cultural: La dinámica étnica en Oaxaca*. Mexico City: Instituto Nacional de Antropología e Historia.

Bartlett Díaz, Manuel. 1995. *Elecciones a debate, 1988: Precisiones en torno a la legalidad, organización y funcionamiento del procedimiento oficial de resultados*. Mexico City: Editorial Diana.

Bartra, Armando. 1992. "La ardua construcción del ciudadano (Notas sobre el movimento cívico y la lucha gremial)." In Julio Moguel, Carlota Botey, and Luis Hernández, eds., *Autonomía y nuevos sujetos sociales en el desarrollo rural.* Mexico City: Siglo Veintiuno.

1996a. *Guerrero bronco: Campesinos, ciudadanos y guerrilleros en la Costa Grande.* Mexico City: Ediciones Sinfiltro.

1996b. *El México barbaro: Plantaciones y monterías del sureste durante el porfiriato.* Mexico City: Instituto Maya, A. C.

Bates, Robert H. 1981. *Markets and States in Tropical Africa: The Political Basis of Agricultural Policies.* Berkeley: University of California Press.

1983. "The Nature and Origins of Agricultural Policies in Africa." In Robert H. Bates, ed., *Essays on the Political Economy of Rural Africa.* Cambridge: Cambridge University Press.

1997. *Open-Economy Politics: The Political Economy of the World Coffee Trade.* Princeton, N.J.: Princeton University Press.

Bates, Robert H., Avner Greif, Margaret Levi, Jean-Laurent Rosenthal, and Barry Weingast. 1998. *Analytic Narratives.* Princeton, N.J.: Princeton University Press.

Bates, Robert H., and Anne O. Krueger. 1993. *Political and Economic Interactions in Economic Policy Reform: Evidence from Eight Countries.* Cambridge: Basil Blackwell.

Benítez Zenteno, Raúl, ed. 1980. *Sociedad y política en Oaxaca 1980.* Oaxaca, Mexico: Instituto de Investigaciones Sociológicas, Universidad Autónoma Benito Juárez de Oaxaca.

Berger, Suzanne, and Ronald Dore, eds. 1996. *National Diversity and Global Capitalism.* Ithaca, N.Y.: Cornell University Press.

Borrus, Michael, François Bar, Patric Cogez, Anne Brit Thoresen, Ibrahim Warde, and Aki Yoshikawa. 1985. Telecommunications Development in Comparative Perspective: The New Telecommunications in Europe, Japan, and the U.S. Berkeley Roundtable on the International Economy (BRIE) Working Paper, No. 14 (May).

Brace, Paul. 1993. *State Government and Economic Performance.* Baltimore: Johns Hopkins University Press.

Bruhn, Kathleen. 1997. *Taking on Goliath: The Emergence of a New Left Party and the Struggle for Democracy in Mexico.* University Park: Pennsylvania State University Press.

Burgess, Katrina. 1999. "Loyalty Dilemmas and Market Reform: Party–Union Alliances under Stress in Mexico, Spain, and Venezuela." *World Politics* 52 (Oct.): 105–34.

Burki, Shahid Javed, and Guillermo E. Perry. 1998. *Beyond the Washington Consensus: Institutions Matter.* Washington, D.C.: The World Bank.

Calderón Mólgora, Marco Antonio. 1994. *Violencia política y elecciones municipales.* Zamora, Michoacán: El Colegio de Michoacán.

Callaghy, Thomas M. 1990. "Lost between State and Market: The Politics of Economic Adjustment in Ghana, Zambia, and Nigeria." In Joan M. Nelson, ed.,

References

Economic Crisis and Policy Choice: The Politics of Adjustment in the Third World. Princeton, N.J.: Princeton University Press.

Camp, Roderic Ai. 1995. *Mexican Political Biographies, 1935–1993.* 3rd ed. Austin: University of Texas Press.

Cantú Peña, Fausto. 1989. "Proyecto de ley para el fomento y desarrollo integral de la cafeticultura en el estado de Oaxaca." In *Primer encuentro estatal de estudio, análisis y capacitación sobre cafeticultura.* Oaxaca: Secretaría de Desarrollo Rural, Gobierno del Estado de Oaxaca.

Carbot, Alberto. 1989. *Fausto Cantú Peña: Café para todos.* Mexico City: Grijalbo.

Cardoso, Fernandeo Henrique, and Enzo Faletto. 1979. *Dependency and Development in Latin America.* Berkeley: University of California Press.

Castillo Palma, Jaime. 1986. "El Movimiento Urbano Popular en Puebla." In Jaime Castillo, ed., *Los movimientos sociales en Puebla.* Vol. 2. Puebla, Mexico: Departamento de Investigaciones Arquitectónicas y Urbanísticas del Instituto de Ciencias de la Universidad Autónoma de Puebla.

———. 1994. "Puebla." In Pablo González Casanova and Jorge Cadena Roa, eds., *La República Mexicana: Modernización y democracia de Aguascalientes a Zacatecas.* Vol. 2. Mexico City: Centro de Investigaciones Interdisciplinarias en Humanidades, Universidad Nacional Autónoma de México.

Castro Aguilar, José Luis. 1995. *Marco historico-juridico de los procesos electorales de Chiapas, 1825–1995.* Tuxtla Gutiérrez, Chiapas: Centro de Estudios Profesionales de Chiapas "Fray Bartolomé de Las Cases."

Cawson, Alan. 1985. "Varieties of Corporatism: The Importance of the Meso-level of Interest Intermediation." In Alan Cawson, ed., *Organized Interests and the State: Studies in Meso-Corporatism.* London: Sage.

Ceceña, Ana Esther, and Andrés Barreda. 1995. "Notas para comprender el origen de la rebelión zapatista." In *Chiapas.* Vol. 1. Mexico City: Ediciones Era.

Centeno, Miguel Angel. 1997. *Democracy within Reason: Technocratic Revolution in Mexico.* 2nd ed. University Park: Pennsylvania State University Press.

Centro de Enseñanza, Investigación y Capacitación Para el Desarrollo Agricola Regional (CEICADAR). 1993. "Diagnóstico." Puebla: Centro de Enseñanza, Investigación y Capacitación Para el Desarrollo Agricola Regional (CEICADAR)

Chalmers, Douglas A., Scott B. Martin, and Kerianne Piester. 1997. "Associative Networks: New Structures of Representation for the Popular Sectors?" In Douglas A. Chalmers, Carlos M. Vilas, Katherine Hite, Scott E. Martin, Kerianne Peister, and Monique Segarra, eds., *The New Politics of Inequality in Latin America: Rethinking Participation and Representation.* New York: Oxford University Press.

Chávez, Elías, and Isidoro Yescas. 1989. "Dividido, el PRI enfrenta problemas en 40 municipios de Oaxaca." *Proceso* 666 (Aug. 7, 1989): 10–13.

Clark, John. 1991. *Democratizing Development: The Role of Voluntary Organizations.* West Hartford, Conn: Kumarian Press.

CNOC-Chiapas. 1995. "Observaciones en relación al funcionamiento del consejo estatal del café." Unpublished document.

221

Cobo, Rosario, and Lorena Paz Paredes. 1991. "El curso de la organización cafetalera en la costa grande de Guerrero." *Cuadernos Agrarios* 3 (Sept.–Dec.): 51–70.

Collier, David. 1976. *Squatters and Oligarchs: Authoritarian Rule and Policy Change in Peru*. Baltimore: Johns Hopkins University Press.

    ed. 1979. *The New Authoritarianism in Latin America*. Princeton, N.J.: Princeton University Press.

    1993. "The Comparative Method." In Ada W. Finifter, ed., *Political Science: The State of the Discipline II*. Washington, D.C.: The American Political Science Association.

    1995. "Trajectory of a Concept: 'Corporatism' in the Study of Latin American Politics." In Peter H. Smith, ed., *Latin America in Comparative Perspective: New Approaches to Methods and Analysis*. Boulder, Colo.: Westview.

Collier, George, with Elizabeth Lowery Quaratiello. 1994. *Basta!: Land and the Zapatista Rebellion in Chiapas*. Oakland, Calif.: The Institute for Food and Development Policy.

Collier, Ruth Berins. 1992. *The Contradictory Alliance: State–Labor Relations and Regime Change in Mexico*. Berkeley: Institute for International and Area Studies, University of California.

Collier, Ruth Berins, and David Collier. 1991. *Shaping the Political Arena: Critical Junctures, the Labor Movement, and Regime Dynamics in Latin America*. Princeton, N.J.: Princeton University Press.

Collins, Joseph, and John Lear. 1995. *Chile's Free-Market Miracle: A Second Look*. Oakland, Calif.: The Institute for Food and Development Policy.

Comisión Intersecretarial del Gabinete Agropecuario. 1995. "Federalización de la SAGAR." Unpublished document.

Concheiro Bórquez, Elvira. 1996. *El gran acuerdo: Gobierno y empresarios en la modernización salinista*. Mexico City: Ediciones Era.

Consejo Consultivo del Programa Nacional de Solidaridad. 1994. *El programa nacional de solidaridad: Una visión de la modernización de México*. Mexico City: Fondo de Cultura Económica.

Consejo Estatal del Café del Estado de Oaxaca. 1994a. "Resumen de inversión por proyectos." Unpublished document.

    1994b. "Relación de obras agroindustriales duplicadas por diferente organización en una misma localidad." Unpublished document.

    1995a. "Construcción de microbodegas rurales para acopio de café." Unpublished document.

    1995b. "Construcción de microbeneficios humedos, ciclo 1995." Unpublished document.

Consejo Méxicano del Café. 1995. "Programa de Credito a la Caficultura, Ciclo 1995/1996: Avances al 13 de Octubre de 1995."

Consejo Poblano del Café. 1993a. Letter from R. Omar Soto Velazco, General Coordinator, to C. Dr. Benjamin Peña Olvera, Director of the Centro de Enseñanza, Investigación y Capacitación Para el Desarrollo Agricola Regional (CEICADAR), Nov. 30.

    1993b. Unpublished document (June).

References

Contarino, Michael. 1995. "The Local Political Economy of Industrial Adjustment: Variations in Trade Union Responses to Industrial Restructuring in the Italian Textile-Clothing Sector." *Comparative Political Studies* 28 (April): 62–86.

Cook, Maria Lorena. 1996. *Organizing Dissent: Unions, the State, and the Democratic Teachers' Movement in Mexico.* University Park: Pennsylvania State University Press.

Cook, Maria Lorena, Kevin J. Middlebrook, and Juan Molinar Horcasitas, eds. 1994. *The Politics of Economic Restructuring: State–Society Relations and Regime Change in Mexico.* La Jolla: University of California, San Diego, Center for U.S.–Mexican Studies.

Coordinadora Estatal de Productores de Café de Oaxaca (CEPCO). 1989. *El Cosechero* 1, no. 1. (Sept.).

Córdoba, José. 1994. "Mexico." In John Williamson, ed., *The Political Economy of Policy Reform.* Washington, D.C.: Institute for International Economics.

Córdoba Gamez, Gabriel. 1994. "Avances del control biológico contra la broca del fruto del cafeto a partir del hongo *Beauveria bassiana.*" *Gaceta Fitosanitaria* 2: 4–7.

Cornelius, Wayne A. 1996. *Mexican Politics in Transition: The Breakdown of a One-Party Dominant Regime.* La Jolla: Center for U.S.–Mexican Studies, University of California, San Diego.

Cornelius, Wayne A., Ann L. Craig, and Jonathan Fox, eds. 1994. *Transforming State–Society Relations in Mexico: The National Solidarity Strategy.* La Jolla: Center for U.S.–Mexican Studies, University of California, San Diego.

Cornelius, Wayne A., Judith Gentleman, and Peter H. Smith, eds. 1989. *Mexico's Alternative Political Futures.* La Jolla: Center for U.S.–Mexican Studies, University of California, San Diego.

Cornelius, Wayne A., and David Myhre, eds. 1998. *The Transformation of Rural Mexico: Reforming the Ejido Sector.* La Jolla: Center for U.S.–Mexican Studies, University of California, San Diego.

Correa, Guillermo. 1995a. "Los turbios negocios de Raúl en CONASUPO, con la complicidad de jefes, parientes, amigos y colaboradores." *Proceso* 996 (Dec. 4, 1995): 13.

1995b. "Ruiz Ferro será llamado por la comisión investigadora de los desvios de CONASUPO, en su calidad de exdirector de finanzas de la paraestatal." *Proceso* 997 (Dec. 11, 1995): 18.

Correa, Guillermo, and Julio César López. 1994. "Legislativo enfrentado al ejecutivo, nuevo rasgo de la crisis institucional en Chiapas." *Proceso* 941 (Nov. 14, 1994), p. 13.

Correa, Guillermo, Julio César López, and Rodrigo Vera. 1994. "Robledo se disfraza, se apodera de banderas ajenas y se cobija con Zedillo, para empezar a gobernar." *Proceso* 945 (Dec. 12, 1994): 16–23.

Cruz Galdámez, Pascual. 1994. "Representates del INI burocratizan la entrega de créditos del café, acusan." *Cuarto Poder* (June 2, 1994): 7.

De Graaff, J. 1986. *The Economics of Coffee.* Wageningen, The Netherlands: Centre for Agricultural Publishing and Documentation (PUDOC).

De Grammont, Hubert C., ed. 1996. *Neoliberalismo y organización social en el campo Mexicano*. Mexico City: Plaza y Valdés Editores.

De la Fuente, Juan, and Horacio Mackinlay. 1994. "El movimiento campesino y las políticas de concertación y desincorporación de las empresas paraestatales: 1989–1994." In Mario Bassols, ed., *Campo y ciudad en una era de transición: Problemas, tendencias y desafíos*. Mexico City: Universidad Autónoma Metropolitana, Unidad Iztapalapa, Departamento de Sociología.

De Soto, Hernando. 1989. *The Other Path: The Invisible Revolution in the Third World*. New York: Harper & Row.

Díaz Cárdenas, Salvador, et al. 1991. "El sistema agroindustrial café y sus perspectivas." In *Memoria del II seminario nacional sobre la agroindustria en México: Alternativa para el desarrollo agroindustrial*. Vol. 1. Chapingo, Mexico: Universidad Autónoma Chapingo.

Díaz Cayeros, Alberto. 1995. *Desarrollo económico e inequidad regional: Hacia un nuevo pacto federal en México*. Mexico City: Miguel Ángel Porrúa.

Díaz Montes, Fausto. 1992. *Los municipios: La disputa por el poder local en Oaxaca*. Instituto de Investigaciones Sociológicas, Universidad Autónoma Benito Juárez de Oaxaca.

Durand, Francisco, and Eduardo Silva, eds. 1998. *Organized Business, Economic Change and Democracy in Latin America*. Miami: North–South Center Press.

Edelman, Marc. 1995. "Organizing across Borders: The Rise of a Transnational Peasant Movement in Central America." Unpublished manuscript.

Ejea, Gabriela, and Luis Hernández, eds. 1991. *Cafetaleros: La construcción de la autonomía*. Mexico City: Coordinadora Nacional de Organizaciones Cafetaleras (CNOC)/Servicio de Apoyo Local, A.C.

Elster, Jon. 1999. *Alchemies of the Mind: Rationality and Emotions*. Cambridge: Cambridge University Press.

Encinas R., Alejandro, Juan de la Fuente, Horacio Macinlay, and Gonzalo Chapela, eds. 1995. *El campo mexicano en el umbral del siglo XXI*. Mexico City: Espasa Calpe.

Escalante Durán, Carlos, Jaime Ruiz Vega, and Jorge Rojo Soberanes. 1994. "Perdidas causadas por la broca del fruto del cafeto (*Hypothenemus hampei*) durante las etapas de producción y beneficiado del grano." *Gaceta Fitosanitaria* 2: 8–9.

Escalante Gonzalbo, María de la Paloma. 1991. "Organización local y regional del poder: El caso de Comitán Chiapas." Unpublished MA thesis. Mexico City: Instituto Dr. José María Luis Mora.

Estrada Castañón, Alba Teresa. 1994a. *Guerrero: Sociedad, Economía, Política, Cultura*. Mexico City: Centro de Investigaciones Interdisciplinarias en Humanidades, Universidad Nacional Autónoma de México.

1994b. "Guerrero." In Pablo González Casanova and Jorge Cadena Roa, eds., *La república Mexicana: Modernización y democracia de Aguascalientes a Zacatecas*. Vol. 2. Mexico City: Centro de Investigaciones Interdisciplinarias en Humanidades, Universidad Nacional Autónoma de México.

Evans, Peter. 1992. "The State as Problem and Solution: Predation, Embedded Autonomy, and Structural Change." In Stephan Haggard and Robert R.

References

Kaufman, eds., *The Politics of Economic Adjustment*. Princeton, N.J.: Princeton University Press.

1995. *Embedded Autonomy: States and Industrial Transformation*. Princeton, N.J.: Princeton University Press.

1996a. "Introduction: Development Strategies across the Public–Private Divide." *World Development* 24: 1033–7.

1996b. "Government Action, Social Capital and Development: Reviewing the Evidence on Synergy." *World Development* 24: 1119–32.

1997. "The Eclipse of the State? Reflections on Stateness in an Era of Globalization," *World Politics* 50 (Oct.): 62–87.

FIDECAFE. 1994. "Informe de los resultados del padrón de productores de Fidecafe." Unpublished document.

Fierro Leyva, Martín. 1994. "Los campesinos del sector social ante el deterioro de la caficultura: Zona cafetalera de Atoyac de Alvarez, Gro." Unpublished MA thesis. Acapulco: Universidad Autónoma de Guerrero, Extensión Acapulco.

Fox, Jonathan A. 1993. *The Politics of Food in Mexico: State Power and Social Mobilization*. Ithaca, N.Y.: Cornell University Press.

1994a. "Political Change in Mexico's New Peasant Economy." In Maria Lorena Cook, Kevin J. Middlebrook, and Juan Molinar Horcasitas, eds., *The Politics of Economic Restructuring: State–Society Relations and Regime Change in Mexico*. La Jolla, Calif.: Center for U.S.–Mexican Studies, University of California, San Diego.

1994b. "Latin America's Emerging Local Politics." *Journal of Democracy* 5 (April): 105–16.

1994c. "The Difficult Transition from Clientelism to Citizenship: Lessons from Mexico." *World Politics* 46 (Jan.): 151–84.

1996. "How does Civil Society Thicken? The Political Construction of Social Capital in Rural Mexico." *World Development* 24: 1089–1103.

1999. "The Inter-Dependence between Citizen Participation and Institutional Accountability: Lessons from Mexico's Rural Municipal Funds." In Kerianne Piester, ed., *Thinking Out Loud: Innovative Case Studies on Participation Instruments*. Washington, D.C.: The World Bank, Latin America and Caribbean Region Civil Society Papers.

Fox, Jonathan, and Josefina Aranda. 1996. *Decentralization and Rural Development in Mexico: Community Participation in Oaxaca's Municipal Funds Program*. La Jolla, Calif.: Center for U.S.–Mexican Studies, University of California, San Diego.

Fox, Jonathan, and L. David Brown, eds. 1998. *The Struggle for Accountability: The World Bank, NGOs, and Grassroots Movements*. Cambridge, Mass: MIT Press.

Fox, Jonathan, and Gustavo Gordillo. 1989. "Between State and Market: The Campesinos' Quest for Autonomy." In Wayne A. Cornelius, Judith Gentleman, and Peter H. Smith, eds., *Mexico's Alternative Political Futures*. La Jolla, Calif.: Center for U.S.–Mexican Studies, University of California, San Diego.

Fox, Jonathan, and Julio Moguel. 1995. "Pluralism and Anti-Poverty Policy: Mexico's National Solidarity Program and Left Opposition Municipal

Governments." In Victoria E. Rodríguez and Peter M. Ward, eds., *Opposition Government in Mexico*. Albuquerque: University of New Mexico Press.

Foxley, Alejandro. 1983. *Latin American Experiments in Neoconservative Economics*. Berkeley: University of California Press.

Foweraker, Joe. 1993. *Popular Mobilization in Mexico: The Teachers' Movement, 1977–87*. Cambridge: Cambridge University Press.

Frieden, Jeffry A. 1991. *Debt, Development, and Democracy: Modern Political Economy and Latin America, 1965–1985*. Princeton, N.J.: Princeton University Press.

Friedman, Milton. 1990. "Four Steps to Freedom," *National Review* (May 14, 1990): 33–6.

Gama Santillán, M. de la Luz. 1992. "Guerrero durante los últimos 30 años." In *La transición democrática en Guerrero*. Vol. 1. Mexico City: Editorial Diana.

García Aguilar, María del Carmen, and José Luis Pontigo Sánchez. 1993. "La política cafetalera y sus efectos en las organizaciones de productores del sector social del Soconusco." In Daniel Villafuerte Solís, ed., *El café en la frontera sur: La producción y los productores del Soconusco, Chiapas*. Chiapas: Instituto Chiapaneco de Cultura.

García de León. Antonio. 1985. *Resistencia y utopía: Memorial de agravios y crónica de revueltas y profecías acaecidas en la provinica de Chiapas durante los últimos quinientos años de su historia*. Vol. 2. Mexico City: Ediciones Era.

Garrett, Geoffrey. 1998. *Partisan Politics in the Global Economy*. Cambridge: Cambridge University Press.

Geddes, Barbara. 1995. "Challenging the Conventional Wisdom." In Larry Diamond and Marc F. Plattner, eds., *Economic Reform and Democracy*. Baltimore: Johns Hopkins University Press.

Gibson, Edward L., and Ernesto Calvo. In press. "Federalism and Low-Maintenance Constituencies: Territorial Dimensions of Economic Reform in Argentina." *Studies in Comparative International Development*.

Gobierno Constitucional del Estado de Guerrero. 1983. *Plan Guerrero*. Chilpancingo: Gobierno Constitucional del Estado de Guerrero.

1995. "Plan estatal de fomento y desarrollo de la actividad cafetalera en Guerrero (1995–2000)." Unpublished document.

Gobierno Constitucional del Estado de Puebla. 1988. "Decreto del H. Congreso del Estado que crea el Consejo del Café en el Estado de Puebla." *Periodico Oficial* 239:40 (Nov. 15).

1993. "Decreto que crea al 'Consejo Poblano del Café'."

Gobierno del Estado de Chiapas. 1993. "Decreto por el que se crea el Consejo Estatal del Café." *Periodico Oficial*. Feb. 24, 1993: 10–17.

Gobierno del Estado de Oaxaca. 1989a. *Primer encuentro estatal de estudio, análisis y capacitación sobre caficultura*. Oaxaca: Secretaría de Desarrollo Rural, Gobierno del Estado de Oaxaca.

1989b. "Decreto Num. 8." *Periodico Oficial* 71 (Aug. 7, 1989).

1990. "Decreto Num. 27." *Periodico Oficial* 72 (April 4, 1990)

1992a. *Del Oaxaca mágico al encuentro con la modernidad: Seis años de transformación y desarrollo, 1986–1992, marco legislativo*.

References

1992b. *Del Oaxaca mágico al encuentro con la modernidad: Seis años de transformación y desarrollo, 1986–1992, resumen general.*

1992c. *Del Oaxaca mágico al encuentro con la modernidad: Seis años de transformación y desarrollo, 1986–1992, resumen estadístico.*

Goldthorpe, John H., ed. 1984. *Order and Conflict in Contemporary Capitalism.* Oxford: Clarendon Press.

Gómez Cruz, Patricia Jovita, and Christina María Kovic. 1994. *Con un pueblo vivo, en tierra negada: Un ensayo sobre los derechos humanos y el conflicto agrario en Chiapas, 1989–1993.* San Cristobal de las Casas, Chiapas: Centro de Derechos Humanos "Fray Bartolomé de Las Casas."

González Esponda, Juan, and Elizabeth Pólito Barrios. 1995. "Notas para comprender el origen de la rebelión zapatista." In *Chiapas.* Vol. 1. Mexico City: Ediciones Era.

Gourevitch, Peter. 1986. *Politics in Hard Times: Comparative Responses to International Crises.* Ithaca, N.Y.: Cornell University Press.

Gracida, Cecilia, Armando Gúzman, and Carlos Moreno. 1990. "Solidaridad en Oaxaca: Una experienca de concertación con los productores de café." Unpublished manuscript.

Graham, Lawrence S. 1971. *Mexican State Government: A Prefectural System in Action.* Austin: LBJ School of Public Affairs, University of Texas at Austin.

Green, Duncan. 1995. *Silent Revolution: The Rise of Market Economics in Latin America.* London: Cassell.

Grindle, Merilee S. 1977. *Bureaucrats, Politicians, and Peasants in Mexico: A Case Study in Public Policy.* Berkeley: University of California Press.

1996. *Challenging the State: Crisis and Innovation in Latin America and Africa.* Cambridge: Cambridge University Press.

Grupo Operativo Nacional del Programa Emergente de Apoyo a Productores de Café del Sector Social. 1992. "Cosecha 1992/93." Unpublished document.

Guillén Rodríguez, Diana Lucrecia. 1994. "Estructuras tradicionales de poder y modernización política en América Latina: El caso chiapaneco." Unpublished PhD dissertation, Facultad de Ciencias Políticas y Sociales, Universidad Nacional Autónoma de México.

Guzmán, Armando, and Fernando Ortega Pizarro. 1994. "Cabal Peniche se convirtió en un poder paralelo en Tabasco: Todo lo compraba, todo lo corrompía." *Proceso* 941 (Nov. 14, 1994): 16–23.

Haggard, Stephan. 1990. *Pathways from the Periphery: The Politics of Growth in the Newly Industrializing Countries.* Ithaca, N.Y.: Cornell University Press.

Haggard, Stephan, and Robert R. Kaufman, eds. 1992. *The Politics of Economic Adjustment.* Princeton, N.J.: Princeton University Press.

1995. *The Political Economy of Democratic Transitions.* Princeton, N.J.: Princeton University Press.

Haggard, Stephan, and Steven B. Webb, eds. 1994. *Voting for Reform: Democracy, Political Liberalization, and Economic Adjustment.* New York: Oxford University Press.

Hagopian, Frances. 1996. *Traditional Politics and Regime Change in Brazil.* Cambridge: Cambridge University Press.

1998a. "Democracy and Political Representation in Latin America in the 1990s: Pause, Reorganization, or Decline?" In Felipe Agüero and Jeffrey Stark, eds., *Fault Lines of Democracy in Post-Transition Latin America*. Miami: North–South Center Press.

1998b. "Negotiating Economic Transitions in Liberalizing Polities: Political Representation and Economic Reform in Latin America." Working Paper Series, No. 98–5. Cambridge, Mass.: Weatherhead Center for International Affairs, Harvard University.

Hall, Peter A. 1997. "The Role of Interests, Institutions, and Ideas in the Comparative Political Economy of the Industrialized Nations." In Mark Irving Lichbach and Alan S. Zuckerman, eds., *Comparative Politics: Rationality, Culture, and Structure*. Cambridge: Cambridge University Press.

Harvey, Neil. 1994. "Rebellion in Chiapas: Rural Reforms, Campesino Radicalism, and the Limits to Salinismo" (revised and updated). In *The Transformation of Rural Mexico*. No. 5. La Jolla, Calif.: Center for U.S.–Mexican Studies, University of California at San Diego.

1998. *The Chiapas Rebellion: The Struggle for Land and Democracy*. Durham, N.C.: Duke University Press.

Hedström, Peter, and Richard Swedberg, eds. 1998. *Social Mechanisms: An Analytical Approach to Social Theory*. Cambridge: Cambridge University Press.

Hellman, Joel S. 1998. "Winners Take All: The Politics of Partial Reform in Postcommunist Transitions." *World Politics* 50 (Jan.): 203–34.

Hernández Navarro, Luis. 1992. "Cafetaleros: Del adelgazamiento estatal a la guerra del mercado." In Julio Moguel, Carlota Botey, and Luis Hernández, eds., *Autonomía y nuevos sujetos sociales en el desarrollo rural*. Mexico City: Siglo Veintiuno.

1994. "The Chiapas Uprising." In *The Transformation of Rural Mexico*. No. 5. La Jolla, Calif.: Center for U.S.–Mexican Studies, University of California at San Diego.

Hernández Navarro, Luis, and Fernando Célis Callejas. 1994. "Solidarity and the New Campesino Movements: The Case of Coffee Production." In Wayne A. Cornelius, Ann L. Craig, and Jonathan Fox, eds., *Transforming State–Society Relations in Mexico: The National Solidarity Strategy*. La Jolla, Calif.: Center for U.S.–Mexican Studies, University of California, San Diego.

Herrigel, Gary. 1996. *Industrial Constructions: The Sources of German Industrial Power*. Cambridge: Cambridge University Press.

Hollingsworth, J. Rogers, and Robert Boyer, eds. 1997. *Contemporary Capitalism: The Embeddedness of Institutions*. Cambridge: Cambridge University Press.

Huber, Evelyne, and John D. Stephens. In press. *Political Choice in Global Markets: Development and Crisis of Advanced Welfare States*. Chicago: University of Chicago Press.

Hutchcroft, Paul D. 1998. *Booty Capitalism: The Politics of Banking in the Philippines*. Ithaca, N.Y.: Cornell University Press, 1998.

Immergut, Ellen M. 1992. *Health Politics: Interests and Institutions in Western Europe*. Cambridge: Cambridge University Press.

References

INI-Solidaridad. 1994. "La reforma del estado, cafeticultores en solidaridad." Mexico City: Dirección del Programa de Apoyo a Productores de Café, Instituto Nacional Indigenista. Unpublished document.

INMECAFE (Instituto Mexicano del Café). 1989a. "Reestructuración del Instituto Mexicano del Café: Presentación a la Comisión Gasto-Financiamiento." Unpublished document (Aug.).

—— 1989b. "Programa de transferencia de instalaciones industriales al sector social." Unpublished document (Nov.).

—— 1990a. "Convenio de concertación para el cambio estructural del INMECAFE." Unpublished document (Jan.).

—— 1990b. "Desincorporación de la planta agroindustrial: Programa de acciones básicas." Unpublished document (April).

—— 1992. "Estratificación de los predios por estado." *Censo Cafetalero 1992*. Mexico City: Instituto Mexicano del Café.

Instituto de Estudios para el Desarrollo Rural Maya, A.C. 1987. "Seguimiento y evaluación. Programa 'Credito a la Palabra.'" Mexico City. Unpublished document.

Instituto Nacional Indigenista, Delegación Estatal Chiapas. 1995a. "Propuesta de transferencia de recursos del programa estatal de apoyo a productores de café del sector social, ciclo 1995, al Consejo Estatal del Café." Unpublished document.

—— 1995b. "Programa fomento a la cafeticultura, ciclo 95/96: Avance actual y reglas generales de operación, 13 de Octubre 1995." Unpublished document.

—— n.d.a "Programa especial de apoyo a productores del sector social INI-Solidaridad." Unpublished document.

—— n.d.b "El Consejo Estatal Chiapaneco de Café." Unpublished document.

Instituto Nacional de Solidaridad. 1992. *El liberalismo social*. Mexico City: Instituto Nacional de Solidaridad.

—— 1993. *Reforma del estado*. Mexico City: Instituto Nacional de Solidaridad.

Instituto Nacional de Estadística, Geografía e Informática (INEGI). 1994. *El ingreso y el gasto público en México, edición 1994*. Mexico City: INEGI.

Interamerican Development Bank. 1994. "Fiscal Decentralization: The Search for Equity and Efficiency." In *Economic and Social Progress in Latin America: 1994 Report*. Washington, D.C.: Interamerican Development Bank.

International Council for Educational Development. 1994. *A Productive Future for the Benemérita Universidad Autónoma de Puebla: An Evaluation by the International Council for Educational Development*. Puebla, Mexico: Benemérita Universidad Autónoma de Puebla.

Jacobs, Ian. 1982. *Ranchero Revolt: The Mexican Revolution in Guerrero*. Austin: University of Texas Press.

Jiménez Huerta, Fernando. 1992. *¿El vuelo del fenix? Antorcha Campesina en Puebla*. Puebla, Mexico: Benemérita Universidad Autónoma de Puebla.

Johnson, Chalmers. 1982. *MITI and the Japanese Miracle*. Stanford, Calif.: Stanford University Press.

Kahler, Miles. 1990. "Orthodoxy and Its Alternatives: Explaining Approaches to Stabilization and Adjustment." In Joan M. Nelson, ed., *Economic Crisis and*

Policy Choice: The Politics of Adjustment in the Third World. Princeton, N.J.: Princeton University Press.

Karl, Terry Lynn. 1997. *The Paradox of Plenty: Oil Booms and Petro-States.* Berkeley: University of California Press.

Katzenstein, Peter J. 1984. *Corporatism and Change: Austria, Switzerland, and the Politics of Industry.* Ithaca, N.Y.: Cornell University Press.

——— 1985. *Small States in World Markets: Industrial Policy in Europe.* Ithaca, N.Y.: Cornell University Press.

Kaufman, Robert R. 1988. *The Politics of Debt in Argentina, Brazil, and Mexico: Economic Stabilization in the 1980s.* Berkeley: Institute of International Studies, University of California.

Keck, Margaret E., and Kathryn Sikkink. 1998. *Activists beyond Borders: Advocacy Networks in International Politics.* Ithaca, N.Y.: Cornell University Press.

Keohane, Robert O. and Helen V. Milner, eds. 1996. *Internationalization and Domestic Politics.* Cambridge: Cambridge University Press.

Kitschelt, Herbert, Peter Lange, Gary Marks, and John D. Stephens, eds. 1999. *Continuity and Change in Contemporary Capitalism.* Cambridge: Cambridge University Press.

Kohli, Atul. 1987. *The State and Poverty in India: The Politics of Reform.* Cambridge: Cambridge University Press.

Krippner, Greta. 1997. "The Politics of Privatization in Rural Mexico." *Politics and Society* 25 (March): 4–33.

Laothamatas, Anek. 1992. *Business Associations and the New Political Economy of Thailand: From Bureaucratic Policy to Liberal Corporatism.* Boulder, Colo.: Westview Press.

Legorreta Díaz, María del Carmen. 1994. "Chiapas." In Pablo González Casanova and Jorge Cadena Roa, eds., *La República Mexicana: Modernización y democracia de Aguascalientes a Zacatecas.* Vol. 1. Mexico City: Centro de Investigaciones Interdisciplinarias en Humanidades, Universidad Nacional Autónoma de México.

——— 1995. "Chiapas." In Gloria Vázquez Rangel and Jesús Ramírez López, eds., *Marginación y pobreza en México.* Mexico, D.F.: Editorial Ariel.

Levitsky, Steven, and Lucan A. Way. 1998. "Between a Shock and a Hard Place: The Dynamics of Labor-Led Adjustment in Poland and Argentina." *Comparative Politics* 30: 171–92.

Lijphart, Arend. 1971. "Comparative Politics and the Comparative Method." *American Political Science Review* 65: 682–93.

——— 1975. "The Comparable-Cases Strategy in Comparative Research." *Comparative Political Studies* 8 (July): 158–77.

——— 1984. *Democracies: Patterns of Majoritarian and Consensus Government in Twenty-One Countries.* New Haven, Conn.: Yale University Press.

Linz, Juan J., and Amando de Miguel. 1966. "Within-Nation Differences and Comparisons: The Eight Spains." In Richard L. Merritt and Stein Rokkan, eds., *Comparing Nations: The Use of Quantitative Data in Cross-National Research.* New Haven, Conn.: Yale University Press.

References

Locke, Richard. 1995. *Remaking the Italian Economy*. Ithaca, N.Y.: Cornell University Press.

López, Yolanda. "Exigen choles de 4 municipios créditos para cafeticultores." *La Jornada*, June 3, 1994, p. 5.

López Hernández, Max Arturo. 1988. *Proyecto político y planeación estatal, 1984–1987: Caso estado de Guerrero*. Chilpancingo: Universidad Autónoma de Guerrero.

——— 1994. "Análisis político contemporáneo del estado de Guerrero (1960–1993)." In *Estudios regionales: Ensayos sobre cinco estados de la República*. Tlaxcala, Mexico: Universidad Autónoma de Tlaxcala.

López Obrador, Andrés Manuel. 1995. *Entre la historia y la esperanza: Corrupción y lucha democrática en Tabasco*. Mexico City: Grijalbo.

Lujambio, Alonso. 1994. "Régimen presidencial, democracia mayoritaria y los dilemas de la transición a la democracia en México." In Alicia Hernández Chávez, ed., *Presidencialismo y sistema político: México y los Estados Unidos*. Mexico City: Fondo de Cultura Económica.

Lustig, Nora. 1992. *Mexico: The Remaking of an Economy*. Washington, D.C.: The Brookings Institution.

Mackinlay, Horacio. 1996. "La CNC y el 'nuevo movimiento campesino' (1989–1994)." In Hubert C. de Gramont, ed., *Neoliberalismo y organización social en el campo Mexicano*. Mexico City: Plaza y Valdés.

Mainwaring, Scott, and David Julian Samuels. 1998. "Federalism and Democracy in Contemporary Brazil." Unpublished manuscript.

Manjarrez, Alejandro C. 1991. *Puebla: El rostro olvidado*. Cholula, Puebla: Imágen Publica y Corporativa.

Marshall, C. F. 1983. *The World Coffee Trade: A Guide to the Production, Trading, and Consumption of Coffee*. Cambridge: Woodhead-Faulkner.

Martin, Scott B. 1997. "Beyond Corporatism: New Patterns of Representation in the Brazilian Auto Industry." In Douglas Chalmers, Carlos M. Vilas, Katherine Hite, Scott B. Martin, Kerianne Peister, and Monique Segarra, eds., *The New Politics of Inequality in Latin America: Rethinking Participation and Representation*. New York: Oxford University Press.

Martínez Assad, Carlos, and Álvaro Arreola Ayala. 1987. "El poder de los gobernadores." In Soledad Loaeza and Rafael Segovia, eds., *La vida política mexicana en la crisis*. Mexico City: El Colegio de México.

Martínez Borrego, Estela. 1991. *Organización de productores y movimiento campesino*. Mexico City: Siglo Veintiuno Editores.

Martínez Nateras, Arturo. 1992. "Guerrero: Violencia y cambio, de Atoyac a Jaleaca." In *La transición democrática en Guerrero*. Vol. 1. Mexico City: Editorial Diana.

Martínez Vásquez, Víctor Raúl. 1990. *Movimiento popular y política en Oaxaca: 1968–1986*. Mexico City: Consejo Nacional para la Cultura y las Artes.

Masferrer Kan, Elio. 1986. "Coyotes y coyotitos: Cambio en los sistemas de intermediación en la Sierra Norte de Puebla." *México Indígena* 12 (Sept.–Oct.): 13–16.

231

Mayhew, David. 1974. *Congress: The Electoral Connection.* New Haven, Conn.: Yale University Press.

McCubbins, Mathew D., and Thomas Schwartz. 1984. "Congressional Oversight Overlooked: Police Patrols versus Fire Alarms." *American Journal of Political Science* 28 (Feb.): 165–79.

McCubbins, Mathew D., and Gregory W. Noble. 1995. "The Appearance of Power: Legislators, Bureaucrats, and the Budget Process in the United States and Japan." In Peter F. Cowhey and Mathew D. McCubbins, eds., *Structure and Policy in Japan and the United States.* Cambridge: Cambridge University Press.

Melgar, Mario, ed. 1990. *Juego sucio: El PRD en Guerrero.* Mexico City: Editorial Diana.

Méndez Arcos, Pedro. 1994. "Secuestran a empleados del INI." *Hoy,* June 2, 1994, p. 40.

Migdal, Joel S. 1988. *Strong Societies and Weak States: State–Society Relations and State Capabilities in the Third World.* Princeton, N.J.: Princeton University Press.

Migdal, Joel S., Atul Kohli, and Vivienne Shue, eds. 1994. *State Power and Social Forces: Domination and Transformation in the Third World.* Cambridge: Cambridge University Press.

Moguel, Julio. 1987. *Los caminos de la izquierda.* Mexico City: Juan Pablos.

——— 1994. "The Mexican Left and the Social Program of Salinismo." In Wayne A. Cornelius, Ann L. Craig, and Jonathan Fox, eds., *Transforming State–Society Relations in Mexico: The National Solidarity Strategy.* La Jolla, Calif.: Center for U.S.–Mexican Studies, University of California, San Diego.

——— 1995. "Apéndice (1994)." In Gloria Vázquez Rangel and Jesús Ramírez López, eds., *Marginación y pobreza en México.* Mexico City: Editorial Ariel.

Moguel, Julio, and Josefina Aranda. 1992. "Los nuevos caminos en la construcción de la autonomía: La experiencia de la La Coordinadora Estatal de Productores de Café de Oaxaca." In Julio Moguel, Carlota Botey, and Luis Hernández, eds., *Autonomía y nuevos sujetos sociales en el desarrollo rural.* Mexico City: Siglo Veintiuno.

Moran, Michael. 1991. *The Politics of the Financial Services Revolution: The U.S.A., U.K., and Japan.* New York: St. Martin's.

Mota Marín, Sergio. 1994. "Estructura económica de Chiapas." In María Luisa Armendáriz, ed., *Chiapas: Una radiografía.* Mexico City: Fondo de Cultura Económica.

Myrdal, Gunnar. 1968. *Asian Drama: An Inquiry into the Poverty of Nations.* 3 vols. New York: The Twentieth Century Fund.

Naím, Moisés. 1995. "Latin America: The Second Stage of Reform." In Larry Diamond and Marc F. Plattner, eds., *Economic Reform and Democracy.* Baltimore: Johns Hopkins University Press.

Nelson, Joan M. 1990a. "Introduction: The Politics of Economic Adjustment in Developing Nations." In Joan M. Nelson, ed., *Economic Crisis and Policy Choice: The Politics of Adjustment in the Third World.* Princeton, N.J.: Princeton University Press.

References

1990b. "Conclusions." In Joan M. Nelson, ed., *Economic Crisis and Policy Choice: The Politics of Adjustment in the Third World*. Princeton, N.J.: Princeton University Press.

Noll, Roger G. 1989. "Economic Perspectives on the Politics of Regulation." In Richard Schmalensee and Robert D. Willig, eds., *Handbook of Industrial Organization*. Vol. 2. New York: North-Holland.

Nolasco, Margarita. 1985. *Café y sociedad en México*. Mexico City: Centro de Ecodesarrollo.

O'Donnell, Guillermo A. 1977. "Corporatism and the Question of the State." In James M. Malloy, ed., *Authoritarianism and Corporatism in Latin America*. Pittsburgh: University of Pittsburgh Press.

1993. "On the State, Democratization, and Some Conceptual Problems (A Latin American View with Glances at Some Post-Communist Countries)." *World Development* 21: 1355–70.

1994. "Delegative Democracy," *Journal of Democracy* 5 (Jan. 1994): 55–69.

Olson, Mancur. 1965. *The Logic of Collective Action: Public Goods and the Theory of Groups*. Cambridge, Mass.: Harvard University Press.

Paige, Jeffrey M. 1997. *Coffee and Power: Revolution and the Rise of Democracy in Central America*. Cambridge, Mass.: Harvard University Press.

Pansters, Wil. 1990. *Politics and Power in Puebla: The Political History of a Mexican State, 1937–1987*. Amsterdam: Center for Latin American Research and Documentation (CEDLA).

Paré, Luisa. 1975. "Caciquismo y estructura de poder en la Sierra Norte de Puebla." In Roger Bartra et al., eds., *Caciquismo y poder político en el México rural*. Mexico City: Siglo Veintiuno.

Pastor, Jr., Manuel, and Carol Wise. 1999. "The Politics of Second-Generation Reform," *Journal of Democracy* 10 (July 1999): 34–48.

Payan Torres, Jorge Carlos. 1990. "Elecciones en Guerrero, 1986–1989." Unpublished MA thesis. Chilpancingo: Universidad Autónoma de Guerrero.

Paz Paredes, Lorena, and Rosario Cobo. 1992. "El proyecto cafetalero de la Coalición de Ejidos de la Costa Grande de Guerrero." In Julio Moguel, Carlota Botey, and Luis Hernández, eds., *Autonomía y nuevos sujetos sociales en el desarrollo rural*. Mexico City: Siglo Veintiuno.

Perry, Elizabeth J. 1993. *Shanghai on Strike: The Politics of Chinese Labor*. Stanford, Calif.: Stanford University Press.

Pieterse, M. T. A., and H. J. Silvis. 1988. *The World Coffee Market and the International Coffee Agreement*. Wageningen, The Netherlands: Wageningen Agricultural University.

Polanyi, Karl. 1944. *The Great Transformation: The Political and Economic Origins of Our Time*. Boston: Beacon Press.

Pólito, Elizabeth, and Juan González Esponda. 1996. "Cronología. Veinte años de conflictos en el campo: 1974–1993." In *Chiapas*. Vol. 2. Mexico City: Ediciones Era.

Pontusson, Jonas. 1992. *The Limits of Social Democracy: Investment Politics in Sweden*. Ithaca, N.Y.: Cornell Univeristy Press.

Programa de Apoyo a Productores de Café INI-Solidaridad, Fidecafe. 1994. "Bases y normatividad general, 1994–1995." Unpublished document.

Programa de Fomento a la Cafeticultura. 1995. "Reglas generales de operación." Unpublished document.

Przeworksi, Adam. 1991. *Democracy and the Market: Political and Economic Reforms in Eastern Europe and Latin America.* Cambridge: Cambridge University Press.

Przeworski, Adam, and Henry Teune. 1970. *The Logic of Comparative Social Inquiry.* New York: John Wiley and Sons.

Puig, Carlos. 1994. "Cabal contó en el extranjero con apoyo de funcionarios e instituciones gubernamentales; según Salinas, era un ejemplo." *Proceso* 932 (Sept. 12, 1994): 6–14.

Putnam, Robert D., with Robert Leonardi and Raffaella Y. Nanetti. 1993. *Making Democracy Work: Civic Traditions in Modern Italy.* Princeton, N.J.: Princeton University Press.

Ramírez López, Heladio. 1981. "La sindicalización de trabajadores agricolas en México: La experiencia de la Confederación Nacional Campesina (CNC)." Working Papers in U.S.–Mexican Studies 26. La Jolla, Calif.: Program in United States–Mexican Studies, University of California, San Diego.

Rappo, Susana. 1991. "Antorcha Campesina, mitos y realidades." *Cuadernos Agrarios* 2 (May–June): 80–90.

Ravelo, Ricardo. 1994. "Cabal en Veracruz: Un corredor de puertos, con apoyo de comunicaciones y transportes." *Proceso* 932 (Sept. 12, 1994): 17.

Ravelo Lecuona, Renato, and José O. Avila Arévalo. 1994. *Luz de la Montaña: Una historia viva.* Mexico City: Instituto Nacional Indigenista.

Reding, Andrew. 1994. "Chiapas is Mexico: The Imperative of Political Reform." *World Policy Journal* 11 (Spring): 11–25.

Rello, Fernando, ed. 1990. *Las organizaciones de productores rurales en México.* Mexico City: Facultad de Economía, Universidad Nacional Autónoma de México.

Reunión Nacional de Consejos Operativos Regionales de Café. 1995. "Mesa de trabajo No. 1." Unpublished document (Nov. 8).

Reyna, José Luis, and Richard S. Wienert, eds. 1977. *Authoritarianism in Mexico.* Philadelphia: Institute for the Study of Human Issues.

Reynoso, Víctor Manuel. 1995. "Puebla: Orden aunque sea del centro." Puebla: El Colegio de Puebla. Unpublished manuscript.

Roberts, Kenneth. 1995. "Neoliberalism and the Transformation of Populism in Latin America: The Peruvian Case." *World Politics* 48 (Oct.): 82–116.

Rodríguez, Victoria E. 1997. *Decentralization in Mexico: From Reforma Municipal to Solidaridad to Nuevo Federalismo.* Boulder, Colo.: Westview.

Roeder, Philip G. 1993. *Red Sunset: The Failure of Soviet Politics.* Princeton, N.J.: Princeton University Press.

Rokkan, Stein. 1970. *Citizens, Elections, Parties: Approaches to the Comparative Study of the Processes of Development.* New York: David McKay Company.

Rojas, Rosa. 1995. *Chiapas: La paz violenta.* Mexico City: La Jornada/Ediciones.

Ros, Jaime. 1994. "Mexico in the 1990s: A New Economic Miracle? Some Notes on the Economic and Policy Legacy of the 1980s." In Maria Lorena Cook,

References

Kevin J. Middlebrook, and Juan Molinar Horcasitas, eds., *The Politics of Economic Restructuring: State–Society Relations and Regime Change in Mexico*. La Jolla, Calif.: Center for U.S.–Mexican Studies, University of California, San Diego.

Rubin, Jeffrey W. 1996. "Decentering the Regime: Culture and Regional Politics in Mexico." *Latin American Research Review* 31, no. 3: 85–126.

———. 1997. *Decentering the Regime: Ethnicity, Radicalism, and Democracy in Juchitán, Mexico*. Durham, N.C.: Duke University Press.

Rubio Zaldívar, Andrés. 1994. *El movimiento social guerrerense y la lucha armada de Genaro Vázquez Rojas*. Chilpancingo, Guerrero: Equipo Profesional Multidisciplinaro de Apoyo Técnico (EPMAT), A.C.

Ruiz Massieu, José Francisco. 1987. "Política de ideas y de hechos: Discurso de toma de posesión como Gobernador Constitucional del Estado de Guerrero." Chilpancingo, Guerrero: Comité Directivo Estatal del Partido Revolucionario Institucional.

Salazar Adame, Jaime. 1987. *Historia de la cuestión agraria mexicana: Estado de Guerrero, 1867–1940*. Mexico City: Centro de Estudios Historicos del Agrarismo en México.

Sánchez Andraka, Juan. 1987. *¡Hablemos Claro! ¿Que ocurrió en Guerrero durante el gobierno de Alejandro Cervantes Delgado?: Testimonios*. Mexico City: Costa-Amic.

Santoyo Cortés, V. Horacio, Salvador Díaz Cárdenas, and Benigno Rodríguez Padrón. 1994. *Sistema agroindustrial café en México: Diagnóstico, problemática y alternativas*. Chapingo, Mexico: Universidad Autónoma Chapingo.

Schamis, Hector E. 1999. "Distributional Coalitions and the Politics of Economic Reform in Latin America." *World Politics* 51 (Jan.): 236–68.

Schmitter, Philippe C. 1974. "Still the Century of Corporatism?" *Review of Politics* 36 (Jan.): 85–131.

Schmitter, Philippe C., and Gerhard Lehmbruch, eds. 1979. *Trends toward Corporatist Intermediation*. Beverly Hills, Calif.: Sage Publications.

Schneider, Ben Ross, and Sylvia Maxfield. 1997. "Business, the State, and Economic Performance in Developing Countries." In Sylvia Maxfield and Ben Ross Schneider, eds., *Business and the State in Developing Countries*. Ithaca, N.Y.: Cornell University Press.

Schwartz, Peter and Peter Leyden. 1997. "The Long Boom: A History of the Future, 1980–2020." *Wired* 5 (July): 116–29, 169–73.

Secretaría de Agricultura, Ganadería y Desarrollo Rural (SAGAR). 1995. *Informe de Labores, 1994–1995*. Mexico City: Secretaría de Agricultura, Ganadería y Desarrollo Rural.

Secretaría de Agricultura, Ganadería y Desarrollo Rural, Delegación Estatal en Puebla. 1995. "La federalización de la SAGAR, un requerimiento para el desarrollo agropecuario estatal." Unpublished document.

Secretaría de Agricultura, Ganadería y Desarrollo Rural, Delegación Estatal en Puebla, Programa de Atención a Poblaciones Indigenas. 1995. "Programa de desarrollo de la cafeticultura poblana (sector social)." Unpublished document.

References

Shafer, D. Michael. 1994. *Winners and Losers: How Sectors Shape the Developmental Prospects of States*. Ithaca, N.Y.: Cornell University Press.

Shah, Anwar. 1994. "The Reform of Intergovernmental Fiscal Relations in Developing and Emerging Market Economies." Policy and Research Series #23. Washington, D.C.: The World Bank.

Skocpol, Theda. 1992. *Protecting Soldiers and Mothers: The Political Origins of Social Policy in the United States*. Cambridge, Mass.: The Belknap Press of Harvard University Press.

Snyder, Richard, ed. 1999a. *Institutional Adaptation and Innovation in Rural Mexico*. La Jolla, Calif.: Center for U.S.–Mexican Studies, University of California, San Diego.

———. 1999b. "After the State Withdraws: Neoliberalism and Subnational Authoritarian Regimes in Mexico." In Wayne A. Cornelius, Todd A. Eisenstadt, and Jane Hindley, eds., *Subnational Politics and Democratization in Mexico*. La Jolla, Calif.: Center for U.S.–Mexican Studies, University of California, San Diego.

Snyder, Richard, and Gabriel Torres, eds. 1998. *The Future Role of the Ejido in Rural Mexico*. La Jolla, Calif.: Center for U.S.–Mexican Studies, University of California, San Diego.

Sorroza Polo, Carlos J. 1994. "Oaxaca." In Pablo González Casanova and Jorge Cadena Roa, eds., *La República Mexicana: Modernización y democracia de Aguascalientes a Zacatecas*. Vol. 2. Mexico City: Centro de Investigaciones Interdisciplinarias en Humanidades, Universidad Nacional Autónoma de México.

Sotelo Pérez, Antonio. 1991. *Breve historia de la Asociación Cívica Guerrerense, jefaturada por Genaro Vázquez Rojas*. Chilpancingo, Guerrero: Universidad Autónoma de Guerrero.

Stark, David, and László Bruszt. 1998. *Postsocialist Pathways: Transforming Politics and Property in East Central Europe*. Cambridge: Cambridge University Press.

Stoner-Weiss, Kathryn. 1997. *Local Heroes: The Political Economy of Russian Regional Governance*. Princeton, N.J.: Princeton University Press.

Streeck, Wolfgang, and Philippe C. Schmitter. 1991. "From National Corporatism to Transnational Pluralism: Organized Interests in the Single European Market." *Politics and Society* 19 (Feb.): 133–64.

Subcomité Especial de Producción y Comercialización del Café. n.d. "Puntos y sugerencias planteadas al Lic. Estéban Figueroa A., Coordinador del Sub-Comité Especial de Producción y Comercialización del Café."

———. 1989a. "1a. reunión del Subcomité Especial de Producción y Comercialización del Café: Minuta de trabajo" (March 7).

———. 1989b. "2a. reunión del Subcomité Especial de Producción y Comercialización del Café: Aprobación y contenido del programa de trabajo" (March 28).

———. 1989c. Letter to C. Lic. José Patrocinio González Garrido, Governor of Chiapas. (April 11).

———. 1989d. "Chiapas: Sector cafetalero" (Sept.).

———. 1990. Letter from Lic. Estéban Figueroa Aramoni, Coordinator of the Subcommittee, to C. Lic. Norberto de Gives C., Treasurer of the State of Chiapas. (Jan. 16).

References

Teichman, Judith A. 1995. *Privatization and Political Change in Mexico.* Pittsburgh: University of Pittsburgh Press.

Téllez Kuenzler, Luis. 1994. *La modernización del sector agropecuario y forestal: Una visión de la modernización de México.* Mexico City: Fondo de Cultura Económica.

Tendler, Judith. 1997. *Good Government in the Tropics.* Baltimore: Johns Hopkins University Press.

Treisman, Daniel. 1998. "Dollars and Democratization: The Role of Power and Money in Russia's Transitional Elections." *Comparative Politics* 31 (Oct.): 1–21.

Tsebelis, George. 1995. "Decision Making in Political Systems: Veto Players in Presidentialism, Parliamentarism, Multicameralism and Multipartyism," *British Journal of Political Science* 25: 289–325.

Unión Nacional de Productores de Café, CNC. n.d. "Ante la situación que vivimos en la cafeticultura." Unpublished document.

UNORCA. 1987. "A pesar de la usurpación de la CNC la lucha no se detiene." In Nuria Costa, ed., *UNORCA: Documentos para la historia.* Mexico City: Costa Amic.

Varshney, Ashutosh. In press. *Ethnic Conflict and Civic Life: Hindus and Muslims in India.* New Haven, Conn.: Yale University Press.

Velázquez Alzua, Alfonso. n.d. "Elecciones municipales en el estado de Guerrero, 1977–1989." Unpublished undergraduate thesis. Mexico City: Dept. of Sociology. Universidad Autónoma Metropolitana-Iztapalapa.

Velázquez Carmona, Manuel. 1989. Letter to Lic. Patrocinio González Garrido, Governor of the State of Chiapas (Jan. 24).

Vitalis, Robert. 1995. *When Capitalists Collide: Business Conflict and the End of Empire in Egypt.* Berkeley: University of California Press.

Vogel, Steven K. 1996. *Freer Markets, More Rules: Regulatory Reform in Advanced Industrial Countries.* Ithaca, N.Y.: Cornell University Press.

Wallach, Lori, and Michelle Sforza. 1999. *Whose Trade Organization?: Corporate Globalization and the Erosion of Democracy.* Washington, D.C.: Public Citizen.

Walton, John, and David Seddon. 1994. *Free Markets and Food Riots: The Politics of Global Adjustment.* Cambridge: Blackwell Publishers.

Waterbury, John. 1992. "The Heart of the Matter? Public Enterprise and the Adjustment Process." In Stephan Haggard and Robert R. Kaufman, eds., *The Politics of Economic Adjustment.* Princeton, N.J.: Princeton University Press.

——— 1993. *Exposed to Innumerable Delusions: Public Enterprise and State Power in Egypt, India, Mexico, and Turkey.* Cambridge: Cambridge University Press.

Weingast, Barry R. 1981. "Regulation, Reregulation, and Deregulation: The Political Foundations of Agency Clientele Relationships." *Law and Contemporary Problems* 44 (Winter): 147–77.

Weyland, Kurt. 1996. "Neopopulism and Neoliberalism in Latin America: Unexpected Affinities." *Studies in Comparative International Development* 31 (Fall): 3–31.

——— 1999. "Neoliberal Populism in Latin America and Eastern Europe." *Comparative Politics* 31 (July): 379–401.

Widner, Jennifer A. 1994. "Political Reform in Anglophone and Francophone African Countries." In Jennifer A. Widner, ed., *Economic Change and Political Liberalization in Sub-Saharan Africa*. Baltimore: Johns Hopkins University Press.

Willis, Eliza, Christopher Da C. B. Garman, and Stephan Haggard. 1999. "The Politics of Decentralization in Latin America." *Latin American Research Review* 34: 7–56.

Winters, L. Alan, and David Sapsford. 1990. *Primary Commodity Prices: Economic Models and Policy*. Cambridge: Cambridge University Press.

Yáñez Delgado, Alfonso. 1988. *Reforma y violencia*. Puebla: Universidad Autónoma de Puebla.

Yescas Martínez, Isidoro. 1991. *Política y poder en Oaxaca: La sucesión gubernamental de 1986*. Oaxaca: Dirección de Comunicación Social del Gobierno del Estado de Oaxaca.

Yergin, Daniel, and Joseph Stanislaw. 1998. *The Commanding Heights: The Battle between Government and the Marketplace That Is Remaking the Modern World*. New York: Simon and Schuster.

Zermeño, Sergio. 1990. "Crisis, Neoliberalism, and Disorder." In Joe Foweraker and Ann L. Craig, eds., *Popular Movements and Political Change in Mexico*. Boulder, Colo.: Lynne Rienner.

Zuñiga, Juan Antonio. "Los lazos de sangre, tierra, dinero y poder en Chiapas." *La Jornada*, June 2, 1995.

Zúñiga López, Rosa Elva, et al. 1995. "Diagnóstico regional de Los Altos de Chiapas." San Cristobal de las Casas, Chiapas: Maestría en Desarrollo Rural Regional, Universidad Autónoma Chapingo.

Index

239

Index

movement, 38t, 39f, 43f, 70–3, *see also* CEPCO; PRONASOL, 64, 66, 79, 82; State Coffee Council, 41, 45, 74, 86–95, 200–1; teachers' movement, 57, 77

O'Donnell, Guillermo, 9n, 98n, 202n

OIT (Independent Totonaco Organization), Puebla, 188

oligarchs, 12n, 30, 31, 36–40, 39f; Chiapas, 141–2, 143–6; Puebla, 170, 174n, 178; *see also* clientelism, crony capitalism, traditional elites

Olson, Mancur, 214n

Ortiz Salinas, Patricia, 137

Paige, Jeffrey, 17, 30n

PAN (National Action Party), 174n, 176, 183, 210n

participatory policy framework, 22, 43f, 198–201; Chiapas, 160–2; Oaxaca, 87–95

partisan strategy, 43f, 44; Guerrero, 47, 114–26; *see also* democratization, political parties, postelectoral conflict

PCM (Communist Party of Mexico), 102

Peasant Torch, *see* Antorcha Campesina

peasants (*see also* producers' movement), 29–34

Perry, Elizabeth J., 202n

Piña Olaya, Mariano (Puebla), 164, 165–8

Polanyi, Karl, 4n

policy repertoires, 7f, 10–11, 40–2

political parties, 203, 210–12; *see also* democratization, PAN, partisan strategy, PCM, postelectoral conflict, PRD, PRI

populism, 204; Guerrero, 99–106; Oaxaca, 55–8, 62–4

postelectoral conflict: Guerrero, 118–22; Oaxaca, 64–6, 81–5

PRD (Party of the Democratic Revolution), 47, 210, 211;

Guerrero, 110, 116–22; Oaxaca, 66, 81, 83–4

PRI (Institutional Revolutionary Party), 24, 26, 55–6; Guerrero, 117–18, 123; Oaxaca, 65; Puebla, 173, 174n, 189; *see also* postelectoral conflict, state governors

producers' movement: 35–40, 38t, 39f, 43f; Chiapas, 146–51, 154–6, 160–1; Guerrero, 104–6, 112–13, 120–6, 128–9, *see also* Coalition of Ejidos of the Costa Grande; Oaxaca, 70–3, *see also* CEPCO; Puebla, 168–75, 187–90, *see also* CARTT; *see also* CNOC

productivist strategy, *see* disengaged productivist strategy, engaged productivist strategy

Proletarian Line, 147

PRONASOL (National Solidarity Program), 28n; Chiapas, 146; Guerrero, 128–9, 130n; Oaxaca, 64, 66, 79, 82; *see also* INI-PRONASOL, SEDESOL

Puebla: CNC, 169, 183–4, 188; CNOC, 178–9, 188–9; crony capitalism, 166–7, 177–9; disengaged productivist strategy, 169; exclusionary policy framework, 43f, 177–9, 183–7, 186t; federal financial assistance program, 182–90; INMECAFE, 169–71, 171t; New Federalism, 176, 180–2, 189–90, 192; oligarchs, 170, 174n, 178; PAN, 174n, 183; PRI, 173, 174n, 189; producers' movement, 168–75, 187–90, *see also* CARTT; Rural Development Council, 181–2; State Coffee Council, 166–7, 177–9, 184–5

Ramírez López, Heladio (Oaxaca), 40–1, 53, 55, 58–60, 66–9, 198, 209

Index

UCIRI (Union of Indigenous
Communities of the Isthmus),
Oaxaca, 73
UCIZONI (Union of Indigenous
Communities of the Northern
Isthmus), Oaxaca, 68–9, 73–4,
84
UEPC (Economic Units for
Production and Marketing), 35, 69,
77–8; *see also* INMECAFE
UNAM (National Autonomous
University of Mexico), 56n, 59, 61,
101
Union of Ejidos Alfredo V. Bonfil,
Guerrero, 104–6, 111–13, 114; *see
also* Coalition of Ejidos of the
Costa Grande
Union of Ejidos and Communities
"Light of the Mountain,"
Guerrero, 128–9, 132

UNORCA (National Union of
Autonomous Regional Peasant
Organizations), 147, 173
URICAA (Independent Regional
Union of Autonomous Coffee
Producers), Puebla, 170

Vázquez Rojas, Genaro (Guerrero),
100n, 125
Villa Issa, Manuel (Puebla), 181–2
Vogel, Steven, 6n

World Bank, 4n, 64
World Trade Organization (WTO),
215

Zapatista uprising, 46, 152, 154,
159–60
Zedillo Ponce de Leon, Ernesto, 157,
180–1

Scott Mainwaring and Matthew Soberg Shugart, eds., *Presidentialism and Democracy in Latin America*

Isabela Mares, *The Politics of Social Risk: Business and Welfare State Development*

Isabela Mares, *Taxation, Wage Bargaining, and Unemployment*

Anthony W. Marx, *Making Race, Making Nations: A Comparison of South Africa, the United States, and Brazil*

Joel S. Migdal, *State in Society: Studying How States and Societies Constitute One Another*

Joel S. Migdal, Atul Kohli, and Vivienne Shue, eds., *State Power and Social Forces: Domination and Transformation in the Third World*

Scott Morgenstern and Benito Nacif, eds., *Legislative Politics in Latin America*

Layna Mosley, *Global Capital and National Governments*

Wolfgang C. Müller and Kaare Strøm, *Policy, Office, or Votes?*

Maria Victoria Murillo, *Labor Unions, Partisan Coalitions, and Market Reforms in Latin America*

Ton Notermans, *Money, Markets, and the State: Social Democratic Economic Policies since 1918*

Roger Petersen, *Understanding Ethnic Violence: Fear, Hatred, and Resentment in 20ᵗʰ Century Eastern Europe*

Simona Piattoni, ed., *Clientelism, Interests, and Democratic Representation*

Paul Pierson, *Dismantling the Welfare State?: Reagan, Thatcher, and the Politics of Retrenchment*

Marino Regini, *Uncertain Boundaries: The Social and Political Construction of European Economies*

Lyle Scruggs, *Sustaining Abundance: Environmental Performance in Industrial Democracies*

Jefferey M. Sellers, *Governing from Below: Urban Regions and the Global Economy*

Yossi Shain and Juan Linz, eds., *Interim Governments and Democratic Transitions*

Beverly Silver, *Forces of Labor: Workers' Movements and Globalization since 1870*

Theda Skocpol, *Social Revolutions in the Modern World*

Regina Smyth, *Candidate Strategies and Electoral Competition in the Russian Federation: Democracy Without Foundation*

Richard Snyder, *Politics after Neoliberalism: Reregulation in Mexico*

For EU product safety concerns, contact us at Calle de José Abascal, 56–1°,
28003 Madrid, Spain or eugpsr@cambridge.org.

www.ingramcontent.com/pod-product-compliance
Ingram Content Group UK Ltd.
Pitfield, Milton Keynes, MK11 3LW, UK
UKHW020333140625

459647UK00018B/2133